12-Step
Horror Stories

**True Tales of Misery, Betrayal,
and Abuse in AA, NA, and
12-Step Treatment**

Rebecca Fransway

Compiler / Editor

See Sharp Press ◆ Tucson, Arizona ◆ 2000

12-step horror stories : true tales of misery, betrayal, and abuse
in AA, NA, and 12-step treatment / edited by Rebecca Fransway ;
introduction by Ken Ragge. – Tucson, Ariz. : See Sharp Press, 2000.
    248 p. ; 23 cm.
    Includes bibliographical references.
    ISBN 1-884365-24-8

    1. Twelve-step programs - Controversial literature. 2. Alcoholics
Anonymous - Controversial literature. 3. Narcotics Anonymous -
Controversial literature. 4. Gamblers Anonymous - Controversial
literature. I. Fransway, Rebecca. II. Title: Twelve-step horror
stories.
                        362.29186

Cover design by Clifford Harper. Interior design by Chaz Bufe. Interior typeset in
Nebraska, a modern version of Baskerville. Printed in USA by Thomson-Shore, Inc.

Dedication

*To Jack, for solid, reliable, and continuous material
and emotional support.*

*To all the contributors of these stories.
Thank you for your courage and your honesty.
Because of your contributions, freedom might ring for others.*

*To Apple of the AA deprogramming site (www.AAdeprogramming.com),
Charles Bufe, and Stanton Peele for helping me gather stories.*

*Thanks as well to Jack and Lois Trimpey,
for their help in gathering stories
as well as their untiring work in support
of self-recovery.*

Contents

Introduction

Over the past 15 years, there has been a rising tide of criticism of Alcoholics Anonymous. Earlier criticisms (e.g., Stanton Peele's *The Meaning of Addiction*) focused on the divergence between the scientific evidence on alcoholism and addiction and what AA front groups, such as the National Council on Alcoholism and Drug Dependence and the American Society of Addiction Medicine, present to the public as "science." Chaz Bufe dared question whether Alcoholics Anonymous was a cult in *Alcoholics Anonymous: Cult or Cure?* For the first time since the 1960s, critical articles began appearing in the print media. And numerous alternative organizations appeared, including Women for Sobriety, Rational Recovery, Secular Organizations for Sobriety, and SMART Recovery. In this rising tide of direct and indirect criticism of the step groups, one thing that has been lacking is an anthology of personal experiences—individuals' stories of manipulation, abandonment, and betrayal at the hands of those who have been touted as holding the one and only answer to drinking and drug problems.

The reformer and activist who has met the need for such an anthology, Rebecca Fransway, was an AA member for many years and has her own 12-step horror story to tell, not just inside AA, but also outside AA. After leaving AA and doing not just better but extremely well, she began speaking out on addictions issues, both through a university TV station and on the Internet. To say that she was not warmly received by 12-steppers is putting it mildly.

A small number of groupers (12-steppers), not limiting themselves to the usual threats and personal attacks, began a campaign of menace, intimidation, and attempts to get her fired from her job. They even went so far as setting up a web site and Usenet newsgroup, not for the purpose of arguing against the points she made, but rather to ridicule her. Their vendetta against this grandmother was the result of her insisting that people follow medical advice (rather than advice from 12-steppers) for the treatment of depression, for suggesting that the 12-step approach isn't the only way to resolve an alcohol/addiction problem, and for pointing out the inherent hypocrisy and inconsistencies in the 12-step "program." Rebecca has shown great courage in refusing to knuckle under to this pressure. The latest result of her work is this collection of personal experiences from scores of individuals who became caught up in step mania.

These stories are not what one would ordinarily expect from people "in recovery." They are not the Wednesday-night-prayer-meeting-type witnessing typical of AA meetings and of AA members who speak to us in the media behind the mask of "anonymity"; and they are not the glowing testimonials found in AA's "Big Book." While a number of those represented here are still members of 12-step groups, their tales are more similar to the stories of those who have been betrayed by the leaders and congregations of their churches than they are to the usual tent-revival-like tales of wreck and ruin followed by salvation via Alcoholics Anonymous.

Perhaps the most shocking thing about this collection of stories is that these accounts aren't a collection of rarities; rather, these stories illustrate the *common* results of what happens when desperate people go to what they believe is a source of help and are indoctrinated to distrust themselves, to believe that they are "powerless," and to believe that their own defenses—their anger, insight, and reason—are their enemy.

At the time I wrote this introduction, *The Guardian*, an English newspaper, reported that:

> Vulnerable alcoholics seeking help for their addiction are being subjected to sexual and other abuse at the hands of long-serving volunteers from the world's largest alcohol support group. An internal memorandum circulated to every Alcoholics Anonymous group in the country reveals that volunteer members are increasingly being investigated by police forces examining allegations of sexual abuse.

It's of great interest that while knowledge of such abuse has been common in 12-step groups for decades, AA chose to address it—and not publicly—only after it came to the attention of the police.

Similarly, after the data in AA's own triennial membership surveys showed that only a tiny percentage of people with drinking problems "keep coming back" to meetings and that only some of them manage to remain abstinent, AA responded only with an internal report from which no action flowed; and when researchers became aware of that internal report ("Comments on A.A.'s Triennial Surveys") and made public reference to it, AA responded by refusing to release any further copies of it, and by refusing researchers access to the raw data from AA's surveys.

Clearly, one cannot look to AA to put its own house in order.

One hopes that the stories that appear in this book will lend many additional individuals the courage to speak up. One hopes that these stories will draw attention to the very serious problems that AA has attempted (successfully, so far) to sweep under the rug. While reform is not to be expected from within 12-step groups, one now hopes—even expects—that it will come from without. Through this book, Rebecca Fransway is doing a great service to those who are considering joining or are being forced into the step groups; this collection of stories will reveal to them that "the loving hand of AA" is often quite different from its wall-poster image.

The gift that Rebecca and the scores of personal accounts in this book offer is the knowledge that, *no, you are not crazy; no, you are not alone;* and *yes, there is life after leaving the step groups.*

—Ken Ragge
Author, *The Real AA: Behind the Myth of 12-Step Recovery*
July 2000

Foreword

Twelve-Step Horror Stories tells tales of unmitigated horror. And all of them occur either in 12-step support groups or in treatment based on the 12 step of Alcoholics Anonymous.

These stories cover a wide range of horrors. There is abuse by alcoholism counselors—many mentally ill themselves. There are therapists who refer people to AA purely because they themselves are alcoholics and can see no other way of dealing with alcohol problems. They are either incapable of discerning that their patients are having intensely negative reactions to AA or simply can't deal with these reactions—including emotional breakdowns, relapses, and ultimately, in some cases, death. There are AA members who exploit newcomers, both physically and sexually. There are rape victims told to "look for [their] part" and even to "make amends" to their rapists. There are treatment center counselors who recommend jail for coerced clients who, even though no longer drug users, resist 12-step treatment. There are AA members who die after taking "medical" advice from their sponsors or other AA members. There are others who are driven to suicide by the cruel treatment they received in 12 step groups. And there are untreated emotional needs—both of the victims of AA groups and 12-step treatment centers, and of the aggressors in these groups. One comes away from these stories with the feeling that one has had a glimpse into hell.

We can imagine AA advocates and members—indeed, a whole treatment system based on the beliefs of AA—questioning Rebecca Fransway's work here. And, indeed, she will be attacked—has already been attacked—for her efforts.

So why tell such stories? Those who tell their stories in these pages reply, "Because the stories are true." Others add, "Why are we asked to accept at face value all the sugar-coated tales told by AA devotees and long-time members? Why is their reality better than ours?" Still others simply want to get their stories off their chests. By doing so, they break their feelings of isolation—and perhaps help others with similar tales who are still isolated. The diversity of voices in this collection of stories is remarkable, yet the stories paint a consistent picture that underlines their veracity.

In contrast to the reality of the experiences described in these stories, the American public is asked, over and over again, to accept what is patently untrue—that AA and 12-step treatment are invariably benign and helpful. We are asked to believe this because some people fervently believe that AA brought them personal salvation, or because (if they are not alcoholics themselves) they imagine that the United States (and increasingly the rest of the world) has a healthy, successful AA-based system to care for alcoholics.

Nothing could be further from the truth. Since AA and treatment programs derived from it are based on folklore and on religious precepts (like powerlessness, acceptance, guidance from a higher power, confession of one's sins, etc.), there is really no "there" there. The dominant treatment model—and more than 95% of treatment programs in the United States rely wholly (usually) or in good part on the 12 steps—is an emperor with no clothes. It appeals to a relative few, while others are forced to go along for the ride—the over one million per year who attend due to court, employer, or other types of coercion. As for the rest—the overwhelming majority of those with alcohol problems—they stay as far away from AA as possible.

The response from the treatment system and AA true believers to this massive disinterest in, even antipathy toward, AA? They accuse *all* of these individuals of mental illness, of a desire to remain alcoholics, of a failure to note their true alcoholic state, and much more. In essence, they claim that the obvious and massive failure of the American alcoholism treatment system is due to those who are not helped by it.

But we rarely hear from these people. Many would ask, "Who wants to listen to an 'alcoholic in denial,' or a 'dry drunk' [the AA term for sober individuals who reject AA], for goodness sake?" In part, this book is a study of how such jargon, labels, and slogans are used to browbeat both those in AA and those who reject it.

For their part, those in this book are incredibly brave. After reading their stories one can hardly blame them for failing to succeed at 12-step alcoholism treatment or AA (although most whose stories appear in this book have eventually overcome their drinking problems, either on their own or with other forms of help—sometimes almost to spite AA). Instead of sinking into a hole ("jails, institutions, or death") after rejecting AA, as AA told them they would, they've stood on their own two feet and have dared to challenge a sacrosanct American icon.

That is why we should be so impressed with those brave enough to share their stories in this book. Those who contributed the stories here are strong and competent enough to perceive that what happened to them and around them in 12-step bedlam was wrong and harmful, and they had the courage to blow the whistle on it. This is an extremely healthy reaction that should be encouraged by those interested in mental health

Indeed, AA and the treatment industry are so powerful that people generally do not do well when they either buckle under to them or buck them—particularly since people exposed to AA and 12-step treatment are often fragile and in deep trouble emotionally. Most are likely to feel the way this young woman did: "My very first experience with alcoholism treatment and 12-step programs was frightening and intrusive. Today, I would have the confidence to speak up immediately against the verbal and emotional abuse I witnessed. But at age 21, I had not yet learned to trust my own judgment in the face of disapproval. I was afraid of my own feelings, my own anger, and I think it's that very quality which allows the treatment industry to roll over so many people."

Rebecca Fransway is one such brave person. Let us be clear about who Rebecca Frans way is and is not. She is not an ideologue—that is, she did not arrive at AA with a preconceived notion that it was wrong, harmful, or violated her values. Indeed, she is not by nature an activist. She does not approach people and activities with misgivings, as though the world is a place rife with danger and disillusionment and in need of correction. She attended AA in good faith, after she was repeatedly referred there by counselors and therapists who did not bother to mention that they were AA members themselves—the kind of counselors one often meets when seeking help for a drinking problem. If anything, Rebecca and many of the others one encounters in this book were often too trusting and accepting. Of course, on the other hand, they were told over and over again—not only within AA groups and treatment programs, but throughout the culture—that Alcoholics Anonymous is the best way, the only way, to overcome alcoholism.

Thus in these stories we see people put up with incredible affronts to their dignity and their mental health. The worst of these personal assaults involve sexual harassment, sexual abuse, and rape. As one woman describes her ordeal, "I was wheeled into a meeting because, due to a disability, I am in a wheelchair. I asked for a ride home after the meeting, since I had cab fare only one way. One of the ladies, although she meant well, sent me home with a known predator/13th stepper, 'Drew'. . . . For the record, I don't drink now, but the abuse I suffered almost drove me insane. It has been ten years since I've gone to a meeting, and I still have horrific nightmares of the sexual abuse—my screaming, *No! No! No! I don't want this!*" Another woman, who repeatedly attempted to gain support in dealing with her rape by AA members, was consistently counseled to analyze her own role in the abuse she suffered—even when she went to a university-town AA group comprised largely of academics. Instead of support, she was repeatedly told:

"Let it go."
"Turn it over."
"Find out what your part is."
"Make amends for your part."
"Keep your side of the street clean."

She concludes, "The existing message *which the women reinforce with their 'by the book' responses* acknowledges that men hunt down women, and that women must simply *accept it.*"

The use of slogans and jargon, of isolation and denigration of individuals who object to any part of "the program," of reliance on "group think" to wish away the inconsistencies and failures of AA, is a study in group coercion and brainwashing. As one perceptive but wounded woman notes, "I believe that many in AA are hiding horrible pain and trauma, and are using the meetings as an artificial boost to get them through the day. I also believe that AA uses thought reform to steer its members in that direction. The problem isn't members' foolishness or lack of willingness. AA is a machine which promotes repression, denial, and escape through 'spirituality.' It encourages members to fit their lives into the AA myth."

Thus it is that a group lionized for championing the downtrodden, a group believed to be nurturing people and encouraging them to understand and express their experiences and feelings, is in fact far more often a mechanism of oppression. AA long ago ceased being the voluntaristic organization envisioned by the small group of white, evangelical, Protestant, heavily alcoholic males who founded it. AA and, especially, treatment based on it, are now better typified as a system inflicted on the vulnerable and unwilling by an oppressive group of true believers who find it to their advantage to accept the received wisdom of the "Big Book"—and to impose that "truth" on others.

—Stanton Peele
Author, *Love and Addiction, Diseasing of America, The Truth About Addiction and Recovery,* and *Resisting 12-Step Coercion*
August 2000

Preface

Why 12-Step Horror Stories?

Why would you want to put together a book like this?, asked one of many AA members who e-mailed me about this project. Many were none too happy about it. But others said things like, *It's about time. The truth can only help, not hurt, AA.*

And this book is about helping those in AA and NA, not hurting them. We have been very careful to change the names of writers and those they name in stories, as well as the names and locations of treatment centers and 12-step groups.

But the fact is, that as horrifying as many of them are, these stories are not at all unusual, and I am quite certain that many groups and individuals will recognize themselves in these tales. These stories come from all over the world, yet the same scenarios have taken place over and over within 12-step groups and treatment centers right here in my town. And all of these scenarios have very likely happened in 12-step groups and treatment centers in your town.

This book serves several purposes. To me, the most important is that it acknowledges the experiences of hurt and angry AA and NA members and former members, and to reassure them that they should not be held responsible for being abused in 12-step groups or treatment. Another important purpose is to assure them that they can stay clean and sober, or learn to moderate, without treatment and without participating in AA or NA.

One of the most significant wrongs in AA is that if AA members hurt you, or if working the program makes you worse, you will have a great deal of trouble finding anyone within the program who will listen to your story without blaming you, dismissing your story as unimportant, or dismissing you as foolish, crazy, or defective. *Quit playing the victim* is a very common reaction of staunch members to anyone who complains about ill treatment. *Get off your pity pot* is another.

When I became suicidal after five years of working the AA program and being the subject of gossip and abuse by insane sponsors, here is what I heard:

> *How have you set yourself up for all this?*
> *You're so angry.*
> *What did you leave out? (of the program)*
> *Let it go.*
> *Move on with your life.*
> *It works if you work it.*

Some therapists can be less blunt, but more harmful, pathologizing anyone who objects to AA. When members of a list for drug counselors in universities and high schools heard that this book was being prepared, one of them wrote:

> I just wanted to share something I find helpful about people's "resistance" to 12 step programs. I think it provides us with wonderful diagnostic information as to where they are in their addiction and denial and what might be helpful for them in their treatment and recovery.
>
> For example, when someone says, "I don't want to rely on others for my sobriety so I don't like AA, " this might suggest that they are struggling with dependency in relationships or with not being able to trust others or ask for help with getting their needs met.
>
> If someone says, "meetings are too depressing," this could suggest that they have an underlying depression or that they might benefit from sharing some of their pain, hurt, sadness etc. with a therapist or someone before they are able to become more aware of it or address it *with the help of AA.*
>
> If people say, "I don't like the God stuff," it might be that they have had difficulty with family or religion in an authoritarian way cramming morals or dogma down their throats. It could have more to do with authority or a domineering parent. (emphasis added)

In my opinion, this pervasive belief that there is something wrong with anyone who objects to 12-step groups and 12-step treatment is dangerous and destructive to self-esteem, spontaneity, and the capacity to be honest and true to one's inner voice. If counselors won't allow clients to make simple value judgments, or trust their own feelings and beliefs and become independent, who is going to take care of these clients? AA? NA? Read the stories here and decide. Ask yourself and, if you care to take the time, ask the folks at your local addiction counseling center: *What do professionals like these think they are doing?* Doesn't the aim of 12-step treatment—to make those labeled as alcoholics or addicts dependent on 12-step groups for life—run directly counter to the normal therapeutic goal of helping individuals to become self-directed adults free of dependencies?

One example of the anti-therapeutic nature of 12-step groups and treatment is that many drug/alcohol counselors and AA/NA members have forgotten or have never learned the rules for active listening: validate the hurt and angry person; acknowledge the person's objections, and don't belittle them for having objections. The very act of listening to the stories of those who have been hurt, and acknowledging their reality—*Yes, you have every reason to be angry; yes, I too have experienced this, and what happened to you is wrong and should never happen to anyone*—has helped many victims to cross the line from feeling crazy to being able to get on with their lives. Here is a quote from a person who submitted a story:

> *Having someone believe you is definitely a preventive remedy to the onset of insanity. It also helps heal afterwards, and for that I am extremely grateful.*

Several people in 12-step groups have attacked me, stating that I am exploiting people who have been hurt, for money. This could not be further from the truth. The contributors have been empowered, not exploited. Here is what one of them said:

> *Thanks for the opportunity to ventilate! My best expression of myself is in my writing and an open invitation like yours is like water in the desert.*

Another volunteered:

> *I personally am joining the cause. Helping to shed light on dangers of the 12-step movement and the disease-based victimhood which has overtaken our country is my new mission. Sharing my experiences about the other non-alcohol addictions might help someone, and is a good place for me to start. Therefore, I am happy to share my experiences.*

Also, with the limited market for this book, I do not expect to make enough to compensate me for the years of abuse I've received in AA and from AA members (even after leaving AA). I've also donated a great amount of time and some of my own money in the access TV field trying to get the message to people that they are not powerless over their addictions and that there are alternatives to religious recovery. In addition, I've been a member of e-mail lists and have haunted usenet newsgroups long before the plan to publish this book ever came into being.

It's also well to note that as far as making money from addicted people, 12-step treatment is a $10-billion-dollar a year industry which is largely owned and staffed by 12-steppers. (A recent national survey indicates that over 93% of treatment facilities are 12-step facilities.) A great many of these individuals have profited handsomely from addictions. They continue to do so despite the fact that the bulk of the most scientifically valid studies (those with control and comparison groups) indicate that 12-step treatment is no better than no treatment at all. One indication of the uselessness of 12-step treatment is that *over the past several decades, while tens of millions of Americans have gone through 12-step treatment*—the figure for the 1990s was about 2,000,000 per year—*the alcoholism rate appears to have risen*. But this makes no difference to those who profit from 12-step treatment. With virtually no scientific backing, they continue to trumpet 12-step groups and treatment as the *only* means with which to deal with addictions problems; and they have attempted (successfully for the most part) to block alternative forms of treatment and to silence critics—in part by charging that we're "killing people" or are "only in it for the money." The hypocrisy of those making these charges is positively breathtaking.*

Yes, I believe this collection will help others. I'll never forget the way it felt when I wanted to leave AA because neither the program nor the abuse I suffered in it were doing me any good. But to get anyone's blessing on my bid for freedom seemed impossible, and at the time I thought I needed AA to stay sober, and hence, to survive.

I never want a single person to ever again think that he *has* to stay in AA or NA, miserable and depressed, or die drunk or from an overdose. I never want another person to think that she can't get

---

* For a detailed discussion of these issues, see *Resisting 12-Step Coercion,* by Stanton Peele, Charles Bufe, and Archie Brodsky, and *Alcoholics Anonymous: Cult or Cure?* (second edition), by Charles Bufe.

sober unless she checks into an expensive treatment center or abusive county detox unit (when well over 90% of those entering treatment facilities don't need detox). I never want another person to have to suffer the way some of us did.

—Rebecca Fransway
May Day, 2000

The Stories

The names of those contributing stories have been changed, except for the names of those who asked that we use their real names. (All have full names listed.) The names of treatment centers have been changed. We (both compiler/editor and publisher) have made every effort to check replacement names to make sure that those names do not match those of any existing treatment facilities. If by chance one of the names does match that of an existing facility, we apologize. It wasn't intentional.

Other identifying factors, such as locations, have been changed or cut from stories. The names of all individuals mentioned in the stories have been changed, unless otherwise specified.

Some story authors refer to writers or activists in recovery reform. For the most part, these names, such as Charles Bufe, Stanton Peele, Ken Ragge and those of other authors, have not been changed.

Finally, while most of the stories in this book recount horrifying experiences, we have included a number which describe more mundane, but still unpleasant and destructive, aspects of 12-step groups. We've done this in order to provide a more rounded view of life in the 12-step subculture than the horror stories alone would provide.

Glossary

This is a guide to terms frequently used throughout the 12-step subculture. All of these terms appear in at least one story in this book. Thanks to Apple at www.aadeprogramming.com and Chaz Bufe for help compiling these definitions.

12 Steps: The 12 steps are the specific instructions on how to obtain conscious contact with a deity. There is nothing original in these steps; they are merely a codification of principles and practices taken from the Oxford Group Movement, the Protestant evangelical movement of which AA was originally a part. Many AA members, and AA literature, say that one cannot get sober or "clean" without "working" the steps. AA's 12 steps have been borrowed and used with very minor changes by other 12-step groups, such as Narcotics Anonymous, Gamblers Anonymous, and Overeaters Anonymous. (In such groups, only single terms are changed in the first and twelfth steps; the remaining steps are exactly the same as AA's.) These are the steps as written on pages 59 and 60 of the book, *Alcoholics Anonymous:*

1. We admitted we were powerless over alcohol—that our lives had become unmanageable.
2. Came to believe that a Power greater than ourselves could restore us to sanity.
3. Made a decision to turn our will and our lives over to the care of God *as we understood Him.*
4. Made a searching and fearless moral inventory of ourselves.
5. Admitted to God, to ourselves, and to another human being the exact nature of our wrongs.
6. Were entirely ready to have God remove all these defects of character.
7. Humbly asked Him to remove our shortcomings.
8. Made a list of all persons we had harmed, and became willing to make amends to them all.
9. Made direct amends to such people wherever possible, except when to do so would injure them or others.
10. Continued to take personal inventory and when we were wrong promptly admitted it.
11. Sought through prayer and meditation to improve our conscious contact with God *as we understood Him,* praying only for knowledge of His will for us and the power to carry that out.
12. Having had a spiritual awakening as the result of these steps, we tried to carry this message to alcoholics, and to practice these principles in all our affairs.

12 Traditions: The traditions were written by Bill Wilson, were accepted by the AA membership at a convention in Cleveland in 1950, and are supposed to be the guide for individual groups and AA as a whole on how to manage themselves. Unfortunately, a great many groups, and AA as a whole, ignore or only pay lip service to at least some of these traditions:

1. Our common welfare should come first; personal recovery depends upon A.A. unity.
2. For our group purpose there is but one ultimate authority—a loving God as He may express Himself in our group conscience. Our leaders are but trusted servants; they do not govern.
3. The only requirement for A.A. membership is the desire to stop drinking.
4. Each group should remain autonomous except in matters affecting other groups or A.A. as a whole.
5. Each group has but one primary purpose—to carry its message to the alcoholic who still suffers.
6. An A.A. group ought never endorse, finance, or lend the A.A. name to any related facility or outside enterprise, lest problems of money, property, or prestige divert us from our primary purpose.
7. Every A.A. group ought to be fully self-supporting, declining outside contributions.
8. Alcoholics Anonymous should remain forever nonprofessional, but our service centers may employ special workers.
9. A.A., as such, ought never be organized; but we may create service boards or committees directly responsible to those they serve.
10. Alcoholics Anonymous has no opinion on outside issues; hence the A.A. name ought never be drawn into public controversy.
11. Our public relations policy is based on attraction rather than promotion; we need always maintain personal anonymity at the level of press, radio and films.
12. Anonymity is the spiritual foundation of all our Traditions, ever reminding us to place principles before personalities.

13th Step: Sex between AA members, usually between a newcomer and a more experienced program member.

The AA Way of Life: Mentioned several times in *Alcoholics Anonymous*. Living a God-controlled life. A routine that encompasses all AA activities—meetings, step work, fellowship outside meetings, working with others by visiting hospitals and institutions, etc. The Big Book alludes to dire consequences for not adopting this way of life, e.g.:

"One poor chap committed suicide in my home. He could not, or would not, see our way of life." (p. 16)

Acceptance: According to page 449 of *Alcoholics Anonymous,* acceptance is the "key" to attaining the much desired state of "serenity." In addition, the word "accept" is considered a key part of the Serenity Prayer which is often used to start or end meetings. Some AA members translate this into a doctrine that any treatment that others subject us to, or anything that happens to us, must be accepted. This is especially true if the one who must accept bad treatment is someone else.

Alcoholics Anonymous: Published in 1939, *Alcoholics Anonymous*, the "Big Book," is the fundamental text of AA. It is almost entirely a restatement of Oxford Group Movement beliefs. Many AA members consider it a divinely "inspired" text, thus placing it on the level of Scripture, and its author, AA co-founder Bill Wilson, on the level of the Old Testament prophets.

Anniversary Medallion: A coin given out at 12-step "birthday" meetings to acknowledge the specified amount of time the celebrant is said to have abstained from the abused substance. In some areas, "medallion" is interchangeable with the word "chip." In other areas, the "chip" is picked up month by month, or in the actual "birthday" month, and the "medallion" is not picked up until an annual "Birthday Meeting."

Basic Text: The NA equivalent of the Big Book.

Big Book: A common AA synonym for the book, *Alcoholics Anonymous*.

Bill W. (Bill Wilson): Co-founder of AA, writer of *Alcoholics Anonymous, 12 Steps and 12 Traditions,* and other AA literature.

Birthday: In the 12-step subculture, the day one began continuous abstinence from the offending substance. If one "slips" or returns to the addiction and then regains abstinence, the birthday is changed and the days, weeks, months, or years of counting start over. Those who are the "oldest," as far as these birthdays go, have the most prestige in meetings. Regular birthdays are differentiated from sobriety birthdays by being called "belly button" or "natal" birthdays.

Character Defects: 1. Faults 2. According to the definitive text of AA, *Alcoholic Anonymous,* these personality traits—"selfish, dishonest, self-seeking, and fear"—are said to block the alcoholic from contact with God . (Chapter 5) Only God can remove character defects. (steps 6 and 7) According to *12 Steps and 12 Traditions,* another definitive AA text, character defects are interchangeable with Christianity's seven deadly sins.

Clancy Group: An ultra-conservative West Coast AA group named after its guru.

Cunning, Baffling, Powerful: Actual traits of alcohol, according to the anthropomorphized description of the substance in Chapter 5, pages 58-59 of the Big Book. At some meetings, "the disease" is also described as "cunning, baffling, and powerful."

Denial: A recovery-house term that has made its way into 12-step groups. This is a term that would have overjoyed 17th-century witch hunters. *Denial* of being an alcoholic or addict is seen as a symptom of the "disease," as strong evidence that an individual has it. The newcomer to counseling, meetings, or anyone who is subjected to an intervention, is asked whether or not they have a "disease" (alcoholism, drug addiction, gambling addiction, etc.). If they *deny* having that disease, that means they *have* the disease. This term can even apply to a family member of an alcoholic who denies needing treatment for a "disease." (In 12-step ideology, family members of alcoholics and addicts are also considered "diseased.")

Disease: A term used to describe the *behavior* of drinking too much. The term is frequently used to describe not only the state of active addiction, but the condition of a person who was once addicted even after abstinence is established. Sometimes character defects, symptoms of depression, feelings of rebellion against the program, sponsors, or meetings are described as "the disease talking."

Dr. Bob (Robert Smith): Co-founder of AA with Bill Wilson.

Drunkalogue (also Drunkalog): A derisive term for a type of "share" in meetings, generally a long, rambling account of past drinking exploits.

Dry Drunk: A derisive term describing someone experiencing strong emotions. Can also be a term describing symptoms of depression, or a dismissive term applied to abstinent critics of AA.

Earth People: Anyone who is not addicted. Sometimes can mean anyone who was once addicted but abstains without a 12-step program. (Synonym: Normies)

Ebby Thatcher: A drinking buddy of AA co-founder Bill Wilson. Thatcher brought the message of the Oxford Group Movement, a Protestant evangelical group, to Wilson, leading to the establishment of AA when Wilson rewrote the Oxford Group's methods and ideology into the 12 steps and Big Book and brought that message to other alcoholics.

Geographic (also Geographic Cure): Moving to a new location to help one stop drinking or to get away from other problems.

Going Out: Returning to drinking or using after a time in AA or NA.

Grapevine: An AA periodical.

Gratitude: A desired attitude throughout the 12-step subculture, and often the topic of meetings.

HALT: Hungry, Angry, Lonely, Tired—said to be signals of possible relapse. See the AA booklet, *Living Sober.*

High Bottom: A term used to describe a drinker whose drinking behavior never caused serious problems—one who was "saved" by AA before his "disease" "inevitably progressed."

Higher Power: 1. A power greater than the addict or alcoholic, who can be prayed to (step 11), who requires humility (step 6), and who can remove "character defects" (steps 6 and 7). 2. A deity.

Hot Seat: A type of attack "therapy" in which an individual is singled out and attacked, sometimes for hours, by the facilitator and other group members. The purpose is to reduce the victim to a heap of quivering jelly, to destroy his or her defenses, so that he or she may be more easily reprogrammed into the group's belief system. This type of "therapy" is commonly employed in 12-step treatment centers.

Inventory: An account of one's resentments and personal character defects, undertaken in steps four and ten. Sometimes this account of one's defects will be taken by a sponsor or someone else in AA; although this is not supposed to be acceptable, it *is* accepted, depending on the length of "Time" possessed by the one taking the inventory.

John Barleycorn: Alcohol.

Low Bottom: A term applied to a drinker whose drinking caused serious life problems, as in "low bottom drunk."

Newcomer: A new person at meetings. In some areas it can also mean someone who is not actually new to meetings, but who has had a "relapse" and then returned to meetings. (Synonym: Pigeon)

Normies: Anyone who is not addicted and who is not part of the 12-step subculture. (Synonym: Earth People)

Old-Timers: Those in any given group with the most "Time" abstinent.

One-Stepper: A pejorative term for an AA or NA member who admits to being powerless as per the first step, but who does not work the rest of the steps.

One-Year Piece: A one-year medallion or chip, significant because it marks the point at which, according to conventional AA lore, it becomes permissible to begin having sexual relations.

Out: See "Going Out."

Oxford Group Movement (OGM): A Christian evangelical group of which AA's co-founders, Bill Wilson and Dr. Bob Smith, were members. AA borrowed its ideology (as codified in the 12 steps) and many of its practices directly from the Oxford Group Movement, and AA was in fact part of the Oxford Groups for the first several years of its existence. At its heyday, around the time AA was formed, the OGM fell into disrepute after its founder, Frank N.D. Buchman, a Lutheran minister, "thank[ed] heaven" for Adolf Hitler in 1936. AA left the Oxford Group Movement in 1939.

Pigeon: In some areas, another term for "newcomer."

Pink Cloud: A feeling of elation typically lasting three to six months following the cessation of alcohol or drug abuse.

Powerlessness: An addict's or alcoholic's alleged helplessness over the urge to drink or use substances in an addictive way. Some in the 12-step subculture say that they are also powerless over "people, places and things."

Program: The AA method of achieving conscious contact with God. Achieved by "working" the 12 steps.

Qualify: In AA, to "qualify" for the third tradition, mainly by telling one's story of past drinking and claiming the desire to stop drinking.

Real Alcoholic (in NA, "Real Addict"): The terms imply that anyone who can get clean or sober without AA or NA was never an alcoholic or addict to begin with, and that therefore AA and NA are the *only* way for alcoholics or addicts to deal with their addictions problems.

Relapse: A treatment center term for returning to "the disease" of addiction. AAs also refer to this as having "a slip" or "going out." Grueling arguments between established members often take place within the AA subculture in an effort to determine whether individuals who have "questionable relapses" should be stripped of their all-important Time. Examples of "questionable relapses" include accidentally swallowing alcohol-containing mouthwash, taking a single swig of cooking wine while preparing food, eating a few liqueur-filled chocolate-covered cherries, or (very commonly) taking doctor-prescribed pain medication or antidepressants.

Rigorous Honesty: Said in Chapter 5 of *Alcoholics Anonymous* to be a prerequisite to recovery from alcoholism. Those who fail in AA are often said to "lack honesty," because the AA program is perfect, and it *always* works if you properly "work it."

(The) Rooms: AA or other 12-step meetings.

Serenity: A much-desired, emotionally correct state of being. Placid, undisturbed, content, emotionally flat.

Serenity Prayer: "God, grant me the serenity to accept the things I cannot change, the courage to change the things I can, and the wisdom to know the difference." Since the 1940s, a great many AA and other 12-step meetings have started with this prayer. Ironically, authorship of this prayer is often ascribed to Protestant theologian Reinhold Niebuhr, an acerbic critic of AA's spiritual father, Oxford Group Movement guru Frank N.D. Buchman.

Sharing: Talking when called on at meetings. Also known as "sharing experience, strength, and hope."

Slip: A temporary lapse in established abstinence. This results in a major loss of prestige (accorded to those with "Time"). In AA, this loss occurs no matter what the nature of the "slip," and a member who consumes a single beer will lose his prestige just as surely as a member who goes on a full-blown, five-day bender.

Slippery Place (sometimes also called "Slippery Slope"): A place where a slip is liable to happen—bars, outings with drinking buddies, etc. The term can also mean an emotional state, such as anger, resentment, or fear, that supposedly can lead to drinking.

Slogans: Homilies frequently used in 12-step groups and thought of as wisdom, such as "Keep it simple, stupid," "Fake it 'til you make it," "Utilize, don't analyze," "One day at a time," etc.

Sober: A more desirable state of abstinence than simply "dry." Denotes serenity, emotional correctness, "working a good program," and/or a high spiritual state.

Sobriety: The most important thing an AA member can possess, and something that goes well beyond what is meant in standard English (being unintoxicated). In AA, "sobriety" means not only absolute abstinence, but also "working a good program." (Those who are abstinent but reject AA and/or the steps are often derisively referred to as "dry drunks.") Many AA members insist that they would be better off dead than if they lost their sobriety. The biggest accomplishment an AA can make is "dying sober." In the AA subculture, for all intents and purposes, it doesn't matter what else a member does or does not do in his or her life as long as he or she keeps the supremely valued "sobriety."

Sobriety Chip: Same as anniversary medallion

Spirituality: The state of God-consciousness obtained by practicing step 11. Some in 12-step groups consider serenity impossible without spirituality.

Sponsee: A person being indoctrinated by a more experienced 12-step-group member.

Sponsor: An abstinent member of a 12-step group who counsels, guides, and indoctrinates a less experienced member.

Synanon: Originally an AA group, this California-based 12-step drug treatment program later turned into a major American religious cult.

Terminal Uniqueness: 1) A contemptuous and ominous dismissal of newcomers who openly disagree with 12-step doctrines and try to preserve some essence of their own identity. Examples might be refusal to admit to being an alcoholic, powerless, in need of a Higher Power, or in need of a sponsor; 2) A "disorder" from which certain alcoholics "suffer" because they see themselves as being different in some ways from their alcoholic peers, when in fact, according to AA lore, all alcoholics are the *same* (i.e., diseased, defective and frequently in denial). The phrase that often follows "terminal uniqueness" is "we're all the same." This implies that AA should, by default, work for everyone, since all alcoholics have a Borg-like similarity.

Time: Claimed long-term continuous sobriety or abstinence. The primary measure of prestige in AA, NA, and other 12-step groups.

Tough Love: Abuse of a type particularly gratifying to the abuser, in that it combines the pleasures of sadism with those of self-righteousness. Commonly employed and widely admired in 12-step groups and treatment.

Two-Stepper: A derogatory term for an AA or NA member who has admitted powerlessness as per the first step, and who "carries this message" as per the 12th step, but who has not worked the steps in between.

White Knuckling: A state of abstinence that is considered to be difficult or unhappy, as opposed to "sobriety," which coupled with "serenity" is the supposed reward for those who "work a good program."

Winners: The term refers to those who achieve (or claim to have achieved) long-term sobriety through "working a good program," and who look and sound good at AA meetings. It is commonly used in the prescriptive slogan, "Stick with the winners."

Work (or "work it"): Take the steps; follow the 12-step program of recovery.

1 ▲ Robert
Rejected by AA

I'm a psychiatric social worker, 21 years out of graduate school. One of my first jobs was as an alcohol and substance abuse counselor in a large community mental health center in the Midwest. Back in 1978, I had one of my first encounters with AA. I made the suggestion that there might be some similarities between alcohol abusers and substance abusers. This was greeted with wholesale disdain among the AAs. At that time, substance abusers were viewed as the scum of the earth by the AA crowd, while they tended to see themselves—when they were alcohol abstinent—as model citizens in touch with some kind of secret knowledge that non-alcohol abusers would not and could not ever know. They used this secret "knowledge" to disqualify anything said by someone who was not a *recovering alcoholic.*

At another time, I started working with a young, very attractive single mother who had recently gotten divorced and had a little daughter. She'd had some problems with alcohol abuse during the time of her stormy divorce, and had come to me for support during her transition into single motherhood. She also made the mistake of going to a couple of local AA meetings.

While at the meetings, *she was told that she was clearly an out-of-control alcoholic* and that *if she was serious about recovery she would have to attend 90 meetings in 90 days.* As a newly single mother trying to raise a daughter and transitioning back into the work force, she told them that she would be unable to do that, as the babysitting costs would be more than she could afford, and the meetings would take time away from her daughter, who was about three years old, and who was also transitioning to life without daddy.

Essentially, this woman was told that she wasn't serious about recovery and that she would undoubtedly relapse and get worse and worse. She was told not to think about coming back to another AA meeting until she was *ready to get serious about her sobriety* and do 90 meetings in 90 days.

This woman reacted to all of this with severe discouragement, and about a week after the rejection by the local AA group indeed started to drink again. About three days after she started drinking, she got herself and her daughter into a head-on accident on a local country road. The woman's little girl was fine, but the woman herself went through the windshield face first. I saw her in the ER, and her face was all messed up. Her jaw, as I recall, was broken, as was one cheekbone. She had severe lacerations all over her face, and was told she would require extensive plastic surgery to remove all the scarring.

I've always remembered seeing that formerly very attractive woman with her face all bandaged up talking to me about the rejection she faced at the local AA meeting.

2 ▲ Berenice

Don't Be Angry, It's Not Spiritual

Shortly after I came into the rooms of Alcoholics Anonymous, I was raped by two men. I was a young woman of 24 who had just finished college, graduating with a bachelors degree and a drinking problem. I landed in a "low-bottom" meeting, and suddenly, in AA as a newcomer, I was the lowest on the totem pole. The other AAs with more time enjoyed higher status

"Take the cotton from your ears and put it into your mouth,"
they said...
"shut up and listen."

I learned that since I was the new arrival, I was sick indeed. Insane, they said.

"You have a disease."
"It's a disease of the perception."

I befriended a group of young people in my first year; one girl in particular, a wild and happy MTV type, took me under her wing. We went to meetings, sober dances, day trips to the city. She introduced me to the various AA members at the clubhouse, including a young man named Chuck, who lived near the AA club. He had five years clean and sober. He told me his sad story. Chuck had been adopted by one of the wealthiest families in the United States as a white baby boy. They were not aware that he was really a mixed-race child, but as he got older he "turned black." Because of this, and some behavioral problems which manifested only later in life, he had been banished by his family to live in a low-supervision group home near the AA club. I felt sorry for him after hearing his tale of woe. But luckily he was on the right track now . . . he was "working a program." Despite his living arrangements, he seemed to be more gentle and together than the other people at that meeting, who appeared quite bizarre and were speaking in contradictions.

"Defeat is victory."
"Powerlessness is empowering."
"The more dependent we are on the program,
the more independent we actually become."

My early days in AA were confusing to say the least. I got a sponsor, a young woman who spoke to me a few times on the phone, then ran off with one of the men from the meeting, never to be seen again. Most of the other women seemed angry, and many of them were dating the men in the group. Since I had never been to AA, I had no way of judging this. I had heard "men with the men and women with the women," but it was not repeated often, and the members modeled behavior which went contrary to this catch phrase. In fact, a lot of the behavior went contrary to what was preached. Nevertheless, I figured that people date and opposite genders mingle in the outside world, so it didn't seem wrong to me . . . besides, they weren't drinking. That's what I cared about.

The AA members kept asking if I would go to any length to get what they had; but despite their claims of happiness and serenity, many of them seemed worse off than my drinking friends. I relapsed several times in the beginning, for two reasons. First, I really couldn't accept that I would have to go to these meetings and be among these people for the rest of my life, even if it was *one day at a time.* Second, I had fully internalized step 8—*made a list of all persons we had harmed and became willing to make amends to them all.* I felt so much guilt and shame over having hurt my parents with my drinking that I felt an overwhelming compulsion to make it up to them. The looming steps, as written on the banner hanging on the wall of the meeting room, seemed to tower over me and remind me on a daily basis of the pain I had caused my family by rebelling against their values. (This is a normal developmental stage for any adolescent, as I later learned.)

This time around, I made a promise to myself that I would obey all the family rules. After all, I had learned from an early age that it is *God's will* to *honor thy parents,* and I now learned in AA that, as a recovering alcoholic, I was to do *God's will,* which was not-so-subtly hinted to be that which is taught by Christian religions.

And so I did. But living life that way was extremely stressful. (Perhaps this is why I had rebelled in the first place.) It was so stressful that relapse was inevitable. The relapses came, and they were coupled with the usual guilt and shame, but I kept returning to AA because I knew of no other answer to my drinking problem. AA did a good job of indoctrinating fear into me, the newcomer, someone who was already coming from a fearful place.

"An alcoholic's fate is jails, institutions, or death."

My new friend Chuck didn't object to my relapses. He would come with me to bars to keep me company while I drank. It felt kind of strange that an AA member with five years should be coming with me to bars, but I let it go—after all, he wasn't pouring the drinks down my throat.

Life was tough in early sobriety. Very tough. And one night I relapsed on some rum at my parents' house, where I was living. I decided to leave the house before it took effect, since the last thing I wanted to do was break their hearts again by having them see me drunk. I just wasn't prepared to face the shame of such an encounter again. I was acutely aware of

"all the persons I had harmed"

and knew that my task was to

"make amends" and
"humble myself with prayer in order to remove my character defects"

I was completely riddled with *Guilt.*

My MTV AA girlfriend had run away to the West Coast by this time, and Chuck was my only friend left, so I drove in my father's car to Chuck's home hoping to sober up there. Seeing me arrive in a drunken state, he appeared to have no intention of letting me wait there until I sobered up. He appeared to have a different agenda, and was behaving in an uncharacteristically aggressive way. I had never seen him this way. (I learned later that he had gone off his meds.) He tried to physically drag me into the house. I was scared and I fought him, trying to get away. My car keys got lost in the struggle. Out of nowhere, a truck arrived at the scene and Chuck's friend, Lenny, got out. (Lenny was not a resident of the home, just a friend of Chuck's.)

Seeing the struggle, he got a baseball bat from his truck and beat Chuck in the head until he was covered in blood. I remember seeing the dark blood running down Chuck's face; it glistened in the moonlight. I was horrified at what had happened and scared out of my wits, but I was also happy to have been rescued, as Chuck was acting like a madman and I was terrified of him.

Good ol' HP had sent one of his "angels" to rescue me.

"I am so grateful to my Higher Power who was looking out for me!"
"There are no coincidences!"

Since I had no car keys, and Chuck's home was in a remote area in the woods, I had no choice but to go with Lenny. I was afraid of running, because there was nowhere to go, and Chuck might come after me. I got into the truck and was taken away. Lenny tried to calm me down by talking to me. Then he stopped at a liquor store and picked up a six-pack. We got to his house, and he told me to sit down. He then went into another room with the beers. He brought me back a glass of beer. I remember taking one sip, then losing consciousness immediately. (In rape crisis counseling I found out that there is a high likelihood that the drink contained a date-rape drug, since it was fixed in another room and because it knocked me out so quickly). I regained consciousness in his bathtub, with this man raping me and doing bizarre things to me. Immediately, I pushed him away and got dressed, feeling completely sickened and degraded. This was a new level of shame that I had never before experienced. Luckily, he cooperated, but not without telling me what a "great time" I'd had with him. "Heh, heh, heh," he laughed in a victorious, psychopathic cackle. I will never forget it.

But there was an up side. AA had taught me that repeated humiliation would help me achieve the requisite state of *humility* which I needed in order to maintain my new sober lifestyle. Cool!

Lenny then drove me back to Chuck's house to get my car. As I mentioned, the car keys had dropped onto the ground during the earlier struggle. Chuck and I found the key and he agreed to drive me home since I was terribly shaken up, and still coming off of whatever Lenny had slipped me, as well as the alcohol. I realized I was in no condition to drive. We returned to my house, and I told Chuck to go sleep in the guest room (it must have been 4 a.m.), and I lay down in my bed. I woke up a few hours later because I felt someone's presence in the room. Chuck was in my bed. I whispered angrily and instructed him to get out, but he would not leave. He insisted that I have sex with him—otherwise he would tell my parents about my relapse.

The last thing that I wanted was to hurt my parents again, because I love them more than anything in the world. I could not face the shame of them finding out.

So, I gave in angrily, knowing that I was already just a worthless hole. Anything to keep my parents from finding out. When he finished, Chuck went back into the guest room. A few hours later my mom and dad woke up. I made up a story about why Chuck was at our house. Despite the fact that I was furious and disgusted with Chuck, I now had to drive him home. (I had been raised with the rule that it is the polite thing to take care of one's house guests.) By the time I returned home from dropping Chuck off, he had done what I feared most—he had *called my parents* and *told them in detail* about the drinking and the "sexual escapade" I'd had with his friend Lenny.

I was sickened and furious beyond belief!

Only he did not mention the dubious circumstances surrounding the events, nor did he mention his coercive sexual encounter with me. He framed his call as if it were coming from a place of concern!—that he was calling because he was looking out for my welfare! "You had better watch your daughter. . . . she's got some problems . . ." Having learned all this from Chuck, my mother sat me down and called me a disgusting tramp who had better sober up and shape up. I was completely at a loss for words. I literally could not speak. I have never, ever, ever in my entire life felt so betrayed, humiliated, used and misunderstood. *Never!*

The rape and humiliation, topped by the reaction from my mother, completely crushed me. I felt like a dead piece of wood. A few days later I started to feel a large lump of emotions well up inside me. I had no idea what to do with it. I knew that as an alcoholic I wasn't allowed to be angry. That was The Word, as written in the Big Book. Anger was labeled as dangerous for alcoholics, an unsuitable emotion for someone with my affliction. I remember swallowing that large lump of emotions. If only I had been working my program better, perhaps I wouldn't have felt it at all. . . .

I didn't know how to even start to fix my life, but I knew that I had to take care of my alcohol problem.

"First things first."

So I went back to AA, but in a different town.

The rape and subsequent events had hurt me deeply, but I had grown up in an old-world European family, where we handled deep emotional pain in the same way that I learned to handle it in AA.

"I turned it over . . . I let it go . . . I gave it to God . . ."

After the rapes, Chuck continued to call my house and come by dropping off gifts and letters. Sometimes it was once or twice a week; other times two months would go by and I would think it was over, but there would be another call or there would be another "gift" in the mailbox or on the front step. This continued for a period of two years. He attempted to convince my father to talk me into rekindling my friendship with him. Years later I found out that Chuck had told my dad that I slipped a drug into my own drink, causing my loss of consciousness prior to "having sex" with Lenny.

"Let it go."
"Turn it over."
"Give it to God."
"Work a fourth step on it."
"Find out what your part is."
"Make amends for your part."
"Keep your side of the street clean."

My mom and dad were furious at their drunken daughter, and I was too filled with shame to discuss the situation with them, so I didn't say anything. I spent the next few years making "amends" for all the "harm I had caused" them through my drinking by working extremely hard in their family business. I workaholiced my way through early recovery. The rapes, the stalking, and all of the feelings that went along with it were left unaddressed, or, should I say, they were left to God.

Many things didn't sit right with me in AA on a core level, but AA had such a good public name that I figured that there must be something of merit there. . . . Also, I knew of no other solution to my alcohol problem—everyone knows that alcoholics must go to AA.

Also, there were plenty of fear-inducing tactics that kept me there.

"There are those too who do not recover, those who cannot
completely **give themselves to this** *simple* **program."**

"Meeting makers make it."
(meaning if you don't go to meetings, you *won't* make it)

"Rarely have we seen a person fail, who has
thoroughly **followed our path."**

and I was to

"just sit back and listen."

The steps were offered as the solution to my alcoholism and my resentments; and it was crucial to eliminate my resentments. According to AA, I was to do this by finding "my part" and making amends to the people against whom I held resentments. According to AA, I was in the wrong for feeling anger toward Chuck and Lenny, and I was to make amends to them for holding a grudge. It was critical that I forgive everyone who had wronged me in the past. It did not matter that the rapists had shown no signs of remorse. It did not matter that, given the chance, they would probably do it again. It did not matter that according to the statistics I learned in counseling they probably *will* do it again; according to AA, I was in the wrong for being angry, resentful, and unwilling to forgive, and that was that.

In AA, *resentments* are poison and they can only be eliminated by forgiving the people who wronged us. To challenge this notion is impossible, because it is akin to challenging the word of God. I also learned that the grouch and the brainstorm are not for us alcoholics, so being grouchy or thinking too much is dangerous.

Unfortunately, the rape and the ongoing stalking by Chuck became unbearable. No matter how much I prayed, there was no real relief. I felt disgraced and humiliated (which was helping me to get humble according to AA), and I felt so much rage that it was as if someone had injected a metric ton of anger into my system. It wasn't blood that was circulating in my veins, but rage. Pure rage.

Nevertheless, it was repeated over and over that I must avoid anger, and that I must forgive, Forgive, *Forgive.* My emotional truth and the things that I was learning that I needed to do to maintain sobriety were at odds. After one Big Book meeting, when the chapter on justifiable anger was read, I raised my hand to share. I objected heavily to the advice against anger, even citing an example: "I cannot imagine that the program wants us to be devoid of anger. What if someone senselessly murders my child," I asked. "Isn't anger the natural response?"

After the meeting, the Elder Members, the ones with lots of Sober Time, lovingly encircled me, chuckled knowingly, and encouraged me to keep coming, that someday I would "get it." The implication was that the program contained some mystical element that had the power to eradicate anger from the human experience, because this was an emotion that alcoholics could not afford to have.

No matter how much I listened, I felt that I would never "get it." I felt like shit. But AA stepped in again with some handy slogans:

"Fake it till you make it."
"Act as if."

Finally, I got tired of practicing acceptance, and started to feel that my Higher Power didn't give a shit about me, so I took my will back and filed court papers against Chuck for the endless stalking. I knew what the legal climate for rape victims was in this country, and I had no "evidence" to prove my case, so I didn't even attempt to file charges.

"Spread your legs ma'am, we need <u>evidence</u>."
"Innocent until proven guilty."
"How ya gonna prove it?"

Nevertheless, I did have evidence of the stalking—a big bag full of stuff Chuck had been dropping off at my house. Enough was enough!

I marched down to the police station to file a complaint and to get the ball rolling. The nice policeman who assisted me groaned and asked me if I was sure that I was being stalked. He had to make sure that I wasn't just one of those hysterical women who makes up this kind of stuff.

I filed the papers, but unfortunately they could not be served because Chuck had become homeless. As far as Lenny was concerned, I had no idea of his last name or address. So, I was back to square one.

"Let it go."
"Turn it over."

At my new meeting, through many tears and sobs, I shared with the group in broad terms what had happened during my last relapse. I told them how I fought off an attacker, and that I had been rescued by someone else, and that my "rescuer" did something to me which was worse than what I was fleeing from!

After the meeting, no one responded to me. No hug, no kind words. I was breaking down emotionally, and no one seemed to give a shit. In retrospect, I think they were probably too afraid to be around someone who was experiencing such strong feelings, since being in the proximity of such a person is disruptive to their serenity, and thus a threat to their sobriety. If it wasn't my experience, strength and hope as it pertains to alcohol, it didn't seem to belong in AA. The silent message was that members are expected to take their unsightly emotional messes elsewhere, or to work the steps on them.

I experienced firsthand that in AA it is impossible to point the finger without "three pointing back." Based on this philosophy, it was clear who was in the wrong: *me*. If I hadn't drunk, if I hadn't befriended a male, and if I hadn't gone to his house to flee my own shame at home, I wouldn't have been raped. (The message to the men? Drunk women are fair game; a woman who befriends you is fair game; and any woman who comes to your home is fair game.)

Wow! If three fingers are pointing at me, it only follows that I should probably go to jail for my own rape.

AA is a place where we look for our part, make amends for our part, and we disregard the other person entirely. I was in pain, so I "owned" the problem. It was my fault for having *expectations* that I wouldn't be raped. End of story. What about Chuck and Lenny? I was to avoid taking their inventory, and keep the focus on myself. According to AA, my duty was to pray for them. I was to think of them as sick children of God, and I was to get on my knees night after night and pray that good things happen to them. I was to keep doing this until my resentment went away. Maybe it was my "diseased" mind, but this sounded like a good way to fuel a resentment rather than a way to get rid of one. The idea of it made me sick.

According to AA's prescription for serenity, in my heart I was to treat them with the same patience and tolerance that I would grant a sick friend who has pneumonia. Boy, it's a good thing that the sentencing judges who put away Charles Manson, David Berkowitz, Ted Bundy, and Jeffrey Dahmer weren't well-indoctrinated AA members!

According to AA, my feelings were the problem. The problem is not that two men are freely roaming the world, having satisfied their own power and sex needs by raping a woman without any thought whatsoever of her feelings or the effects on her life. The problem isn't that they have experienced no consequences whatsoever for their actions. The problem was my feelings, which I was to change by using prayer.

I learned that I was to pray for them. But who was to pray for me? No one of course—how selfish of me to even ask. Could I at least feel sadness over what had happened? No! Why that would put me on the *pity pot*—a place reserved for *dry drunks*. It felt wrong, it all felt so very, very *wrong*. I simply couldn't meet AA's emotional demands no matter how hard I tried. I felt like a failure.

In retrospect, I ask myself why I didn't go to a rape crisis center sooner, but I can now see that going for therapy or seeking outside help was subtly shamed in my family as well as in AA. We were strong Europeans who pulled ourselves up by our bootstraps. Come to think of it, every time I went out the door to go to AA, I felt shame. But I went because I wanted my parents to see that I was doing something about my problem.

Soon thereafter, I got myself a new sponsor. She was the young "happy, joyous, and free" type. She had what I wanted: a big smile and lots of friends. I had neither. I called her nightly in the obligatory way. I got the answering machine most of the time, but, finally, I needed to discuss the rape, so I confided in her. Her response? She told me to read page 449 of the Big Book ten times to get rid of my resentment. Dutifully I turned to that page:

> And acceptance is the answer to all my problems today. When I am disturbed, it is because I find some person, place, thing or situation— some fact of my life—unacceptable to me, and I can find no serenity until I accept that person, place, thing, or situation as being exactly the way it is supposed to be at this moment. Nothing, absolutely nothing happens in God's world by mistake. Until I could accept my alcoholism, I could not stay sober; unless I accept life completely on life's terms, I cannot be happy. I need to concentrate not so much on what needs to be changed in the world as what needs to be changed in me and my attitudes.

I almost puked. In essence, my sponsor was telling me that what I needed was an attitude adjustment. This is the advice I got about the rapes—from a woman!

I stopped trusting people in AA. I tried to distract myself from my feelings by taking a coffee commitment. Maybe "what's at the bottom of those urns" would help me. (In AA, the practice of preparing caffeinated beverages for one's peers is highly touted as a remedy for emotional pain.) The overwhelming message was that I needed to get out of myself. Accordingly, I made coffee, I scrubbed urns, I bought cookies. I ritualized my life, and slowly and methodically managed to repress, reframe, and deny the truth of both the incident and the rest of my life.

I felt broken and desperate, and could have used some love, empathy, and support, but I couldn't find any at home or in the rooms. With my parents, I simply didn't have the psychological or emotional strength to sort out the situation and tell them what had really happened.

Nothing in AA validated my feelings; in fact, everything about it countered my internal truth. My internal truth produced symptoms of rage and depression which were chalked up as "disease symptoms" for which more meetings were the remedy. I knew I needed to stay sober, so I kept going to AA. The whole world seemed to support this organization, and I knew of no other way.

Fortunately for me, my Higher Power stepped in again, and a dashing AA prince who was very well liked in the meetings became interested in me. I felt fortunate indeed that someone like me, a woman who was damaged goods for sure, could win the attention of such a well-liked Sober Man. He took me on several dates to fine restaurants. I was completely swept off my feet. Everyone who met him was charmed. Shortly after we started being somewhat physically intimate, he stopped taking me to fine restaurants. In fact, he stopped saying hello to me at meetings, and one night when we were set to go out, he drove me behind a convenience store. He parked his car by the dumpster and said he just wanted to "make out." So I did, thinking that this was the best I could get. (As you can tell, I had lots of experience with humility.) Nevertheless, my feelings were hurt. I felt him slipping away from me, and knew I had to look for and fix my part. My part must be that I am too fat. That's it! So I responded in the usual way, by losing weight. I dropped from 125 to 105 in a month or so. If I was prettier, he would treat me better. I also got a cassette and workbook on improving my relationship skills. I had been used by this Sober Man, and I blamed it on my relationship skills. I listened to the tapes while I jogged, trying to burn off my nonexistent fat. Everything about the gender messages embedded in my culture reinforced this response as being the appropriate one.

At that point, I needed to be cared for so badly that I was willing to go to any lengths to keep this Wonderful Sober Man. However, I could not ignore his change in behavior and my subsequent hurt feelings, so I decided that I had to talk to him. We went to a restaurant where I told him, "Jim, it really hurts my feelings that you used to take me to nice places, but now you park beside a dumpster and you only want to make out, and you won't even say hello to me at meetings." He responded by pulling out a Big Book from underneath the table. He said, "Sweetheart, you have to remember that you are *powerless* over my behavior, but here are some steps that you can work to change the way you feel about it."

His attitude toward women seemed to be "take what you want and leave the rest." I felt like a piece of toilet tissue, used and disposed of once again. I felt incredibly bad, hollow, broken, unlovable and lost. Even though I had learned that "God never gives you more than you can handle," I relapsed.

Not on alcohol, because I didn't want to get raped again. But on cough syrup. That way I could change the way I felt while maintaining some sense of control.

I found another sponsor. I picked one of the "career sponsor" types, someone who was big on "helping others" and really seemed to grasp and revere the Big Book. I must do it by the book, I thought. I must follow the rules (thinly veiled as "suggestions"). Please keep in mind that during this time I had even started to reframe the rapes because of the responses I had gotten from others as well as the 12-step programming. *We can only look at our part,* was drummed into my head at repeated meetings, and with each repetition of the Lord's Prayer, I was reminded to *forgive those who trespass against us.* Meanwhile, I was to avoid strong emotions, as they were implied soul poisons.

No matter how hard I tried to "fake it till I make it," my new sponsor detected that I was an angry person, so we made plans to remedy the situation immediately. I would have to work The Steps—the fourth step in particular. She handed me some forms and explained what to do. I was to write down the names of all the people against whom I had a resentment, and then find "my part" in each situation. She even gave me an example from her own life. Many years ago, she had an incident with a police officer who had acted as a peeping Tom. This cop had spied on her and her boyfriend as they made love in a parked car, late at night in a public park. My sponsor explained to me that the steps helped her reveal her part, and thus allowed her to get rid of her resentment. She explained that if she hadn't *put herself in that position*, the cop would have had nothing to peep at. Technically, there seemed to be *some* truth to this, but it still rang of abuse of power to me. I did not understand why that aspect was completely ignored. The idea of excusing Chuck and Lenny in this fashion made me sick beyond belief.

I stopped using that sponsor.

I didn't understand why my alcoholism demanded a thorough and fearless moral inventory in which I only looked at *my* part. What about everyone else's part? The more I thought about it, the more it seemed that throughout my life I had been on the receiving end of other people's immorality. Why am I the sick one for feeling angry over hurtful treatment? Is this logic bi-directional? Does it mean that I can hurt anyone I want and it's their fault? If a newcomer male goes to a bar and relapses, can I follow him there, slip a date-rape drug into his drink, sodomize him with a Vaseline-coated baseball bat, take Polaroid pictures of the act, mail the photos to his children, invade his personal life and terrorize him psychologically, and it will be *his* fault?

The answer? In AA I found that I sure can do that (although it works much better if women are on the receiving end because our culture tolerates this type of behavior toward women much more readily than toward men)!

My experience reflected the sickening fact that in AA, as long as the perpetrator maintains a *serene* exterior, offers an *optional* meaningless amends to whomever he's hurt, and confesses his wrongs to a supernatural being as well as to his sponsor, he will be let off the hook.

Sponsee: Shucks Joe, I got a little rough with *another* newcomer this weekend, if ya know what I mean . . .

Sponsor: It's OK Lou, so did I . . . couldn't help it . . . my *character defects* got the best of me.

Sponsor & Sponsee to newcomer: Sorry hon, forgive us. Don't be *angry*. It's not *spiritual*.

The perpetrator will be absolved and he will be accepted into the group. He will receive the social reward of pats on the back and hugs for having *gotten honest*. At the same time, the perpetrator's victim will be shamed, shunned, and expelled from the herd for reacting with anger and for feeling resentful over the abuse. She will be expected to react in a "sober way," without strong emotions. She will be pressured to forgive, and she will be blamed for having put herself in the position to be hurt.

Throughout this entire ordeal, it was virtually impossible to find a healthy response within the herd. Hardly anyone said: "How horrible that these people raped you!" "How horrible that they're using date rape drugs these days!" "How sick!" "Shame on them!"

Why did I stay so long in AA? Fear, desperation, and a very powerful force which I later learned to be a form of mind control. After leaving, I read several books on cults and psychological manipulation, and learned that the AA theology is replete with contradictions and circular logic which serve to make the program look perfect, and that AA employs many devices for psychological and emotional control which are characteristic of the ones used by cults. The more rigidly one works the program, the more powerful the mind-control effect.

Despite the dubious aspects of much of its lore, AA also has a very powerful human element that keeps people sucked in. Relationships are formed, friendships are forged, and meetings satisfy a voyeuristic desire. By hearing the struggles of others, I was kept riveted to my seat. This kind of personal exposure is hard to find anywhere else. It is very alluring. The promises were the carrot and the steps were the stick. There was an evangelical power to the meetings which was mixed with a strong "spell" that was cast on us all.

Knowing nothing about mind control when I entered, I was not able to identify what was happening. I intuitively knew something was wrong, but I couldn't put my finger on it. For this reason, I fell under the AA spell. Being desperate and therefore willing to entertain almost any new idea certainly contributed to it. AAs openly say that "the Program is brainwashing, but out brains *needed* washing." Well, they are at least half right.

Another reason I kept coming is that there was a climate of shame at home. I was still in the doghouse with my family, so naturally I gravitated to my new AA family, even if it employed similar dysfunctional methods for keeping me "in line." I kept on coming, trying to make the best of it.

The resentments I had against Chuck and Lenny took their toll. I refused to do the fourth step in the fashion presented to me. I was seen as a bad seed in AA—the rebellious alcoholic. Over and over, I was warned against being willful. Compliance and obedience were rewarded with social approval; free thought was met by rejection. I learned through repetition that those who do not take the "suggestions" do not make it. I was to concede my will to the better judgment of my sponsor or the group. I was to take her suggestions.

But I just couldn't do it. The thought of it made me sick. If I refused the "suggestions," I would be shunned by the group. If I took them and felt worse, it was my fault for taking them since they were "only suggestions." Because of my broken state, I could not at the time recognize this as circular logic which is used to make the program look perfect at the cost of members' sanity. I learned that nothing happens in God's world by mistake. "Why," I wondered, "does God want me to live like this?"

The internalized rage took its toll, and I developed a pathological compulsion to both abuse men and find one who would protect me. Even if I learned that a Big Benevolent Supernatural Patriarch was there to protect me, provided that I bow to him with humility, he didn't seem to be picking up the signals from my prayer antenna.

Nevertheless, I had scraped together a few years of sober time. Not because of any thorough moral cleansing, but simply because I was terrified of having to go through an incident like the rape again.

What was the culmination of these events? It wasn't good. Often, sexist behavior by the men in the rooms would trigger hostile, reactive behavior on my part. This is not my natural state, but was a result of the internalized trauma.

I wanted men, especially men in AA, to be attracted to me and to suffer because of it. I wanted them to want me, and then get absolutely nowhere. Ever. I was young and attractive enough to pull this off, and since I had become completely sexually dysfunctional, I was able to be "just friends" with almost any man, with no feelings of missing out on my part. The trauma affected me in so many ways. The more I internalized it, the more powerful its influence became.

I felt a pathological compulsion to lash out against men who were openly misogynistic, and who openly objectified women. Fellow AA members witnessed this behavior, and to this day some of them think that it was this behavior which invited the rape, and not the untreated rape which resulted in this behavior.

What I had turned into was not good. As yesterday's victim, I was now driven to be the victimizer. This behavior seemed to flow naturally because I had not found any empathy or compassion for the original trauma. No one felt sorry for me, so why should I feel sorry for anyone? This behavior continued until I finally crossed paths with someone who fed me a dose of my own medicine, and I could taste how bitter it was.

Without the necessary healing, the therapy, the human compassion, the empathy, and the support of my loved ones and peers, I became completely wacky. I tried and tried to turn it over to God, but "it" must have been tied to a boomerang, because back it came every time. And when it came back, I would feel like a failure for not being able to turn it over like the others seemed able to do. This contributed to my feelings of shame. I even lost my best friend in the rooms because I was "too angry" to be around, and because I wasn't "nice" to men. At the time I couldn't explain why, because I had internalized the whole incident.

Instead of healing me, many of the slogans wounded me, and the platitudes I heard, which were supposedly quick fixes to deep emotional pain, were more like salt thrown on a festering wound. The steps . . . well, they claimed to lead to a peaceful place, but for me, emotionally, they seemed to descend into hell. I felt so out of place. I couldn't share my experience, because mine wasn't a good experience, and sharing bad feelings was seen as being "whiny" or unaccepting of God's world. (This is why the atmosphere of meetings often seems so positive and uplifting despite the fact that alcoholics are often hiding extremely painful histories—because revealing the true nature of deep emotional pain is often discouraged.)

I wanted so much to be part of the in group. The *happy* recovering drunks. The grateful AAs who were part of the in crowd. But I had one thing going against me: I was never good at hiding my feelings. If I was angry on the inside it would show. For this, I was shamed, sometimes subtly, other times not so subtly, for not working the program.

I still hadn't given up on AA, because its control over me was powerful, and I did see people who seemed happy, and I wanted so much to be like them. I got another sponsor. This time, when I told her my story, I knew that blaming Chuck and Lenny would get me a reprimand, so I reframed the event entirely to blame it on myself. This fit the program better, and this is what got me the approval which I needed so very badly. Of course, my sponsor gently reminded me that I needed to share my experience, strength, and hope, and that she found no strength or hope in my story. That was because I didn't have any. I continued to go to her home group and to call her. She was gentle and kind, and I appreciated that. Nevertheless, she went off to pursue higher education and no longer had the time to sponsor me. My bulimia was acting up very badly by then. I couldn't even sit through a meeting without going off to puke up the cracker I had eaten for lunch. I knew that if I was skinny that men would be nice to me and they wouldn't hurt me anymore, because I would be too pretty and valuable. I was driven to correct "my part."

I learned that *in AA the greatest possible transgression is not the rape or exploitation of newcomers.* It is not robbing, cheating, or lying and making a meaningless amends afterwards. *The greatest possible transgression is challenging the Big Book and AA lore.* A person who transgresses in this manner will be labeled as a sick and diseased person. The rejected member seldom has any friends outside of the program by the time this happens, because the group encourages its members to cut ties to others, and because it encourages members to stick with the "winners"—the winners being people who "work a good program," who are serene and content because of the program, and who experience a shallow emotional range because of the serenity they derive from the program. Period.

Finally, I went back to my first home group. I felt like a big loser. I would never be able to attain the upbeat gratitude of the cheerleader types in AA. These girls seemed to be clones of the same peer group who rejected me in high school. The "fake it till you make it" crowd. I went back to the club where the lower level of drunks seemed to gravitate. I went and took the seat which had been waiting for me. The one with the invisible sign: *loser.*

Over time, I stuffed away the trauma in a little corner of my mind, and managed to not even think about it much. Occasionally, when running or driving, memories would come back and I would burst into tears. It became incapacitating. But ordinarily, especially at meetings, I would "confess" to the group that it was I who treated men badly. My behavior was now a "disease" symptom. The group would nod in agreement and give me their approval for my "getting honest."

(Note that this "getting honest" was the *highest form* of dishonesty. It required that I go against what my insides were trying to tell me for years. This truth was not my truth or even "the truth." It was the AA "truth," which was a result of AA's power to reframe memories.)

By this time I had absorbed the indoctrinated idea of personal powerlessness to such a degree that several years had passed, and I was still leeching off my parents (living rent free), having long overstayed my welcome. Since I did not seem to be moving out, my parents decided that they would move out. They left for California, taking the family business with them. I was now out of a job and a home. I helped them with the packing and moving, in accord with the *do for others* mantra and out of residual guilt as well as genuine concern for their welfare, but I had failed to plan adequately for myself. Luckily, I found a place to live at the last minute, and one of the men whom I had known for years from the AA club offered to assist me. Why a man? Well, he had a large truck, adequate upper body strength, and enough free time to help me move my personal belongings to my new abode.

Help he did. The help with moving turned into help with finding work, and to help with a bevy of other tasks. In retrospect (hindsight is 20/20 isn't it?), I see that I should not have accepted so much help, but 1) I really needed it; 2) on some level, I felt that men "owed me"; and 3) he seemed willing to give it. Nevertheless, I was very grateful for his kindness. My Higher Power had sent me a real jewel this time! I kissed and hugged my new hero! I truly appreciated his help and his company. But the sweetness of affection soon turned to control through kindness and then control through fear. A violent outburst resulted in my drawing the line and his responding by leaving at least 25 apologetic messages on my answering machine. I was seriously concerned about this behavior, but my AA head took precedence over my gut and I forgave him. Big mistake! By doing this I had given him back his power, and the controlling behavior and violent outbursts started up again. The more I resisted, the more he persisted, until once again I was faced with a stalker. This "excitement" went on for about a year and a half this time.

Meanwhile, memories from the rape were flooding back, and I was dying on the inside. I went through a phase of heavy prayer. I bought many religious candles, read the Bible, bought meditation books, read the Big Book. I was trying to use prayer to tamper with my emotional reality. It worked! I was able to deny the facts about my life by praying for several hours per day. Bingo! I had finally "gotten it"! I proudly went back to the rooms to speak in praise of spirituality and prayer. I had stumbled upon a marvelous discovery, one that mankind has employed for centuries. The use of prayer and religion to escape the pain of reality. How marvelous!

I got myself another sponsor. She was very pleased with my spiritual ways. But I had a troublesome habit of asking too many questions. Questions that were often answered with "read the book." I read the book, but I still had questions. I did my fourth step. I'm amazed today that the rapes appear on the fourth step as some minor inconvenience. This is evidence to me of the power of the program to alter memories and perceptions. Nevertheless, we determined during the fourth step that I had been raped, and while my sponsor asked me, mustering all of her tough love, *"Now what was your part?"* (I could have slapped her), she also suggested that I go into therapy. I promised that I would pursue it. Ultimately, I figured out that therapy was what I needed all along. It was only by releasing the rage and working through the anger in therapy that I finally felt the leaden overcoat lift from my soul.

During the time that I was attending crisis intervention for the rapes, the harassment by the man who had helped me move had gotten way out of hand, even to the point of requiring police intervention on more than one occasion. My life seemed to be a never-ending terror flick with men as the monsters. Feeling fearful and powerless, I did what I knew, and started to pray to my Higher Power to help me.

My street-wise roommate, who had grown up in a major city, was quick to point out that only nincompoops pray in response to threats such as those I was receiving, and she talked me into feeling my anger so that I could take proper measures to defend myself. She was absolutely right. I had discarded the emotion of anger in accordance with *working a good program,* and I literally could not find it when I needed it! I was then able to see how, once again, AA's indoctrination had done me a great disservice, in this case, by tampering with my natural fight-or-flight response. Instead of the healthy response of anger—the primal survival response—I had been programmed to pray and forgive! Boy was I shocked when I made the connection!

Immediately, I made efforts to procure a weapon for self-defense, which I carried with me at all times. I also went down to the court-house to request a restraining order, hoping to secure some peace of mind, but the judge (a woman), didn't find the latest transgression serious enough to warrant a restraining order. (It is always issued based on the latest incident.) She said she would have gladly issued it based on the incident before last. I asked her for special consideration, explaining that I was currently in therapy for rape, telling her that the harassment on top of it was psychologically unbearable, but she declined my request with the following comment: "I'm sorry, miss, that you've had problems with your previous relationships [!] as well, but I will not grant you the restraining order." By this time I had become used to such responses, so I left the courtroom quietly.

When at last the therapy was successful in breaking down the wall of denial which I had built with the help of AA, I began to see how it had been the AA theology which had hindered the natural healing process. This was why I had accumulated five years of "sobriety" in the program yet I was bursting into tears at regular intervals. I had a moment of clarity at that time, which I felt compelled to confirm.

I decided that either I was crazy or AA was crazy. I knew that it was time to find out. I was attending a meeting in an Ivy League town, which was frequented by doctors, lawyers, university professors, and other upper-crust drunks. I decided that I would march down to the old meeting hall and drop a bomb on them. The speaker qualified for ten minutes, some other people shared, and I raised my hand. They called on me, and I stood up and walked right into the middle of the circle and told them.

I told them everything, using my own words and using all of my emotional truth without any of the AA step-talk that I always had to tag on to receive their approval. I wasn't grateful for anything, and I wasn't looking for the hidden blessing sent by God. I was hurt and I was mad!

I told them where I came from, what happened, what it was like now. I told them the truth! I showed them the pain, I showed them the confusion of banging up against yet another brick wall in the rooms of AA. It was one of the most important days of my life, because I broke through. I broke through the mind control of the AA program, and I could see the men sitting in the circle. Not one of them thought it was funny. In fact, Paul, the 13th-step guru, started shaking visibly. Something that I said had really hit home! None of the other men laughed the way the rapist had laughed. "Heh, heh, heh"—"Don'tcha remember how much *fun* we had?" I'll never forget it.

One of the women from the meeting had connected with my story, and she crossed the room to give me a hug. It was so wonderful to finally have one human being understand! Finally . . . someone . . . The meeting continued, albeit in a semi-shocked state. I wanted to run out of there; my heart was thumping like a bass drum. But a very kind social worker that I had met in the rooms encouraged me to stay. He was a newcomer so he wasn't under the "spell" yet. I will never forget either of them.

Many people, both men and women, gave me a hug and offered kind words after the meeting! I was amazed and thrilled! Compassion at last! The kind people seemed to be the quieter ones, not the ones who "talked the talk" but the ones who were more human—the ones who weren't too *programmed.*

But I can also attest to the sickness in the rooms. A notable portion of the meeting (the Party Liners it seemed) focused on how I had disgraced myself and compromised my dignity by revealing this story. My dignity would have been preserved with silence—the very same silence which protects the rapists and gives power to the crime. I later learned through the gossip mill that the kind woman who crossed the room during the meeting to offer me a hug was reprimanded by an old-timer for doing so! The reasoning was that it went against meeting format! Can you imagine! Reprimanding someone for exhibiting kindness because it breaks the Goddamned format! Also, some men, whom I had known from the meetings for years, reacted to my story by pointing and laughing at me as they elbowed each other in the ribs! I know what they think: "You reap what you sow, baby." Never mind that our culture infects women with a horrible double message: to find love, be sexy and alluring, but if anyone rapes you it's your fault because you were sexy and alluring. Never mind that women are called whores, tramps, and sluts for engaging in *the same* sexual activity which elevates men to the status of "stud," and that almost no such derogatory terms even *exist* to describe male sexual behavior. Never mind that Christianity, the religion which laid the groundwork for our culture as well as the AA program, flat out tells us that woman was fashioned from *the rib* of a man . . . *man* who was created in God's image.

And you ask me why I drank.

I can't even begin to describe the sexist behavior I have witnessed in the rooms over the years. I remember one father and son team in particular who were both in AA. I learned from one of my girlfriends who was living in the local halfway house that the son had made the moves on her in a big way, even before he had gotten his "one year" piece. The father, an old timer, had told him it was OK to have sex with the halfway house girls as long as he didn't get into an *emotional* entanglement. It's OK to screw 'em as long as you don't feel anything above the waist. Of course this makes him the stud and her the slut. He gains and she loses. This double standard is so deeply embedded in our culture—not to mention AA—that it goes by without the wink of an eye.

"And acceptance is the answer to all my problems today."

I remember bands of men assembling for private Big Book meetings. These "spiritual" sessions would result in the pack members acting as if anything they did was excusable because anyone who they hurt had "put themselves" in the position to *be* hurt. I remember one guy (a grandfather, for heaven's sake) who was sponsoring eight or more guys at once. He used to throw parties at his house, after which the younger women from the club (ages 17–20) would be invited to sleep over. One of the girls, just a few years past the age of consent, ended up becoming his girlfriend. I really didn't think much of this at the time, but today I shudder, because this grandpa is one of the men who laughed upon hearing about my rape. His attitude is that rape is no more than slightly aggressive sex that the woman didn't plan on having that day! (Our legal system defines it as a felony, but the Big Book seems to override legal definitions in the rooms, since it's held up to be "spiritually inspired" and therefore the word of God.) The psychological fallout, which can last for years, is just an overreaction in their eyes. It's up to the women to mop up the emotional mess, so the men never have to see what effects such crimes have on women.

And you ask me why I drank.

In their defense, however, I must say that the natural socialization of males is bullshit as well. Since childhood, men are desensitized to pain. They are encouraged to kick, hit, conquer, and to be aggressive. They are discouraged from crying, and are encouraged to swallow (repress) their pain which ends up coming out as violence, controlling behavior, and aggressiveness against anyone who is lower in the hierarchy. AA does a great job at keeping men's pain repressed. Instead of becoming angry at a father who shamed him, a peer group that ridicules him, and a culture which demands macho behavior, a man is encouraged to deal with his own pain with the same useless platitudes: *Give it to God. . . . Turn it over. . . . Practice acceptance.*

When the AA house of cards tumbled, I could see the abuses against women which were happening right under everyone's nose. In addition to the lost and confused garden variety alcoholic, there were also predators lurking in the rooms. The pressed shirts and crisply pleated slacks couldn't hide it any longer. When my Big Book blinders fell to the ground I could finally see what was going on. I could finally see that the AA gurus were "spiritual leaders" of the TV-evangelist kind rather than the kind-hearted "trusted servants" that they were pretending to be. I could see that these charlatans were actually driven by a thirst for power over their peers rather than true philanthropy. I could also see that they operated from the belief that their status of self-appointed leader entitled them to special privileges with young and naive women. Get 'em while they're hot . . . preferably the same day they get their one-year piece!

I could see how certain men scanned the rooms for naive or severely codependent women in order to exploit them for sex. "Accept the fact that you're powerless" has a very different meaning when administered to a codependent woman with extremely low self-esteem than when it is administered to a bull-headed, arrogant, power-abusing male, the type for whom the AA program was originally written.

I saw the racket the predators were working: Do anything you want to them . . . they will be shamed by the group for reacting with anger. They've been socialized to be "good girls"—to follow the rules. You can have ultimate control over them by convincing them that they need to give up control. Their self-esteem is so low it doesn't matter anyway. Just tell them they're powerless! They'll have to forgive you. The group will shame them if they don't. Their sponsors will tell them they put themselves in that position! To challenge the game, they'll have to challenge AA, and nobody in their right mind would do that!

We all know that the Big Book specifically states:

"Even when a situation was not entirely our fault, we find that somewhere early on, we made a decision based on *self* that placed us in a position to be hurt."

What does this mean? If I had been thinking of the welfare of my group, none of this would have happened? That I can actually control unpredictable events by restricting my life to the scrubbing of coffee urns?

When the wall tumbled I couldn't believe what I was seeing. I spoke out against the 13th-stepping. I told the meeting that in the rooms lurks:

**"Sober Man . . . he's got so much Time in the Program . . .
he comes to the beginners' meeting to S-P-R-E-A-D the good word
of recovery to the young and the newly sober women."**

But I made a grave tactical mistake when I spoke out against 13th stepping: I had anger in my voice! The AA cement that is packed into everyone's ears—another thin layer is added with every meeting —blocks out anything that is delivered with anger. In most cases, the longer one attends, the thicker the layer of cement. I asked to be escorted out of the meeting, and two members did so. They had no clue what I was raving about. One of them told me to remember that *I am my own worst enemy!* Imagine that! Me! I'm the one I should be afraid of! What a frightening way to approach life! If my children are gunned down by hoodlums in the street, if politicians take away my rights, if my doctor abuses his power, assaults me during a routine examination, and the police fail to protect me, I should remember that I am my own worst enemy?!? Like hell I am!

I saw a woman react when I spoke up against the predators. I saw her facial expression change from the usual smile to horror. I called her that night to ask if she had ever run into a predator. The tone in her voice was a dead giveaway: she made a hasty and reactive effort to compare and not identify . . . "Nope . . . nope, not me . . . I never *put myself* in that position." The "nos" were too quick, too defensive. She was hiding something. What could it be? And what could be the message to the predator in such a response? Anyone whom the predator exploits "puts herself" in the position *to be* exploited. It doesn't matter if the predator preys on a newer member's innocence, ignorance, or vulnerability; it's the victim's fault for not being all-knowing and all-seeing. Essentially, for not being God.

Two other women whom I encountered had similar disturbing reactions. One of them offered her phone number because she too had been raped. But the way she dealt with it was by "letting it go" the

AA wave-of-the-hand way. She also mentioned that her artwork reflected a powerful sexual theme. (I learned later in art therapy that this is normal in the case of unresolved trauma, since it cannot be hidden from the subconscious and will come out in dreams, art, creative writing, etc.) Luckily, I knew that this response was not healthy.

Another gal, I learned, had been attacked on her way home from her very first AA meeting. A man had followed her out of the meeting and pushed her into some bushes to do God knows what. Fortunately she was able to get away, but she too "let it go" the AA way, without signs of strong emotion, in accordance with what is modeled in AA. What next? Will armies someday be able to slay our children while we will remain emotionlessly "serene"?

I know today that it will be only a matter of time before their memories come crashing down on these two women. It happens like clockwork, just around the four- or five-year mark. People in step groups who are hiding abuse issues suddenly find themselves feeling crazy, severely depressed, or suicidal.

I can see why AA members don't want to acknowledge this. It's hard to do so in a weakened state, and reality is quite frightening when we stop "keeping it simple" for a moment and really take a long hard look at the bigger picture. AAs are discouraged from probing into the mechanics of the program anyway:

"Utilize, don't analyze!"
"Keep it simple, stupid!"
"Resign from the debating society."
"Your thinking is stinking."

Acknowledging abuse problems shatters the illusion that finally, in AA, we have found a safe place. People are so desperate to find a safe place at last that they delude themselves into believing that they have. It is precisely because of this delusion that AA is decidedly unsafe. Until people start looking at these problems and taking action, the predators will have the power in the rooms. The existing message *which the women reinforce with their "by the book" responses* acknowledges that men hunt down women, and that women must simply *accept it.*

"Nothing happens by mistake in God's perfect world."

This is why predators continue to revel in their remorseless exploitations.

It took a long time and a lot of therapy to be able to write this down. When I told my last sponsor that I felt I must speak out, she exclaimed that I should do no such thing! She said, *We can't reveal this story to the newcomer!* This is a very revealing statement. It is exactly this lack of willingness to expose the dangers within AA that makes AA such a dangerous place. Reporting these facts is not an attempt to dismantle the institution of AA. It is simply a way of cleansing it of some of its vermin. Personally, I've had enough of hiding. I don't think that the newcomer is helped by hiding this information. I knew when I heard my last sponsor's stern attempt to silence me that it was my cue to speak.

This is a piece of my life. I've cried a bucket full of tears over this. When I first wrote down my story, I sent it to *The Grapevine*. The original version had a gung-ho, pro-AA message about women not turning it over and empowering each other. But *The Grapevine* returned my story with a form letter saying they didn't have enough room in their publication for it.

When I left the last meeting I attended, I told everyone that I would write a book. Well, I may not have written an entire book, but I did write this story. I went onto the Internet to find someone I could speak to, and amazingly ran into a woman in cyberspace who was collecting AA horror stories of misery, betrayal, and abuse. I certainly had one. Apparently so did many others. I hope this helps someone out there.

If you are reading this and you are an AA member who loves the fellowship, please use this information to help others. Not all groups are bad, and I believe in the people who make up the program. Many women who have rape in their history end up leaving AA. It's too much work to re-educate the world, and rape just doesn't fit well into the AA belief system. For this reason, there are few women to catch the newer women when they begin reliving the pain.

I believe that many in AA are hiding horrible pain and trauma, and are using the meetings as an artificial boost to get them through the day. I also believe that AA uses thought reform to steer its members in that direction. The problem isn't members' foolishness or lack of willingness. AA is a machine which promotes repression, denial, and escape through "spirituality." It encourages members to fit their lives into the AA myth. The myth is that we drank because we were selfish and self-centered. (Says who?) That we need a moral inventory. (Some do, some don't.) That we must abandon the self. (Whatever that means—sounds like the ultimate form of self-hatred to me)

The real answers lie in the truth and not some artificially implanted myth. Most people simply don't have an awareness of what mind control is, and how powerful it can be. (Read up on cults and mind-control. You'll be amazed at the similarities to AA!) I showed my story to a couple of friends who are still in AA. One of them said "Nope . . . nope . . . sorry you were raped; this has nothing to do with the program." Most of them don't speak to me anymore because I don't go to meetings, and because I am speaking out against the injustices I found. Think again if you believe I'm exaggerating the power of the programming in AA. It's called a "program" for a reason. It's like new software loaded onto the hard drive of your brain, overwriting what was there.

Why are so many AA members marching in line in this strange parade of lemmings? First, abject loneliness and a hunger for social contact in a world in which community and family is disintegrating contribute to the success of AA. Second, so much in our society encourages and rewards individuals for obedience and compliance. Child rearing, education, and workplace dynamics all have strong elements of this. Throw fear into the mix, and reward "faith" in the form of unquestioned obedience, and you have a huge, fear-powered recovery machine which possesses the characteristics of a totalist movement.

"The movement has all the answers."
"Everything you need to know is in the Big Book."
"We have the monopoly on the truth. "

The bottom line is this: In order for the love-starved newcomer to receive peer approval, s/he must "work the program." The more the member employs a totalist approach to the program in her life, the more she works the program in *all areas* of her life, the more she is seen as working a *good* program. Crimes such as rape simply cannot be defined within this totalist approach. It is not possible to blame someone else for our pain while simultaneously applying the AA theology in a totalist fashion. It is not possible to experience anger, rage, and indignation (the healthy responses to rape and similar transgressions) while simultaneously applying the AA theology in a totalist fashion. The Program Code simply does not allow it. Challenging the Program Code is heresy, and it often results in peer rejection—something the desperate newcomer cannot afford. For these reasons, rape, exploitation, and similar abuses *do* happen within the AA subculture and the perpetrators of such transgressions are often able to hide behind the *Program Code*, e.g., "she put herself in that position." I find this extremely frightening.

Care should be taken by current or would-be predators, because this logic may be used in reverse. The predator should keep in mind, that somewhere, sometime, one of his conquests (even if she is a newcomer) may have the blood of Lorena Bobbitt surging through her veins. Even if hunting down newcomers seems like a safe pastime, and even if the rooms of AA appear to be a consequence-free rape safety zone for predators, there are women within the fellowship who have had enough of that kind of treatment. And if just such a woman should become possessed by the Spirit of Lorena, it will be the predator who will be left to his own twisted theology in order to cope with his feelings:

"I am grateful that at least my testicles are still attached to my body" doesn't look so good on the ol' gratitude list, does it Mr. Predator?

In summary, I do not think that the various women who reacted to my story in the disturbing ways that they did, did so out of malevolence. I simply feel that they were looking for the answers within the theology of the AA program. The ritual of daily meetings makes for *very intense* indoctrination. It is hard to remain rational when a singular belief system, especially one which is as problematic as the one espoused by AA, is thought of as the be-all and end-all of how we should define reality.

If you are an AA member who is suffering while trying to work the program but are finding no real relief, you may try *not* working the program to see if it helps. It helped me. I have parted ways with that dreadful organization, am staying sober just fine, thank you very much, and, most important, my self-esteem has soared.

The lessons that I learned from this multi-year ordeal are as follows: 1) If the rules seem ludicrous or harmful, don't follow them. (Remember, tens of thousands of Germans participated in the extermination of millions of Jews, and none of them felt personally responsible; after all, they were just following orders—i.e., *obeying the rules.*); 2) My brain is my best friend, and not my worst enemy—no one has the right or authority to interpret reality for me; 3) I should never, ever, ever go against my gut feelings, even if a great many people or revered institutions encourage it (and they will). The messages from deep within are my survival instincts. To ignore them is insanity.

3 ▲ Mr. Texas
Bait & Switch

Sometime last spring, I was finally able to convince myself that I was an alcoholic and had to do something about it. I had no idea what treatment centers were like. Also, I had never had any dealings with AA.

I checked myself into a local treatment center, with my insurance paying for the excursion. The center was self-contained, with doctors and nurses on board. A package deal. However, as I was soon to find out, it also doubles as a mental health facility. There was no room in the alcoholic unit, so they put me in the mental care unit. I stayed there for two days. Finally, I was moved in with the drunks and druggies.

The center was a very loose operation. You could go to meetings, or not. You had free access to the whole campus. You could leave if you so wished, but I had no intention of leaving. Not until after I attended about six AA meetings.

I soon found out that the folks who run these places preach a bunch of garbage with little, if any, facts to back it up. For instance, I heard *if you surrender your heart and soul to God,* He, I guess, would cure you of this awful sickness. I also soon found out that the folks in the audience were not prime examples of this surrender they talked about. I had never heard so much cursing, vulgar language, threats and damnation from one single group of people. One of the classes I went to was devoted to sex, with rubber play toys to enhance the presentations.

The doctor I was assigned to looked, talked, and acted like he needed to look in the mirror. The director of treatment was an old, very hateful and sarcastic Ph.D. Many, many times he left people in tears. I would not put up with it. I pulled him aside one night and told him I was going to put the biggest Texas ass whupping on him he had ever seen. Boy, do they believe in drugs! Fill you up on a moment's notice.

My counselor had never had a drink in her life. And she was trying to stuff all this Big Book, 12-step holiness down my throat. I stayed maybe six days. When I walked out the door, I stopped at the nearest bar and had a few drinks. Five grand down the tubes and still a drunk. Thanks, AA.

The next place I checked myself into was a pre-packaged deal also. I went through the yellow pages calling drug treatment places at random. If you have good insurance or a huge credit limit on your VISA, and pay in advance of course, then you are in the door. This was a total lockdown facility, which I did not realize until the door was closed. It was an AA preaching facility, which I knew up front. I figured I'd gotten a bunch of loonies at the other place, and that this one would be OK. Wow, was I wrong! They searched every bit of my luggage, including personal belongings. They strip-searched me. Several items were confiscated, including my cell phone. They also searched my wife's purse. The AA people at this place were three times as loony as those at the other place. God this, Jesus that, Holy Spirit this *and* that, higher beings all over the place. We were totally locked down to one wing. They even took shoe laces out of people's shoes. If we had to go outside the ward, for food for instance, we were escorted by guards. But there were very few meetings, for which I was thankful. The most fun we had was playing volleyball in the gym, under the watchful eyes of two guards. I lasted two days at this place. I had to leave, or I was going to get into trouble. And believe me when I say that I did not want, and still do not want, to be in a Texas prison. Four grand gone this time. Thanks, AA.

My third and most recent try was a resort-type lodge setting in the Texas hill country. Damn, was that salesman good! My dumb butt did it all over again. Except this time it was 300 miles from home. The salesman said this place was the Betty Ford of Texas, only better. He said it was in a beautiful setting and that nothing would be forced down my throat. This guy should sell used cars. At check-in, everything I brought was searched, and I was strip-searched. I soon found out this place was 100% pure AA. They had meetings eleven hours a day. You had a set schedule and had to carry a punch card. We were preached hell and damnation (jails, institutions, and death) twelve to fourteen hours a day. When I resisted, I was brought in for counseling. They did bed and spot checks, and would call the guards if you were not in your bed—note, I said *bed* not *room*—at curfew. You were required to be in bed with the lights out.

As this center was coed, there were, of course, flings and romances. And boy did the staff *not* like that! You could get kicked out for it, no less. Most thought this was dumb. Hell, if you are a consenting adult paying fifteen grand a month, it ought to be your choice to have a romance.

The meetings were so religious in nature that I walked out on many of them. We were required to stand in a circle, hold hands, and say the Lord's Prayer. I stopped doing that also. The intern counselors would try to trick us by saying the meetings were spiritual, not religious. This did not work on me. I am an engineer, and you have to have your act together or I will put the cards on the table and call you a dumb ass. The staff did not like this at all.

Thanksgiving night, the AA chapter in a nearby small town was there to present a meeting. At this meeting there was a raging war going on between the visiting AA loonies and the local AA loonies. I sat back and laughed so hard it hurt. They almost came to blows. It was the best time I had there.

Later that evening there was another meeting at a place called the "Bell." People go there and leave mementos—mainly, religious memoirs. It is, indeed, a gorgeous place. They immediately announced, *no pairing off.* I assume the jailers would put us on lockdown for talking to a member of the opposite sex. Then the praying and story-telling started. And these upright Christians almost got into another fight. I left and was accosted by a guard, who, when I told him about my Texas ass whuppings, backed off. I left the center the next day and just dared anyone, and I meant anyone, to stand in my way. Fifteen grand gone. Thanks, AA.

Now I am at a stage where I really couldn't care less. Had AA and their cronies tried to fix me rather than preach at me, perhaps one of these treatments would have worked. Maybe, maybe not. But I place the blame squarely on the arrogant program of AA.

Of course, I take full responsibility for my drinking. No one held me down and made me drink. That's my own decision, and my own failure. But I believe in playing the ball where it lays. I do not care about all this religious crap. I am not paying you a grand a day to convert me. Hell, I can turn on Sunday morning TV for that—and it's free. Would my outcome have been different without all the crap? I don't know, because I didn't have the chance to find out.

Here is a letter I wrote to one of the treatment centers:

Mr. Thaddeus Rattnut
Administrator
Hope Mountain Center
Sassafrass, Texas

Dear Mr. Rattnut:

This is in reference to my abbreviated stay in November 1998.

As I do for my employees, I will give you and your center a per-
formance evaluation. Do with it as you wish. It is not meant to be
either critical or helpful. It is just fact. Use this as toilet paper, line
your cabinets, or maybe even take it as constructive. Whichever, rest
assured I could not care less.

In descending order, here are the reasons I left your center:

1) The endless pounding of religion. God, Jesus, and a higher power.
Every other word that came out of faculty's mouths tried to slam this
into me. An immediate turn-off. I was there to receive help with my
drinking problem, not go to a series of church revivals.

2) Prison-like conditions. For $15,000 a month, I could stay at the San
Francisco Airport Hilton and live like a king. They would even bring
in a preacher if I so desired. Hell, they would bring in AA if I wanted.
Your accommodations from the outside look fantastic. From the
inside they are in shambles. Bare bones living. The telephone is not
really a telephone, bed checks, search and seizure of personal belongings, screening of mail, screening of telephone messages, restricted telephone use, and Gestapo-like raids. Also, brainwashed (or
brain-dead) counselors. If there is a God, these guys and gals think
they are him, and they are giving him a bad name.

3) I have not been treated like your place treated me since the
military. However, an extended trip to Nam put me in my place. I
came out alive, and there ain't anyone going to act like god to me
again. I mean, *ever!*

4) I was amused by your policy of non-fixation with the other sex.
This, in my opinion, is stupid. If both are consenting adults paying

$15,000 a month to park their butts at your place, exactly who cares? Although I did not participate, I assure you your prison did not prevent this from happening. Happened all the time. We are animals, Rattnut—live with it.

5) Restricted to post: Since when do I have to ask, or even report to someone, to leave the premises? Remember, *I* was paying *you*. Not the other way around. My wife of 41 years came to visit the Friday after Thanksgiving, and a group of three counselors told me that I could leave for only an hour or so. I told them: *Guys, let me rephrase. I am leaving for the weekend. Any questions?* You see, Mr. Rattnut, I paid *you*. When you pay me, I will do as you say.

6) We—my wife and myself—were not aware of the Gestapo prison-like conditions. If we had been aware of them, I would not have come.

I think the Big Book is a crock of crap written around the turn of the century. I also think AA is a crock of crap. A bunch of people telling other folks their sob stories, and no one could care less. Perhaps, just perhaps, someone will come up with a rational treatment plan that does not hit you up side the head with Southern Baptist God, Jesus, Holy Ghost, and higher beings. As one of the inmates, believe me when I tell you most of the others did not believe any of this junk.

You nursing staff was the best part of a lousy wasted two weeks.

Mr. Texas

––––––––––––––––––

Later down the road I went to a shrink MD thinking he might be able to help me with this booze problem. After all, that *is* his speciality. He told me, and I quote: *You must get religion and let God take care of your life. Then go to AA and let them guide you.* Honest injun, that's what this moron said. I am an atheist. That is like asking a Baptist to become Catholic. Just ain't gonna happen.

In my opinion, AA is one sorry organization, nothing more than a bunch of religious bigots.

4 ▲ Nancy

My Dad, Abused in Treatment

My very first experience with alcoholism treatment and 12-step programs was frightening and intrusive. Today, I would have the confidence to speak up immediately against the verbal and emotional abuse I witnessed. But at age 21, I had not yet learned to trust my own judgment in the face of disapproval. I was afraid of my own feelings, my own anger, and I think it's that very quality which allows the treatment industry to roll over so many people.

My father had been in treatment for alcoholism at a VA hospital. The year was 1975. Several of our large family—I, my mother, my sister and her husband, and three of my brothers, loaded into mom's station wagon and we drove to the West Coast town where the VA hospital was to visit Dad.

Zoomers was what Dad called the mentally ill patients who were housed near the alcoholism treatment wing of the hospital. Some walked up and down the concrete paths. You could tell they were zoomers because of the way, due to medications, they paced, heads down, traveling the walks. They wore orange, foam-rubber slippers. I would glance here and there, anywhere but at their faces. Although Dad was not a zoomer, I would feel, by the end of the day, that they might be receiving infinitely better treatment than an "alcoholic" would in that hospital.

I don't remember much about the lunch we had in the cafeteria, except that we were hungry, and talk seemed different with Dad sober. He didn't talk very much.

After lunch, we had to hurry back to the ward with Dad, because there would be a meeting, a *family group*. He had invited us here at this particular time specifically for that group. Immediately, I was nervous. I did not like the idea of sitting in a group of strangers and talking. What would we talk about? Dad? How could we sit and talk about Dad with strangers? I told Dad I'd go, but that I did not want to talk. He said that would be okay; we didn't have to say anything.

We were herded into a sunny day room. There was a wall with windows open to the spring day, and there were a few bookshelves lined with paperback novels and hardcover books with titles that sounded religious. On the wall were charts; some looked like chore lists, and others discussed "alcoholism." About 30 folding chairs had been placed in a huge circle, and the chairs were soon filled with a motley assortment of folks, some of whom Dad had already described to us. There weren't enough chairs, so more were brought in. Folks settled in. The energy of the room was frenetic. I would come to recognize that energy in later treks in and out of such rooms. (In fact, in the recovery subculture, such gatherings are called *the rooms*.)

The facilitator of the group, a man in his thirties I'll call "Rollin," sported a clipboard and intense, quick eyes. I had never been in a therapy group. I did not realize what was happening was *attack therapy* until Rollin and the others began to *attack* people.

He'd start out asking a person how he or she was doing. If she said "fine," or words to that effect, Rollin would say *bullshit!* and then the attack would begin. The word *bullshit* flew about the room quite often, along with defensive explanations, angry diatribes, tears, and much melodrama. I became petrified, because it was apparent that Rollin picked people for group focus out of the blue, and that to say you were okay was the wrong answer. My mind quickly began to search for something I could say was wrong with my life that would be okay to tell these people. The fact was, I worried about whether my own drinking was abnormal, but no way would I say that in this verbally abusive situation.

Besides, I was not drinking at the time, was going to community college, making good grades, dating a nice guy, and really did feel fine most of the time. But now I felt hot, close, sweaty, and embarrassed to be there and see Dad there. Rollin, and then some of the others, began to yell at one man in particular.

"Bill" had been sent to the VA alcohol program while awaiting sentencing for manslaughter. He had been drinking and driving, and had killed an innocent person. He said he could not remember the accident. *Bullshit!*, Rollin nearly screamed, a lock of brown hair flipping over his eye. *That's pure bullshit! You remember—admit it! You remember everything about that accident—admit it!* Bill's head was hung. Others joined in. I was reminded of the flock of chickens which we had while I grew up. When chickens are under stress, and one of them gets hurt, the rest move in and peck it to death.

While Bill was being verbally pummeled for not remembering the accident he caused while driving drunk, I realized that, according to the information about "alcoholism" hanging right there on the wall, *blackouts,* in which the alcoholic has no memory of events taking place while drinking, were supposed to be common occurrences. Why did they not believe him? I did. I wanted to speak up and defend him. But suddenly that felt unseemly. After all, he had killed someone. Yet the death surely was an accident. Was alcoholism a disease or a willful behavior? If Bill had a *disease* in which *blackouts* were common, why were they yelling at him?

I was confused and frightened. I decided I did not know enough about what was going on, so I said nothing. Later my dad told me he didn't think Bill remembered anything about the accident either, but that *attack therapy* consisted of *tough love* designed to crush people's *egos.* It was *big egos,* he said, that stood in the way of alcoholic recovery.

They harangued Bill for quite awhile, then Rollin continued around the room. Folks' personal thoughts, feelings, and lives were pried into, and the accusation *bullshit* flew freely.

I knew this behavior was all wrong, but I didn't know why. Years later, I would understand that my fear and discomfort were correct, healthy emotional responses to the intrusive verbal abuse known in the recovery subculture as *tough love.* In that group, and in many alcoholism/addiction treatment centers, as well as 12-step groups, people's emotional or ego boundaries are deliberately violated in the name of *tough love.*

I had, at that time, fairly good boundaries. But over the next few years at AA meetings I would be taught that my own judgment was not to be trusted, and that if I wanted to stay sober and not end up like my dad, I would need to be *rigorously honest* and confess my *character defects,* which included *anger, dishonesty,* and *fear.* "Dishonesty," besides lying and cheating, means failing to admit to group members personal weaknesses and failing to reveal family information. Not only would my own healthy boundaries be torn down, but I would join in tearing at the boundaries of others.

Rollin's eye finally landed on me. He asked questions about my dad. How did I feel about Dad? Wasn't I angry? Rollin's eyes flashed fanatically. He looked intelligent and scary, as if he really did know everyone's deepest secrets, and was only asking to test your *honesty.* Problem is, I didn't have any feelings concerning Dad that I wanted to talk about there, right in front of them and him.

Nervously, my eyes darted to my brother, Mike. Rollin noticed. He took a new tack. *I see you glance at your younger brother often. Are you worried about him?* Smiling, trying to be pleasant, I felt myself turning red. I wasn't worried about Mike; I'd just needed a familiar person to look at, and Mike was nearby.

Yes, I guess I do worry about him.

Why? pried Rollin

I felt about for words, terrified. I'm sure my voice shook. *I . . . when I agreed to sit here, I really didn't know what this was. I'm sorry, but I would rather just listen and not talk,* I finally burbled.

Rollin nodded. Then, he excused me and my whole family, including Dad, from the group. It was done in a supercilious way, which I would later come to call the Recovery Dismissal: *Well, we certainly wouldn't want to interfere with your day. Recovery is for those who want it. Have a nice visit.*

I left that room knowing those people thought there was something terribly wrong with us just because we were part of Dad's family. Whatever that might be, I had no inkling. I thought we were as good as anyone else.

Upstairs, Dad showed us where he bunked with several others. The room was like one in any other hospital ward, with six narrow bunks, though a little warmer perhaps, because the people who lived there weren't really sick (or were they?) and had the time and energy to decorate the walls and to enjoy little pillows, afghans, and photos from home, as well as their own clothes.

Some, however, were required to wear orange uniforms as punishment for infractions, such as running away, refusing to do their KP duties, or not showing up at the scheduled meetings. Other punishments included shaved heads. I noticed one woman in the group whose head was shaved, and she wore an orange uniform. Dad told us she had fled the ward, gone downtown, and gotten drunk. She was not allowed back unless she submitted to having her head shaved.

I asked Dad if they ever did anything like that to him. He said that the first two weeks he was there he was required to wear a sign around his neck, scrawled with the words *I'm Important.* Because he had once held highly responsible jobs as a hospital administrator and served on local school boards, the counselors decided that wearing such a sign would be the best way to attack his ego. I got angry.

You know what, Dad? This place is awful! You should get out of here. You should come with us right now! These people are crazy!

But Dad wouldn't come. He had lost everything and would have needed to live with one of his grown kids until he got on his feet. In his mind, he was better off getting back on his feet in the VA program, and making a new life without becoming a burden to us.

I left there with the distinct impression that for all their big talk about *recovery,* such treatment centers provide little more than humiliation for drunks.

5 ▲ Kevin Yriondo
A Saga of Real Honesty

My first experience with drug treatment came early in life. I went through high school using drugs moderately, for the most part, sometimes every day, other times not at all. My grades fluctuated, but not necessarily because of my drug use; I lacked interest in school as well.

When I was 19 years old I met a girl who liked using cocaine intravenously. So I probably used cocaine intravenously 30 or 40 times—not occasions, but doses, rather. However, I realized this had an addictive hold on me, and I didn't think that was right, so I asked my parents if I could talk to them—not that I have a close family. They were kind of stunned that I wanted to talk to them both at the same time. I told them that I had a problem and I wanted to do something about it.

My parents decided they would go see what help was available. They ended up speaking to the people who were running a therapeutic community—one of these programs that last two years. These people convinced them that unless I attended this program I was doomed, as they say in 12-step programs, to "jails, institutions, or death." They told my parents they needed to give me an ultimatum —get out of the house or go to this two-year program.

Out of the house seemed a lot more attractive at the time, so I left my home and lived at friends' houses for awhile. When I got tired of that, I took a car that didn't belong to me and went back to my home town in Mississippi. While down there, I got arrested for the stolen car and put in jail.

Meantime, my mom had talked to folks at another program that seemed a little more mellow—they said I would only have to stay in that program for two weeks. They didn't have a max. The program was called Notsostraight, Inc.

Unfortunately, that's where I went. When I got in there, these people held me by the belt loop in a big room filled with people. This was for confrontational "therapy" where newcomers had to get in front of a group of about 120 people. One by one, these folks raised their hands, and when they were called on, they screamed at you in front of the other people—they got right in your face. After about four hours of this, your face is covered with spit. Victims got extremely mad or broke down crying. Most of them broke down crying.

I realized that after you release all these emotions, that's your weakest and most vulnerable time, a time they then use to start brainwashing you. They break you down to the point where you don't know what's going on anymore—you're totally malleable.

So I decided I wasn't going to break down. I decided I'd try to treat it like a bad acid trip. I was watching what was happening to all these new people, and thinking, *wow, this is really weird, this couldn't really be happening*. I tried to think of it that way, since I knew what their intent was.

So after they got done with me, the counselor, because I didn't cry, etc., asked what I had to say for myself. I told him I was an adult, I was over 18, I didn't want to be there anymore, and that he had a legal and moral obligation to release me. So he starts talking all this shit. He told that group of about 120 people, *You know what this guy did? He stole a car, and got caught. He can't do* shit *right*. The counselor kept it up, trying to humiliate me in front of all those people.

I didn't show that bothered me—I just sat there smiling. Then he asked the people holding me to move back. He asked if I wanted to hit him. I said *No, I don't want to hit you. I want to leave*. He kept pressing the issue, kept asking if I wanted to hit him. Well, it was true that by that time, I did want to hit him. So I did hit him, and broke his nose. They jumped on me, and as a result, years later, I still have a knot on my forehead, which had crashed on the hard floor.

And they wouldn't let me out of there.

Four days later I stole a pair of scissors. I broke the scissors in half, so I had a pointed piece and a curved piece. They had the doors barricaded with mattresses and so forth, and bars on the windows so people couldn't get out. But I got out.

On the way to the parking lot, I was accosted by one of them. I had to put the scissors up to his throat. It even drew a little blood—not a lot of bleeding, not bad. When they saw how serious I was, they let me out of there. They didn't call the police or anything, because they knew they were wrong to start with. I was justified in whatever I had to do to get out of there. I was an adult being detained illegally.

I got in a little more trouble after that. My troubles, in fact, persisted for another two years. Eventually, I was arrested in Alexandria, Virginia, for possession of cocaine with intent to distribute. This made the *Washington Post* as well as the *Fairfax Journal*. I got arrested with a sizable quantity of cocaine and $18,000 dollars. I was sentenced to 18 years in the penitentiary.

I went to Virginia state pen. During my years in prison, I became extremely good at prison legal work. As a result, I got out after six years. Also, I had no drug problem by then. I had not used drugs the whole time I was in prison—no AA, no NA, just didn't use. While in prison, I had been forced to go to AA and NA, but I didn't like it. I told them I thought it was cult-like, and it wasn't for me, and because of my own religious preferences I did not think it was right for them to force a male monotheistic God or any other religious structure on me. So I was barred from those meetings for speaking my mind.

I was clean all on my own when released from prison. I did well, bought a house, and got married to my former prison counselor.

During mid-1984 I got depressed, which had actually been my problem all along. I now take antidepressants, but at that time I didn't know what I needed. So I got very depressed, and whenever I got depressed, I'd want to use drugs. The options would sort of narrow down for me—take drugs to numb the pain, or commit suicide. When I was depressed like that, the drugs would seem the lesser of two evils. It's not that I was attracted to drugs or that my life was centered around drugs—I just didn't know what else to do. It wasn't an ingrained behavior—it was just an option. And I had access, through someone I knew, to a lot of opiates.

I started using opiates. Eventually, I forged several prescriptions and got caught in Bay County, Florida. I got caught by the pharmacist, but I knew a warrant would be issued eventually. I told my wife, who did not handle it very well, which I can understand. I told her I had to get out of town.

So I flew to Amsterdam from New Orleans, and from there to Berlin, then to Zurich. At the time my wife was a juvenile probation officer in Florida, so she could check if there were any warrants for my arrest. There weren't any.

So, I flew back to the good old U.S. Within a week, the police called my wife's workplace, my workplace, and our home looking for me. So I departed again. This time I was going to Spain, but I had a layover in Mexico City. My parents talked me into staying there, then taking a bus to San Miguel to see a therapist some relatives knew. He told me he couldn't help me, that I was as close to hopeless as a person could get. I was very addicted to narcotics at that time, to an extreme that most addicts in NA with their little drugalogues never get to, because they rarely have the unlimited access to drugs I had.

Have you heard of fentanyl? It's anywhere from 200 to 1000 times stronger than heroin, depending on the variety. They don't make pills with it—they've got a lollypop now and patches for terminal cancer patients and so forth. It's undetectable—you can't get caught by a urine test. So I was wearing my 400 mcg patches of fentanyl, and getting 80 mg of methadone a day, and shooting dope. I was doing really bad.

My wife made arrangements for me to go into XYZ Clinic, in a university hospital. They detoxed me there. There's a famous doctor there who holds the patents on two prescription drugs. He detoxed me. No 12-step nonsense. I could sign out and leave if I wanted.

I got caught drinking beer there. I had brought two cans of beer back in my coat, and the maid found the empties in my room. The doctor called me in. *Hey Kevin, were you drinking beer in your room?* I admitted it. He then asked, *How many did you have?* I said *two*. He asked me how I felt after two. I told him *fine, a little more relaxed.* Then he said, *well, that doesn't sound like alcohol abuse to me.*

XYZ Clinic is also where I learned that my drug problems were rooted in depression, which is, of course, treatable.

However, the law wasn't through with me. After the arrest on the prescription forgery charges, I went to jail for six months. The probation people then ordered me into a six-month drug treatment program called "Clinton." It was run by a company called Doesn't Work Programs, Inc. They get state contracts for drug treatment. The whole thing is based on 12-step nonsense. So from the time I went in, I was, because of my opinion of the 12 steps, public enemy #1. From the beginning I had a hard time in there.

They told me I had to call myself an addict, or I would be kicked out. I didn't want to be dishonest in that way, and I didn't feel like I should say this as long as I wasn't using addictive drugs. But then I realized I could probably say I was honestly addicted to nose spray, since I needed to use it constantly to keep my sinuses from getting swollen and my nose from running all the time. So I figured, *well, I'm addicted to nasal spray, so I can honestly say I'm an addict.* I would go through mental gymnastics like that so I could feel like I was being honest with these people and still be able to stay in the program and avoid going back to jail.

Verbal abuse in Clinton was very common. They had unbridled discretion to discharge anyone, which, since they relied on probationers to fill their beds, gave them god-like power over their patients. This was an excellent set-up for Nazi-like rule enforcement, since discharge for any probationer meant prison for that person. They could get away with forcing obedience to a lot of very stupid rules, and could inflict a lot of emotional abuse. Anyone who spoke out against their 12-step program who hadn't the ability (unlike me) to file a lawsuit could easily be discharged. Selective enforcement of rules was a tool they frequently used to discriminate against people who spoke out against 12-step orthodoxy, or refused to follow it.

On one occasion a counselor at Clinton asked me what I thought of the program so far. I told him I thought AA and the 12 steps were fine for someone who just needed to blindly follow a religion or a superstitious doctrine, but that I thought most people needed something other than that, and that they should be allowed to choose other approaches. I was making this speech, and the program director came in and started raging at me. She had totally misinterpreted me. I was promoting tolerance, but she kept raging. I said, *Excuse me, but since you're interrupting me, can I interrupt you for a minute? You've managed to not only interrupt me, but misinterpret me, which takes a real talent.* After that she didn't like me at all.

I had one problem after another like that. Anything I said like that, even joking, would become a gigantic issue at Clinton. Once I joked that maybe if Bill W. was born in a manger on Christmas, the wise men would bring him coffee, cigarettes, and literature, and oh they blew a hole about that.* Then I made a fake flyer for the *Billapallooza* concert, with the band *Serenity* playing their hit, *Think, Think, Think,* and I put it on the bulletin board. Oh, they raged about that, too. These things were jokes—if there's no humor in the way you live your life, you've got to rearrange something. But they didn't understand; they thought I was making light of this serious, serious issue. When they kept talking about this disease, I'd say, *Look, there's no disease cured by drinking coffee and talking in a smoky church basement.*

If this were a viable modality of treatment for anyone who was sick,

---

* Bill W., the revered co-founder of AA, was severely addicted to tobacco. He continued smoking even after he began suffering from emphysema and eventually died from the disease. And coffee-drinking, is, or course, endemic at AA meetings.

I'd send them to a church basement, give them 25 cigarettes, and talk to them—they'd get better, right? I'd tell them, *What it is, you guys have a social support network, and the problem with that social support network is that you encourage each other to stay sick.*

I went through the program, but I ended up threatening to start a lawsuit against them for violating the Establishment Clause of the U.S. Constitution's First Amendment by forcing me to go to these 12-step meetings and hear this religious nonsense. So they exempted me from going to outside meetings, but when I got out the probation department insisted I still go to two meetings a week.

I went to the meetings, but they were horrible. The people didn't like me to start with, because they'd met me while they had been doing H & I (Hospital and Institutions Service) at the inpatient meetings while I was inside the drug rehab. They already knew I would speak my mind. I'd tell them I was only trying to grow up, to find things in my life that were more appealing than drugs to fill the void, rather than this artificial social circle they'd formed in meetings. All a 12-step group really is is a social club that's made for the socially inept, the maladjusted, and the perpetually needy. As long as you're sitting in that social circle and looking to it for the answer to your problems, you're going to stay sick the rest of your life. They did not like that I said that.

By this time, I'd been clean for two years, but still had to go to these meetings. The people I had to listen to were so miserable. It was just one diatribe after another about how horrible their days were. Half of them in there have to create a crisis in order to have something to talk about at the meeting. If you're too happy at the meeting, you're not honest, and if you bitch too much you're on your pity pot.

I'd hear young women at the meeting say, *oh, and my boyfriend said this and this today, but I thought "using is not an option," and I decided I would just let it go and let God.* I'm thinking, *Didn't I just hear this last week? Wasn't it just last week that your mother said something you felt like using over? And you let it go and let God?* It's the same fucking shit, week after week. And they don't learn, because they are trained to think they are going to want to use, and to be needy.

I got really sick of being subjected to that. That's why, once I got off probation, I decided that since I had to have this dogma shoved down my throat week after week, that AA and NA would have to listen to what I had to say about it for an equal amount of time. That's justice. That's why you're reading this now.

6 ▲ Lani

Harmony Home Treatment Center: Punishment for Drunks

When I had been sober in AA for two or three years, I used to go with friends to the nearby treatment center to visit and sponsor some of the clients in AA. This center, besides taking private paying clients, was also county funded. Folks were sent there to undergo alcohol and addiction treatment in lieu of jail, and homeless folks and the poor were charged nominal fees that could be paid off over time. After awhile, I became so disillusioned with the treatment given there that I began to call the center *Hardheart Home.*

Whenever treatment centers are criticized, AA members will often make the excuse that treatment centers are "not AA," and that treatment centers give AA a bad name. I didn't see much difference between AA and Harmony Home. The clients were required to go to AA meetings; they were bused to meetings; they were picked up and driven by sponsors to AA and NA meetings; and one of the biggest meetings in town was held right there at Harmony Home every Sunday night. In addition, clients were encouraged, and some required, to work the first five steps of the 12-step program before leaving the center. AA and NA literature was distributed at the center, and if all that wasn't enough, every single counselor who worked at Harmony Home was an AA or NA member. Officially, they are supposed to be anonymous. I knew they were members, however, and so did everyone else, because we saw them at meetings all the time.

("Anonymity" is why it is so hard to get statistics on how many certified alcohol/drug counselors who work in publicly funded detoxes and treatment centers are also AA or NA members. Because of "anonymity," even states and counties that employ these people do not keep track of AA/NA affiliation.)

The counselors at Harmony Home happened to be among my least favorite AA members. I have never particularly liked most alcohol/drug counselors, although today a couple of my best friends are such counselors. But it seems like the meanest, bossiest, most demanding, angry, and verbally abusive people in AA often gravitate to this kind of career. I realize this statement can be supported only by anecdotal evidence, and a thousand alcohol/drug counselors will probably complain about what is written here, but listen to this roster of the counselors at Harmony Home:

P. Jane: She was the director of Harmony Home during part of the time I visited and sponsored women there. Jane's fashion style at AA meetings, as a university-town AA woman with "good recovery," was loose, unstyled hair, either tennies or plain leather sandals, with pants or shorts, and no makeup on an unsmiling, serious face.

During Jane's reign as director of the center, an especially strict rule against sex was enforced. One day, while visiting with my sponsee, Darcy, at Harmony Home, I noticed that she would not talk to men. Later, I found out why—she had been caught by other clients having sex with one of her male visitors.

Clients were encouraged to snitch on one another, and Darcy's violation was quickly brought to the attention of P. Jane. Jane invited everyone else into the office to hear about what Darcy did, and *to decide what Darcy's punishment should be.* The group decided that Darcy would not be allowed to talk to any men—visitors or clients, or men at meetings—for a week. Darcy had been sent into treatment by the court. If she didn't like it, she could leave and go to jail.

The *no-talk* punishment was dealt out for other offenses, and could be more severe, with no talk to anyone at all except AA sponsors and counselors. But Darcy's ban was particularly humiliating. *Holy scarlet letter!,* I said to some of my friends. I wondered how these kinds of punishments fit in with any scientific view of alcoholism/addiction treatment. But such punishments were accepted at Harmony Home, and still are in the other unmonitored little kingdoms that counselors like Jane reign in.

Besides the incidents at Harmony Home, P. Jane showed other evidence of being, if not emotionally ill, at least a total jerk. It is quite possible that the 12-step world was the only world in which she was accepted.

When I first met her as a newcomer, I had liked what she'd said at a meeting, and went up to greet her and introduce myself. She totally snubbed me; she looked at me like I was a small turd. I get along with almost all people, and could only think, and not until much later, that she would not speak to me because I wore a dress and makeup, my hair was long and curled, and I smiled.

Some AA women think that smiling and being nice to someone is *people pleasing*, a behavior condemned in the recovery subculture. Where I lived, many women in AA rarely smiled, and in the groups I spent most of my time in, wearing makeup and trying to look nice was also suspect. Often you will hear women with "Time" (years sober) boast that, as pitiful newcomers barely sober, they took great pains to *look great on the outside*. Other women will nod understandingly as the speaker adds, *but I felt rotten on the inside*. In AA, feeling bad means that you do not have *good recovery*. It is the sign of not *having a program* or not *working it*. And at some meetings, maybe because of this kind of socialization, it is popular for women to look unmade-up, perhaps even unkempt. It shows that you *value your sobriety* more than how you look outwardly.

Back to P. Jane. This woman, in charge of many newcomers, sounded very good at meetings. But she did not like newcomers—I heard her say that in a meeting while I was a newcomer. She was being *rigorously honest,* according to AA principles, but I was still new enough to think of it as rudeness. I had problems with many people in AA because of this confusion between *rigorous honesty*, or *tough love*, and just plain rudeness.

Many of the statements one hears in the AA community, which are taken as wisdom, are actually nothing but rudeness, or even hostility. For example, take the popular AA cliche, *keep it simple, stupid.* Can any thinking person not find that cliche offensive? AAs repeat that slogan all the time, as well as others like, *take the cotton out of your ears, and put it in your mouth,* and *if you point a finger, you've got three pointing back at you.* These churlish sayings, which tend to discourage folks from critical thinking, and, especially, from voicing critical thoughts, are considered *wisdom* in the step groups.

Jane, queen of such churl in meetings and at Harmony Home, let it be known that she was an attorney. I soon realized, however, that she had never worked as an attorney while sober. I wondered why not. Being the director of Harmony Home, while a position of power in the 12-step community, did not pay well. And the money P. Jane did make had not been used to pay rent, because, for awhile, she had no place to live. She house sat for friends on extended vacations, and stored her furniture for free in the garages of other AAs. One woman complained to me that Jane had used her small garage for free storage for two years. She asked Jane to come and get the stuff because she needed the space, but Jane acted angry and wouldn't pick up the stuff. I said, *Jane's an asshole. Tell her to come and get it or you're putting it on the street.*

My friend was quite taken aback by my bluntness. It is very rare in 12-step culture to criticize anyone with *Time.* That's why so many of the old-timers get away with incredible screwings. But my hypothesis on P. Jane is mental illness. She lived and acted like a mentally ill or personality-disordered person. But the social structure in the 12-step world is such that mental illness is not easily acknowledged. People who are controlling and who avidly seek power over others are often thought of as *tough sponsors,* which some newcomers are said to *need.* Grouchy, angry, possibly depressed people are seen as *rigorously honest,* and *not people pleasers,* particularly if they have *Time.*

What I would like to know is, why were therapists, courts, and agencies sending vulnerable people in the community to be cared for by P. Jane?

Anyway, enough of Jane. She got so sick of newcomers that she left Harmony Home, and along came Big Jon.

Big Jon: He was well known and liked in local NA, and was considered a *winner* because he had nine years *clean,* which was probably a record for NA in our group. The vast majority of people in the NA meetings I attended didn't stay clean for even a year. Also, Big Jon dressed and talked like a biker, with the key chain hanging heavily from the jeans, the black jackets, the jackboots. This look is popular in NA. But I had never seen him on a motorcycle. In fact, no one knew what Big Jon did for a living. He didn't seem to have a job until he became a counselor at Harmony Home.

One day I arrived at Harmony Home to work with a sponsee. However, the whole house and all the clients were in an uproar. The Harmony Home board and county authorities were coming to inspect the house. Funds had been earmarked for painting and other small renovations, which were not yet finished. All the clients were running about, sawing, painting, hammering, cleaning. They were being utilized to do most of the work. No professionals were being used at all.

I don't understand this, I said to Margaret, my sponsee. (Darcy had long since run away.) *Aren't you supposed to be concentrating on recovery?*

Margaret assured me that participating in improvements to the house was part of *recovery*. I asked her if she could take a break to go through the Big Book points we had discussed in our visit the week before. Margaret went into the noisy, dust-filled din and came back with her Big Book and notes.

We sat outside on folding chairs beneath a big oak tree and sessioned for about 30 minutes, until Big Jon came huffing and barreling out, his key chain rattling. He was quite overweight, and had to belt his jeans under his enormous belly. Keeping his shirts tucked in was impossible, so a bit of butt cleavage always showed.

Hey! he called to Margaret, motioning toward the house with his thumb, *Yer needed in there!*

Margaret said goodbye, got up, and ran in. Margaret was a grown woman, but I was reminded of my teenage years, trying to get a few minutes of communication with a girlfriend who was grounded, caught by her angry dad.

For the next two or three weeks, most of the Harmony Home clients' extra time was taken up with house renovations. During that time, Big Jon mainly sat on his office throne, talking on the phone, settling differences between clients, and grazing from a bag of cookies or chips. He did not like to get up, and he did not like to answer questions from outsiders. Once, I went to his office to inquire about whether Darcy would be back. *She's not here,* said Big Jon, looking up from an enormous sandwich a client had brought him from the Harmony Home kitchen.

I know that, but she's been gone for awhile, and I'm wondering when she'll be back. She did not tell me she was going home, or out for any time at all. (Sometimes clients could leave for family emergencies.)

She's not here, repeated Big Jon.

Can you tell me when she'll be back?, I specifically asked. *No,* he said, his mouth and jowls roiling over a big bite of sandwich.

Later I heard that Big Jon had been kicked out as treasurer of the local NA group for stealing the group treasury. I and others were shocked. Usually those who steal from the treasury are newcomers. I could not understand why Big Jon, who at least had a job, would steal from the NA treasury unless he had started using again and needed the money for drugs.

But he was still collecting chips and was at least officially "clean."

I knew he was into porno video, because he used to borrow frequently from a collection an NA acquaintance had accumulated to entertain cranksters in past drug-dealing days. But even if he'd had to rent videos, surely they were inexpensive enough to preclude stealing from the NA treasury. One can only guess why he did it.

What I would like to know is, do professionals who send vulnerable clients to NA and to treatment centers such as Harmony Home understand that the only criteria for being a 12-step role model or *winner* is not necessarily health, nor even a semblance of it, but, instead, *Time?* Big Jon is but a mild example of this strange phenomenon, this worshipful view that once-addicted teetotalers possess special wisdom which qualifies them to hold positions of power and to guide others.

Yet another such counselor in Harmony Home was Glenda.

Glenda: If she worked at any other job—except perhaps as a prison guard—Glenda would have been fired. She was probably the most consistently unpleasant, disagreeable person I had met within the prior five years. She barked at people, started arguments, yelled at clients, slammed cupboards, frowned, sighed, moaned, and dripped sarcasm. She may have been deeply depressed and in desperate need of medication. I wonder if any board members realized how this employee acted at work. They may not have, unless someone made a complaint, which was unlikely. In the recovery subculture, to criticize anyone means either that you are *angry* and therefore not in possession of good recovery, or you *have three fingers pointing back at you.* In other words, noticing and complaining about Glenda's ugly personality being unsuitable in a treatment environment would mean that something terrible is really wrong with *you.*

Two things that made Glenda dangerous are that she sounded good at AA meetings and also possessed at least seven years of *Time.* So, clearly, in AA she was a *winner.* Because of these things, unsuspecting newcomers often got involved with her.

If I thought a decent percentage of people who stayed at Harmony Home stayed clean or sober, I might not be so critical. Again, this is just anecdotal evidence, but in the two years I made frequent visits to Harmony, I recall only one woman who actually stayed sober awhile, continued attending meetings, and got a job and a place to live after leaving Harmony Home. Out of an entire AA group of 200 in town, there were only two old-timers who said they had graduated from Harmony Home.

Anyway, this roster of Harmony Home employees is not comprehensive, because there's no purpose to that. If you would like to gather your own evidence on the pervasiveness of AA and NA members in treatment facilities, call your local county- or city-funded detox, treatment center, or even general mental health center. Say that you would like to recommend the center to a relative, but first you want to find out how many of the counselors are proficient in 12-step treatment and are NA or AA members themselves. If the person who answers the phone can't tell you, they probably will be able to tell you who can. Try it, and please write, care of the publisher of this book, with the results. They'll forward them to me, and I'd like to know what you find.

7 ▲ Danni

They Said My Pain Was My Fault

I was sober in AA for seven years. I have been drinking on and off for the last two years. I went into AA when I reached a desperate time in my life and it really helped me—for awhile. Then I met a man in AA who was a Big Book thumper. He felt that the answer to my every problem was a verse from the Big Book. But he was also very charming and loving, and I married him.

Almost immediately, the problems began. If I was angry that he came home late, it was because I was "expecting something." If I wanted him to spend the day with the family instead of fishing with his buddies, I was controlling. When I went to AA meetings, the others in AA echoed his response. Whatever went wrong in the marriage, was the result of my not working the *program.*

I never had a right to get angry. If I was angry, I wasn't "working the program." If I thought about the future, I was "projecting" rather than "letting go and letting God." One of his favorites was: *Do you know what your problem is? It's self-centered fear.*

In a deep depression, I went to a doctor who put me on an antidepressant. Although my husband did not criticize me for this, many in AA did. In their eyes I was substituting one drug for another. I heard one man say he'd rather put a bullet in his brain than take an antidepressant. I was in so much pain that I wanted to kill myself. However, the medication helped me tremendously.

But the problems in the marriage deepened. I thought, *Well, he's going to meetings and I'm not, so I must be the problem.* After all, he told me so, and so did AA. But every time I went to a meeting, I would hear a lot of self-deprecating talk.

I needed to be built up, not torn down. My feelings were never validated. If I felt bad, it was because I wasn't working the program. When I had a problem, I was told to turn it over.

During this time, I was also in psychotherapy. I am certainly not averse to looking at changes I need to make within myself. However,

I was always told in AA that if I was upset about something, it was my own fault. I had to change my *stinkin' thinkin'* and pray for the person who injured me. Even if they abused me, lied to me, and mistreated me, *I* had to forgive.

In therapy I realized that, yes, I have to take responsibility for my actions, and that I can choose my response to an adverse event. However, I am not a bad person, I am not a stupid person, and I don't deserve to be treated poorly. And it's OK for me to be angry.

Over the past year, I found out that my husband had been indulging in pornography on the Internet almost daily. Since he was not interested in sexual relations with me, I thought he was having an affair. I searched his office and found evidence of almost daily use of the Internet for porn and literally dozens of XXX-rated videos and catalogs that he had received at a post office box. Of course, he was still participating in AA at the time and insisted that this was not an addiction. We separated briefly. He begged for forgiveness, got us into marriage counseling, and attended AA meetings nightly. I finally allowed him to move back in.

Three months after he moved back in, I found out that he had been indulging in porn almost since the day he moved back. When I confronted him with the evidence, he broke down and confessed. To make a long story short, he finally left me because I didn't trust him anymore. I felt he needed help and he didn't. Believe it or not, he is still attending AA meetings nightly.

During this painful time, I started drinking again. It alleviated the deep pain I felt over his betrayal of me. I also felt betrayed by AA. All of my husband's AA friends called here daily, speaking the world of him, because, after all, he's not drinking. He lies and participates in another obsessive behavior, but as long as he's not drinking, well, that's OK.

Over and over again, when I saw problems before we got married, I was told by my sponsor and others in AA that Don was a good man, that he was a really spiritual man, and that I was lucky to have him. And I was stupid enough to marry him and put myself through years of hell. I feel a lot of bitterness over my separation, and the lack of support I got in AA. I am so happy that there are others who have been in AA—particularly women—who feel as I do, and that I've found some of them [via the Internet].

In fact, I have to tell you this. I went to an AA meeting about a year and a half ago. I mentioned to a man that I had attended a women's group the previous evening. He started ranting and raving about how wrong it is to "exclude" men from AA meetings, that the Big Book is for both men and women, and that he has a real problem with "women only" meetings. After talking to him, I realized why I loved women's meetings so much: nobody preached to me!

AA was designed for men with big egos, not for women with low self-esteem. I hope and pray that I will find a means to sober up that doesn't deflate me further.

8 ▲ Belinda
Raped by Old-Timer Sponsor

When I was 23 I left an abusive marriage and started drinking to ease the pain. I kept this up for ten months. My father is an alcoholic and I didn't want to become one, so I went to an AA meeting.

I was wheeled into a meeting because, due to a disability, I am in a wheelchair. I asked for a ride home after the meeting, since I had cab fare only one way. One of the ladies, although she meant well, sent me home with a known predator/13th stepper, "Drew."

I was vulnerable, lonely, and didn't stand a chance from that moment on. Even though at that time I considered myself a lesbian, I was in bed with him before I knew what happened. I suffered several months of what I now consider to be sexual abuse from this man.

He also became my sponsor. I know this sounds crazy, but you need to understand the kind of shape I was in. I was barely hanging onto sobriety, and I was totally open to all kinds of beliefs and views. This man was a sober member of AA, and I was a newcomer. Needless to say, I was not thinking straight.

People with many years of sobriety are viewed as AA gods. They are rarely questioned, and when it comes time for one of them to speak, they are viewed as so spiritually superior that you might hear a pin drop in some meeting halls. Drew had enough time sober to be considered superior. Who would question his judgment? Not me! No one told me of this man's history with newcomers.

I am not simply complaining. I tried hard in AA. I really did. But I was also in awe of Drew, and I had only a few friends.

My family supported my ex-husband, so I was cut off from them for many years. Also, Drew saw nothing wrong with sex; he claimed he was removing a roadblock to my sobriety. He said that if I came out as a lesbian in AA, I would be shunned in the God-based AA program.

But eventually I did gain some strength. When I found out Drew was dating my best friend, I got up the courage to stop having a sexual relationship with him.

But then, on the night I received my one-year chip, he raped me.

For the record, I don't drink now, but the abuse I suffered almost drove me insane. It has been ten years since I've gone to a meeting, and I still have horrific nightmares of the sexual abuse—my screaming, *No! No! No! I don't want this!*

Some AA circles frown on therapy. The day after I had gone to the local battered woman's shelter shortly after I was raped, my therapist asked me about my weekend plans. I said I was going to hit a few meetings and kick back. She responded, *Do you want to drink?* I said, *No.* She then wanted to know why I would attend a meeting. I had to explain that, in my AA indoctrination, I had never been given a choice. Attending meetings was drilled into me.

But that weekend I chose to skip a meeting, and I never went back. I am sober to this day, because I found the answers to my pain through therapy, which has done more to relieve me of the need to self-medicate than AA ever did.

I really want people to know that AA is often filled with very sick people. I, too, was sick, but I never preyed on new people.

One of the ways AA is similar to cults is the doctrine of *90 meetings in 90 days*. I felt that in those 90 days I was torn apart so I might be rebuilt. Really, I was torn apart not just so I could get sober, but so I could be controlled and learn not to think for myself.

You know it is kind of ironic, but had Drew not raped me the night I got my one-year chip, I might never have sought therapy. I guess I really should be grateful.

9 ▲ Lorretta
My 12-step Counselor Stole My Husband

Sparky and I were married on a dismal rainy Saturday in November 1969. Mutual friends had introduced us (blind dates are supposed to make a lasting marriage). We courted in the old-fashioned way (no sex before marriage) and discovered one another with gentleness and respect.

Our first year of marriage marked my first year of teaching in a local public school district. Sparky worked in the computer department of a local university. We spent time together building our garage and house, camping, fishing, organic gardening, raising animals (pigs, chickens, and rabbits), and spending a lot of time together. It was an ideal life and marriage for at least the first five years.

Suzy was born in December 1974, and within a few days I spiraled into a horrible depression from which I never totally recovered. My obstetrician had taken me aside to inform me I was depressed (I already figured that) and would probably benefit from anti-depressants. But I didn't try them. This was in the 1970s, the choice of antidepressants was limited, and I didn't want to put strange chemicals into my body.

Sparky and I began to drift apart after Suzy's birth. He drank more and more, and I focused on Suzy and my art—painting and basket making. At this time I started giving private art lessons in my home. I used art, jogging, natural food supplements, and Suzy to alleviate my depression. It worked, somewhat, for awhile.

I saw the relationship between us weakening and thought I would drink with him in order to be with him. I could never keep up with him—that was never the intent—although he decided that was what I was doing. I just wanted the return of his closeness, but it was already too late. We began having more verbal fights and mis-understandings.

In 1983, our summer schedule was usually divided between the house and our cabin in the country. I gave a private class on Wednesday mornings, and following class I'd pack the cat, dog and Suzy into the car and go to the camp to wait for Sparky to join us.

On one occasion it was 7:30 p.m. before he arrived, and boy was he drunk! While waiting patiently for his arrival I had one drink while I ate supper with Suzy. She was around six or seven years old and was in the habit of going to bed early, even in the summer.

Playing solitaire at the kitchen table, I watched for his coming from the window. As his truck lumbered into the clearing and crept toward the buildings I knew he was drunk. He walked into the cabin weaving and wavering. Picking up his guitar, he struggled with strumming and trying to sing. Then he wanted me to sing to the tunes he strummed. He played so badly that I got pissed and told him to get someone who knew how to play. I muttered something regarding his drunkenness and before I knew it he flew at me. I anticipated his wrath and got up before he could strike.

We went at it like we had never done before. I ran toward the back door which was in the bedroom, but he caught me. He picked me up and threw me onto the bed where my head slammed against the brass headboard. It hurt! He punched and hit me. I got up and jumped into his truck to try to get out, but I was unfamiliar with his vehicle and couldn't start it. He yanked me out by the hair and we tussled on the veranda of the cabin. He dragged me into the pond and shoved my head under the water a few times, then pushed me up the hill close to the camp where he slammed a flashlight on the back of my head, splitting the scalp. Dazed, I staggered to the ground.

Suzy woke up (she had been sleeping through all the commotion), saw my bloodied head, and started crying. I stayed calm for her sake. Night had come, and the light from the kerosene lamps glowed dimly as Sparky washed away as much of the coagulating bloody mess as possible.

I was feeling quite dizzy and generally bad. I asked him to stay the night in case I slipped into a coma as I might have had a concussion and, if that was the case, Suzy wouldn't be left alone. He did stay and we slept together.

He left for home about 6 a.m. I slept a little longer. When I got up and looked in the mirror, my face and head were swollen. I wasn't sure who was in the reflection. Bruised and aching, I moved slowly in both body and mind. Suzy helped collect the animals and pack my car. I rarely had a drink after that and soon quit altogether.

I had my first experience with alcohol counseling in the Spring of 1984. I wanted Sparky to stop drinking, and on the recommendation of acquaintances went to a local alcoholism counseling facility that I'll call The Alcoholism Agency. I found the counseling to be abusive and knew it wasn't what I needed. Even in my undiagnosed depression I knew I didn't need to be heavily confronted or constantly thrown off balance. Sparky had been doing that for quite some time now, and this counseling reeked of the same. I left after three or four sessions with some information on how I could "detach from the alcoholic."

My first counselor also diagnosed me as having depression, but *did not* refer me to an agency appropriate to that health issue. When I didn't return to what I perceived as inappropriate and abusive counseling, I was accused of being in denial and unwilling to deal with *my* "alcoholism."

We tried couples counseling with other agencies for four years. These efforts were to no avail as they did not deal with the alcohol issue. Sparky continued to drink and suffered adverse consequences.

Case in point: Sparky was in the throes of his drinking. On this particular occasion we were at the camp. A gentle summer rain was falling, yet he had gone into the woods to cut dead standing trees for firewood. In the camp I listened to the buzz of the power saw and knew all was OK as long as I heard it. Suddenly it stopped. My heart rose to my throat. All was ominously quiet.

Suzy came to say she could hear her father calling weakly from the bush, "Help me." I told her to stay at the cabin, as I didn't know what I would find and didn't want her traumatized further. I walked into the wood lot, called to him, and a garbled "here" answered. I soon found him, dazed, sitting on the ground, his glasses off, a lens out, a big gash along his brow ridge and his jaw immobile. The tree he had been cutting had kicked out and, as it fell, the butt end caught him in the face. I helped him back to the camp, stumbling over deadfall and tanglewood. After assessing the damage, I took him to the ER for initial treatment. A week later he had surgery to have his jaw wired.

Surgery was done in a city about a hundred miles away. We came home the same day, when I began my job as acting 24-hour nurse. Loyal as a dog, I slept on the floor beside him, as he slept on the couch. Unbeknownst to me, when all he could eat was puree, even while on pain killers, he continued to drink beer through a straw! What insanity!

I returned to The Alcoholism Agency in the Fall of 1988 as a last resort. The one-on-one counseling seemed to go better than the first time, but I was still depressed. I ran away with Suzy in February 1989 to the local women's shelter. The household insanity had become too great. The accusations, the drinking, the passing out, the quiet rage all made life in the house impossible to endure. I was urged to get my "ducks in a row," stash money, leave home, make a plan, and in effect to create a crisis. This leaving was subtly encouraged by the counselor, who used the words, "I support you." The Agency forced my husband into its intensive outpatient program. I was put into their women's group in March 1989. The women were from all walks of life, some alcoholic with any number of chronic illnesses, and some depressed and codependent as I was. Some were very confrontive and created issues out of the most insignificant matters, just as the counselors did.

I was vilified in the name of healthy confrontation by the head women's group counselor, a male, Herr Direktor. Get that, a male counselor facilitating a women's group! His reason for being the group facilitator was that the "unhealthy" women would see what a good role model was like! His only admitted addiction was a former cigarette habit. Herr Direktor is a stocky middle-aged man of southern European decent. He reminded me of a little Napoleon, especially when things didn't go his way. He'd tap his foot, then mutter and snort. He was opinionated and a master of head games, which I felt were abusive.

Word is that his wife rules the roost. It appears he has resentment toward women who are outspoken or assertive, and as a result tries to mold them into apologetic and demure Stepford wives. He certainly strove to "modify" my independence and shake my diminishing self esteem. The precepts of the program for which he worked were a throwback to the '40s and '50s. It's no wonder it held to such an archaic idea of how women should behave. At least Herr Direktor thought he knew how I should behave—keep my mouth shut, share feelings, don't try to be in control, and don't expect my opinion to matter. I did as he dictated, thinking maybe it would work. They took control of my life. In order to survive the group experience I had to play his game, in effect, "fake it 'til you make it." It was "his way or the highway," and they dumped many vulnerable clients who were in the midst of a crisis of The Alcoholism Agency's making. So I complied.

I was expected to stop doing my art (supposedly to "get in touch with my feelings"), and at one point had to initiate sex on a weekly basis with my husband. This was excruciatingly difficult as the issues of sexual abuse had not been dealt with. Their intent was to beat down the client (me), to break through the "denial," and then build the client up again. Trouble was I was already beaten down. My boundaries had been trampled first by Sparky and now by Herr Direktor and his crew.

I survived this group therapy, though even on my last day Herr Direktor, in his closure speech, made it sound like I hadn't learned anything from the experience. He intimated again that I was an alkie and would need to deal with that someday. He was still trying to create self-doubt in me. I guess that the more clients they had who were alcoholic, the more funding they got from the state.

They clearly stated that if you had an illness such as depression, it would be resolved only if your "alcoholism" was addressed. They told this lie to every client so that they would "come to believe." Not only were their clients' chronic illnesses a result of alcoholism, (instead of the other way around) but the counselors led the clients to believe that their "character defects and shortcomings" would become easier to deal with by going to many 12-step meetings and through treatment of one's "addictions" and "alcoholism."

Remember, I was depressed, a real medically treatable illness that had never been addressed. When I would tell them that their allegations didn't fit or feel right, I was chastised and told just to "take a look at it." The counselors tried at almost every turn to shut me up. I was accused of being alcoholic. If I didn't deny it, that set me up to be one; and if I did deny it, they'd say "thou protesteth too much" —you're in denial. It was a no-win situation.

My husband was in intensive outpatient treatment for about five-and-a-half months. Upon "graduation" he was asked to be a volunteer. Within a short time I too was asked to be a volunteer, a psychosocial intake person for The Alcoholism Agency. I agreed and was accepted into their world. I soon obtained my F.S.A. (Fundamentals of Substance Abuse Certification). At the same time I was working part time, going back to school for my master's, continuing my art activities and private classes, and being a mother and a wife to the best of my ability.

Within the first year of my "graduating" from the women's group and Sparky's "graduating" from the intensive outpatient program, a different kind of abuse began in the home. Where there had been abandonment, neglect, verbal and some physical abuse, now there was real domestic violence, and the abuse now became intensely psychological in nature. The same type of cold, insidious confrontations, abusive head games and judgmental attacks that had been present in group and one-on-one counseling became a part of our home life.

Sparky would work as a volunteer at least once a week. Often he was called in to volunteer two and three times a week. With all this training he began to "live" this therapy.

Sparky and I returned to couples counseling to deal with issues in the marriage, including our daughter. Initially, the focus was only on him and me, with the assumption being that if we got back on track, so would the relationship with our daughter. While in counseling some things improved. But on the last day of counseling, Sparky said as we left, "don't you ever do that to me again!" I perceived that as a threat! I felt terrified and at a loss for what to do.

I called Herr Direktor, the number one women's group counselor and director of The Alcoholism Agency's substance abuse services, and told him I needed help in dealing with the escalating irrational rages of my husband. His behavior was worse than when he was drinking. No longer did he pass out on the floor or couch; instead he stayed awake and raged about non-issues. At least when he drank our daughter and I could do what we wanted, but now he scrutinized our every move, counted the phone calls and what items were in the root room and freezer, and judged our every action harshly.

On one occasion Herr Direktor invited me in to talk about what was going on. He asked, "what do you have to own?" I told him, "I'm staying in an insane situation again. It's like he's gone nuts, screaming about the most insignificant things." Herr Direktor told me to go home and think about what I wanted in the relationship and to call him in two weeks. This was an emergency! I needed help now! I didn't call back. I felt confused and hopeless. The Alcoholism Agency was not a safe place, but I didn't trust anywhere else, as I had been brainwashed by them to believe no other agency could adequately address our problems. Sparky by then had bought into Herr Direktor's Gestalt therapy and wouldn't consider going to another agency because *he and the agency had all the answers!* . . . "You would get pissed too if your wife wouldn't clean the house" was probably what he thought. The problem was all mine. The counselors had said so.

Sparky's comments at home to Suzy and me had become accusatory. He was on a mission to prove I had an addiction, too. I felt as though I was falling apart. My depression intensified and it was all I could do to get through the day. I felt hopelessly trapped. My marriage was supposed to have gotten better according to The Alcoholism Agency's philosophy. It didn't. In fact, it was going downhill fast. Something hadn't been addressed, and they decided it was me—that I needed to "get honest."

I had become friends with most of the counselors as I was still doing the psychosocial intakes along with attending Al-anon meetings, sponsoring newcomers, working on my master's, teaching publicly and privately, and doing my arts. I was put into one-on-one counseling again, this time with my husband's primary treatment counselor. He didn't even bother to update my file. Not a single entry! He promised to address problems with my husband when the two of them were on break while working in the intensive outpatient program, and he probably did this twice; but the balance of the time nothing happened. I was given instructions to initiate sex weekly, stop sponsoring newcomers, go to more 12-step meetings, stop doing my art, stop taking 12-step calls, and to stay off the phone. That really isolated me, and I began to think of this place as a cult trying to cut me off from the outside world.

Things didn't improve with Sparky. My efforts were never enough! Sparky's moods changed like the wind. One moment he was raving about the mess and the next he was helping with the laundry. It's real interesting that Sparky had never complained about my housekeeping until he got to The Agency. Once he got his teeth into this one he was like a pit bull.

Nothing changed at home except the insanity got worse. No counselor seemed to get it that Suzy and I were trapped in a constant battle zone that had become so bad that I was functioning in a survival mode typical of one who was experiencing battered woman's syndrome (learned helplessness) and a major depression.

After several more years of this, things got so bad that I had to leave. One morning after Sparky left for work I packed my belongings and didn't return home for two weeks. I went to see Herr Direktor after work that day and told him what happened. He asked again what I had to "own" in this and I couldn't give him the "right" answer (the one he wanted to hear, to prove I got *his* program). He did finally suggest that sometimes problems are greater than could be handled by The Alcoholism Agency, and perhaps I should go somewhere else. But I felt abandoned and was hanging on by a thread. Their brainwashing had made me doubt my own judgment and the value of any other mental health agency.

Some of my friends had gone to a hospital in another state to deal with their depression. I called to have an assessment via phone and was accepted. I couldn't get in for another two weeks, but when I did I spent four weeks finally getting appropriate help long past due. Officially diagnosed and finally getting appropriate meds, the depression cycle began to slow down, but never really lifted.

At the first three sessions of group after I returned to The Alcoholism Agency, Herr Direktor loudly yelled at me. He accused me of bad mouthing the counselors (at this time I still blindly loved and trusted them), not working a program (I was attending meetings and workshops), flirting with a male counselor (flirting and sex were the furthest things from my mind), associating with "unhealthy" people (program women and counselors?—they were my support group), and then the kicker: that I needed to start from square one and get a whole new group of people in my life that I couldn't fool by blaming my problems on my husband.

I informed Herr Direktor that I needed to be treated respectfully. I also told him that I believed his confrontational approach was abusive and was like that which my husband had perpetrated on our daughter and me since he had begun volunteering at The Alcoholism Agency. Herr Direktor blew up and started yelling at me.

I had just returned from a hospital with responsible, educated staff, where I had been diagnosed and had been treated for severe clinical depression. Barely a month had passed, I was in a very fragile mental state, and now I was being emotionally battered by a male counselor who was also the program director. I shut down and blocked all feelings.

The schedule and irrational expectations of the Alcoholism Agency "therapy" group wore on me. I felt horribly overwhelmed, and the antidepressant was losing its effectiveness. I was not getting well. All I wanted to do was sleep (but couldn't) or just sit and vegetate, then vaporize.

The Agency eventually told me that I had to go to the ER to get help for my suicidal ideation. I didn't really think that would be necessary, but Herr Direktor stood his ground. I cried hysterically, but I agreed to go under duress. After waiting for what seemed forever, I finally met someone from another agency who would treat me appropriately and help me on my road to a real recovery.

My last group session at The Alcoholism Agency was spent with my recently assigned female counselor reading excerpts from my file in front of everyone in the women's group. I fell right into their trap. I felt shamed, abused, and vilified as the reading progressed with pauses and innuendoes that implied that I had made no progress and that I still needed to deal with alcoholism. There was no mention of the symptoms and dynamics of depression and what had become domestic violence. Herr Direktor suggested that after I dealt with the depression elsewhere, I could come back to be counseled by one of the female counselors, Helga, since I didn't have a history with her. Sorry, but I couldn't imagine how that would happen, since I knew I wasn't an alcoholic.

Months later, I completed counseling with the new agency, and felt ready to work on my relationship with Sparky. I called Herr Direktor to ask if he thought Sparky would be ready too. He said he'd talk to him.

Soon my husband contacted me, came over, and we talked. He was adamant about me not having adequately dealt with all of my issues (the same thing I had accused him of in one of our more recent arguments). He stated that I couldn't be ready for a relationship until I'd dealt with my drinking, and then brought up counseling with Helga. He held the relationship out as the carrot before my nose. I knew it wasn't right, but I agreed to go.

Sparky and Herr Direktor had apparently collaborated and had decided that I was truly in denial and needed to be in *their* treatment. They totally ignored the serious nature of my medical diagnosis and hung onto the erroneous belief that depression is due to drinking alone.

Sparky was supposed to have been in counseling to deal with the abusive way he treated our daughter and me—at least so I thought. Why hadn't the counselors contacted the proper authorities regarding the child abuse? Why hadn't we been referred to domestic violence counseling? Why was this counselor/director so bent on believing that "it always takes two"? How could he be made to see that he endorsed violence without realizing it?

Once again the focus was put on me as being the one who needed help to deal with my denial (maybe my denial of the nature of The Alcoholism Agency and of what our marriage had become). My husband apparently had embroidered tales of our life together, turning me into a wild drunk as he talked of the times when I was so drunk I couldn't know whether I had a highball or a glass of soda. In his mind I was consuming all the alcohol. I had not drank for over a decade, since the early 1980s, and was still accused of "just putting a plug in the jug." I'd had assessments for substance abuse when I first started counseling at The Alcoholism Agency, and again when I arrived at the hospital in another state. Neither indicated substance abuse, let alone substance dependence. So why would my situation now be any different? But they chose to ignore official diagnoses.

In my first session with Helga, she asked me what I thought my issues were. I told her my issue was depression and that the issue with Sparky was that of power and control, that he had to be in control because of what he had learned through being a volunteer in the intensive outpatient program and in Herr Direktor's Gestalt treatment. She snapped at me that I was a "fuckin' drunk" like her. Wow! I felt very disrespected.

I didn't respect her very much, either. Helga is a sorry sort of a person. She's an angry alcoholic who believes the whole world is against her, has a very foul mouth, an abrasive nature, and a voice as deep as a man's. She isn't physically attractive either. She may have a soft side, but I could never find it. Since her alcoholic first husband died at his own hand, she had been "man hungry," and just about anything would do.

Helga expected me to go to closed AA meetings and announce I was an alcoholic. I did as told, knowing my marriage was on the line. My guts rolled each time I said I was an alkie. It was a lie. I jumped through every hoop she put before me, including a "no contact" restriction regarding my husband. (After we separated, he'd occasionally stop by to see how things were going, check if there were any needed household repairs, and then we'd chat and get caught up on personal events.) She told me not to answer his phone calls or let him in the house. Why? I wanted to cut myself, wad up into a fetal position and just disappear. This shit was too much.

She implied in a number of sessions that I didn't need my meds, which she called "happy pills," and said "once a pill popper always a pill popper." I responded by saying "that's not true," and repeated that I wasn't alcoholic. Of course, her tactic was supposed to throw me off balance, but it wouldn't work anymore. I was wise to it. She yelled and swore at me again, said that I was still a "fucking drunk" and had better get honest and start dealing with it or there would be consequences.

Hmmmmm, "consequences"? A flash of what that possibly meant crossed my mind. Divorce! I had seen them use this pressure tactic with numerous clients when they were trying to break through the denial of their alcoholism. What happened to my official medical and psychiatric diagnosis—had they "forgotten," chosen to ignore it, or just blown it off?

In early summer, after I started counseling with Helga, I visited the family camp and sensed a "presence" in the buildings and around the landscape. Sparky had had a woman at "my camp"! I discounted the feeling, still wanting to believe he was loyal to the marriage.

During the time I was in counseling with Helga, Sparky had a difficult time holding eye contact with me. Friends in the program asked if he had ever had an affair, suggesting that his behavior was that of a man who had "something on the side." I said that ours was a marriage of fidelity, but I wasn't so sure about that now.

Sparky called the week before our 26th wedding anniversary to tell me he had filed for divorce. He said he didn't love me and only cared about me in a "program way." He wanted to remain friends and offered to help around the house if necessary. Friends?!!!! What?!!!!

I was devastated!

I got off the phone with him and called everyone I could think of for support, including my counselor. And she wasn't home! Hmmmm . . . I wondered where she was . . . in the background cheering my husband on?

I saw her a couple of days later in session, and was "in crisis" crying about the divorce. She was cold and controlled, said that I would be getting a divorce and that there was no stopping it now. I told her again that I wasn't an alcoholic and that my issues were depression and domestic violence, and that Sparky was supposed to have been getting help! She returned the focus to my unwillingness to "get honest." While my counseling continued with her, I continued to deteriorate psychologically.

In the spring, Sparky decided to have our old dog euthanised. It seemed like Old Jake was the last thing that connected us. He had aged to the point where his legs would give out, and he had trouble hearing and seeing. I didn't want the dog to go, but conceded as he was in a lot of pain. We buried him at the camp, on the hill. I cried as Sparky covered the old boy with dirt. Ace, our cat, also passed away in August of the same year. Even the animals that symbolically bound us were gone.

A few weeks later I had a chimney fire for which the fire department had to be called. In the same week, I accidentally left the gas flame on under an empty cast iron pan for five hours, the water pump burned up (that meant no water to cook, drink, bathe, or flush the toilet), and the furnace had to be replaced. Then I backed out of the garage with the hatch on my van up and managed to break the window (damage of a couple thousand dollars). All this in one week! Yet Helga accused me of "dry drunking" and being on a "pity pot."

A few sessions later she announced that if I didn't want to deal with my alcoholism there was no sense in her counseling me. I'd thought that right from the beginning. Counseling ended in December 1995. She said she was going to discharge me, but would keep my file open, and if I wanted to deal with my "alcoholism" I should call her.

Because of my trip to the ER I had been introduced to an agency that treated me and my illness respectfully. Additionally, someone who counseled Vietnam vets and Post-Traumatic Stress Disorder clients helped me deal with my own PTSD issues and the trauma from the past few years of marriage and the abusive counseling. I also attended domestic violence counseling at the local women's shelter at the same time. As I struggled to heal, some people in the Agency program had the gall to imply I wasn't in recovery because I—who hadn't drank in years—wasn't dealing with my "alcoholism."

Word reached me that *my counselor* and *my husband* had been seen together at numerous AA and other social functions. She had given him a license plate for the front of his truck. On it was a single red rose with the words "a touch of class." This happened on Christmas 1995, during the last month I was in counseling with her. I was in a state of disbelief and shock about how blatantly she behaved!

The next year was a year from hell. There were numerous trips to the attorney. More reports of their affair. The antidepressants no longer worked. More confusion and emotional devastation. No one took my illness seriously, not even my divorce attorney, whose office (I learned later) had connections with The Alcoholism Agency. No fair counsel there either. But he sure wanted his money.

In October 1996, three days after our 27th wedding anniversary, we signed the divorce papers so we wouldn't have to go to trial. Shortly after I got home that evening I received a phone call from a friend who had seen Sparky and Helga kissing in front of an AA meeting place that same evening. The truth was in the open. It was *her* telltale energy that had lingered at the camp, in the sauna, and the surrounding land. She had been seducing him by making herself available when he was confused, lonely and vulnerable, and while she instructed me to have no contact with him.

Within two weeks I presented The Agency with phase 1 and phase 2 of the client complaint forms. I was blown off by Herr Direktor. They lied regarding Sparky and Helga's relationship, and to top things off they attempted to have me banned from the public services available at The Agency. They also tried to charge me an administrative filing fee for services for which there were no established fees policies. When they denied me restitution of any sort I moved on to the next stage of the process, involving the coordinating agency and then the state licensing department.

In December 1996, barely one month after our divorce, word was out that Sparky and Helga planned to marry; in January 1997 it was publicly announced that they would be married. The other counselors at The Agency planned a wedding shower for her. Talk about a betrayal! *My husband, my counselor, and The Alcoholism Agency!* My emotions whirled! I felt overwhelmed and my depression got worse. I couldn't do anything to stop this travesty. I struggled to get through the days at work and the nights at home.

My complaint went through the state process. Before that came to an end, Helga the Horrible, the "garden implement" (ya know . . . a rake, a shovel and a __) and my now ex-husband married in August 1997. The Alcoholism Agency insisted that they "did not start seeing each other socially until September of 1996," barely 10 months after Sparky had filed for divorce. What about early summer of 1995 when there had been a woman at the camp, and what about the license plate with the single red rose on Christmas of the same year? The time frames just don't match, nor does the intensity that the relationship had reached in such a "short time." It's also relevant that Sparky was in counseling in The Alcoholism Agency at the same time I was. Counselors, clients, and spouses of clients are not supposed to have any kind of personal relationship.

People from the AA community, many of whom were my friends (or so I thought), attended their reception with no consideration of how Helga "bagged her buck."

The Ethical Standards Policy states that counselors will not have a personal relationship with a client, or have sex with a client, former client, service recipient, or former service recipient. In order for agencies to receive insurance, counselors are not to have sex with clients or spouses of clients. This applies to *anyone* who has been counseled by *anyone* at an agency. No wonder Herr Direktor lied about when Sparky and Helga's relationship began.

As a result of their lies, Helga still had her job, my husband and my cabin, and Herr Direktor still had his job.

For the most part I have withdrawn from the program. I don't make 12-step calls or sponsor newcomers. I don't trust men or many women. I avoid coming in contact with "friends" who are in the program, and I'm cautious about those with whom I associate.

Periodically I do go to 12-step meetings, only to come away with immeasurable feelings of hypocrisy, disgust, betrayal, and helpless victimization, especially when Sparky and his twin are at the same meeting. They greet me with a sugary sweet, "Hi Lorretta." Oh, gag me! It's as if they're rubbing salt in my wounds. And it's hard not to run into them, as this is a relatively remote area without many meetings.

I no longer have a loving, caring husband who could've stayed at my side through my illness. The marriage might have been saved if my case had been handled responsibly. Things simply did not have to turn out this way.

Untreated depression often deepens. Mine is now resistant to conventional antidepressant therapy. Recently I was told I was bipolar II (cycling depression that never reaches the manic phase and is difficult to treat), yet at The Agency I was treated as though I was a "hard core alcoholic" who needed to "be broken." At times I felt as if I was in the Dark Ages where they cajoled, taunted, poked, and prodded the mentally ill, then put them in small rooms where they lay in their own excrement. Who would've thought that in the 20th century this type of abusive treatment would exist?

The Alcoholism Agency continues to discount real health issues and uses them as a manipulative tool to convince clients they're alcoholic. They take advantage of clients' vulnerability by using their position of authority. In regard to numerous chronic conditions, including depression, anxiety disorders, and anything in between, the counselors tell clients that if they deal with their alcoholism then all their other health problems will cease to exist! This is what my husband bought into and continues to buy into.

I'm sure many clients initially were self-medicating to alleviate the pain of other chronic ailments. I know many who have drunk very little, if at all, who the counselors at The Alcoholism Agency have prodded—in the name of "healthy" confrontation—into believing they were alcoholic. These supposedly professional counselors discount the care that the medical profession has provided their clients, resulting in many of them going off their meds, thus endangering their lives even further.

There has to be some kind of protection or justice for persons who have been victimized in this manner by over-zealous, self-righteous, unscrupulous, self-serving, uneducated, tunnel-visioned counselors and their counseling. Maybe their hearts were in the right place in the beginning, but it appears that they've lost sight of their ethics, ideals, morals, scruples, and objectivity.

10 ▲ Harry

AA or Divorce—
And I'm Not an Alcoholic!

I am a 35-year-old man whose past includes the abuse of alcohol. I no longer abuse alcohol, and I have had a very interesting, frustrating, even perilous journey through AA and a standard outpatient program based on the 12-step model.

First, let me tell you there is no doubt in my mind that I once *was* an alcoholic. There is also no doubt that I am no longer an alcoholic —I am no more an alcoholic today than I am a teenager. But the fact is, I did abuse alcohol in the past, and certainly to the degree that I would have been defined as an alcoholic. The point I'm trying to make is that now that I am no longer an alcoholic, many people in AA will either insist I am in *denial,* or insist that I was never an alcoholic to begin with.

There was an unfortunate point in my life when I'd had it with drinking. I went to a standard 12-step-based program. (When I say *standard,* I mean that with very, very few exceptions, those are the only programs that are available.) I checked myself into a program that was run by a treatment/hospital community in the Midwest. From the very beginning I noticed that what they expected of us was to be *sponges* rather than gold miners, that is, they wanted us to accept everything they told us rather than sift through it for what we thought was useful.

But my drinking had become so problematic that I was delighted to find any way to get out from under it. I became, in a very short period of time—four or five months—a model AAer. I knew the Big Book back and forth. I never carried it around like a Bible because I have Christian beliefs, and I don't confuse the two, but I got a sponsor, worked the steps, and everything was just hunky dory *until* I began to notice certain things about AA.

For instance, some people in meetings would say the same things over and over again. There was one man who would say: *Now I've been sober for twenty years, but I still have an alcoholic mind.* Another would say: *Well I've been sober for ten years, but I still think it's not the drinking, it's the thinking.*

I'm the kind of person who just has to question that. I started with simple questions like, *How can you say you're an alcoholic after twenty years without a drink?* and, *What do you mean, your thinking hasn't changed?*

My questions went further than that. I actually started reading some books. I think I started with Stanton Peele's *Diseasing of America,* and *When AA Doesn't' Work for You,* by Albert Ellis and Emmett Velten, and Charles Bufe's *Alcoholics Anonymous: Cult or Cure?* I read books by Ellis, and just about everything I could get my hands on. Soon, it became clear to me that there is no such thing as an *alcoholic mind.* Alcoholics are no more fearful, angry, or anything else than anyone else is.

So I called a psychologist friend of mine, who has a very long history in the study of alcoholism. He has written several articles and has done meta-studies of alcoholism, some specifically on which treatments work and which ones don't. I posed this question to him: *If you took a thousand alcoholics, and a thousand non-alcoholics, and you put them in a room together and gave them all the same battery of psychological tests, what would the results be?*

He replied: *They'd be indistinguishable. You would not be able to tell who the alcoholics were.* He turned me on to a study done by William Miller at the University of New Mexico back in 1976, which pointed in the same direction.

Well, I made the mistake one day, while listening to one of the *AA Pharisees* preach the AA line to a newcomer at a meeting, of disagreeing with him. I thought what he was saying was pretty heavy handed—he was scaring this newcomer about the prospect of never being able to change his thinking. I spoke up and said: *The fact is, there is no such thing as an alcoholic mind. It doesn't exist.*

That's when the trouble started. I went from being welcome at meetings to being cast out, shouted down. I was told that I wasn't a member of the fellowship, that I was in denial, that I had no *real desire to stop drinking.* After more of this abuse, I left AA. And I felt perfectly comfortable with that.

After awhile, I started having a drink every now and then. And I drank very moderately and successfully for about seven or eight months—and this was after a period of 18 months of abstinence. No one knew. I would have a glass of wine at lunch, or a couple of beers.

Then one day, my wife smelled it on my breath, and I admitted to her, *Yes, I've been drinking moderately.* Well, her father is in recovery and a very heavy duty member of AA. So immediately a number of bad things happened. First, I was told I had *relapsed.* I was told I had broken my promises, and that I had to get back into rehab, because if I didn't, I would be slapped with divorce papers.

I asked her: *On what grounds?* Nevertheless, I was coerced back into treatment. Back at the treatment outpatient meetings, I kept telling these people: *You know, I don't really think that I have a problem. I'm not here because I'm afraid of losing control over my drinking, or because I think I have lost control. I've already shown that I do have control. I'm here to placate my wife.*

They would say: *That's not a good enough reason to be here.*

I'd reply something like: *Now wait a minute. If my goal is to keep my family together, so that we keep having a highly functional, beautiful family as we have had, then yes, that is a good enough reason.*

Of course, I was branded as recalcitrant, and told I was in *denial.* I sat through three outpatient classes a week, where the addictions counselor seemed very good at fitting everyone's emotions, comments, problems and activities into the guidelines of the first 164 pages of the Big Book. I thought, *Oh, gee, this is easy. I should make money in my spare time this way. All you have to do is pull out one cliche after another.* I always questioned these methods. But then they would threaten to go to my wife and say that I wasn't interested in recovery and that perhaps she would be better off serving me with divorce papers. Can you imagine?

Right then and there I decided: *OK. What we're going to do is go along with this. There are good lies and bad lies. I will go along with this to convince my wife. She doesn't have to know I'm doing this just to please her. She can't understand; she's so steeped in this AA-think because of her father's experience. I will do this for all of our benefits.*

I had to fight to stay in the program. I was not only penitent, I was practically mendicant. *Fake it 'til you make it,* right? I had to stay in long enough to convince my wife I was really *in recovery.*

In any event, a little while ago I had a conversation with someone in AA. If you ask the tough questions of these groups—AA, or other parts of the treatment/12-step community—you're going to be dubbed as being *in denial.* Tough questions like this one: "Bill Wilson suggested that 50% of the people who followed the instructions got sober immediately and stayed that way. That's a remarkable figure. How did he come to it? What method did he use to arrive at that conclusion? How come his results are not reproducible? How come nobody else has been able to get near that either before or since? Do you think Bill Wilson could have been pulling our leg just a little bit? If you ask these tough questions, rest assured you will be labeled as being *in denial.*

I've probably e-mailed 50 different AA groups across the country, with probably 100 or 200 different e-mails asking questions like this, and virtually all of the responses are something like: *I'm sorry we can't help you in your denial.*

Another thing I've noticed in the treatment community—they practically command: *You will relapse.* They'd ask: *What are you gonna do if you relapse?* I honestly didn't know. They'd say: *Well that's not a good enough answer. You have to have a plan.* Yes, they demand that you have a plan for relapse. I asked them about that, and they'd always say something like: *Well, we know that most people do relapse; it's the nature of the disease.* I seriously question that. If they've observed this for 50 years, maybe it has something to do with the nature of the *treatment.*

I feel liberated now, compared to how I felt when I was heavily into AA. While I was a true believer, a very big part of the world was closed off to me. Not just bars and liquor stores, but, more importantly, certain avenues of thought. AA teaches its followers not to think about certain things—you *mustn't* question certain doctrines—the nature of "alcoholism," etc. If it can't be reconciled with the Big Book, it's false. And, if you're active in AA, what's the response to every dilemma that pops up? *Call your sponsor. You've got to fourth step your problem; you've got to fifth step it.* This is all reinforced by the professional treatment community. For instance, if they ask: *How do you feel today,* and you reply, *I feel great,* the stock answer is, *What are you masking? Have you talked to your sponsor about this problem you've got masking things?* It's all completely arbitrary. You're absolutely at the mercy of whatever knucklehead you're talking to. And yet, if you try to dissuade them, logically, from their position, it proves all the more that you are *in denial.*

I've heard some of the AA old-timers say stuff like: *You know, every day you don't drink, you're that much closer to the day you do.* And, of course, everyone in AA knows that if you ingest just the slightest bit of alcohol, you're *out;* your choices are death, insanity, or jail. [Awhile back I saw an anguished post on alt.recovery.aa from an AA member who was tormenting himself over having eaten a little cornbread baked with some alcohol in it.—ed.]

So, my horror story is that I am a 35-year-old man who accepted the consequences of abusive behavior and moved on. But because I once said *I'm an alcoholic*—it's like being a speck of dirt that gets sucked up into a vacuum. You'll never get out, and if you scratch and claw your way out of that vacuum bag, someone is going to suck you back in. Now, my life is tenuous. I sit through four or five meetings a week to keep my marriage intact.

I've never believed what Hobbes said about life being nasty, brutish and short, and I never believed that there is power in alcohol. When I was forced back into treatment, I told them up front that I would not do a first step; I would not "admit" I was powerless over alcohol. I am not powerless. And they can't convince me otherwise.

11 ▲ Charlotte
Two Years of Hell

Two years ago, when I was 26, I decided I wanted to spend my time differently, drinking less alcohol. I went to an AA meeting because I thought there would be non-drinking activities such as dances. I wanted to meet people who had fun without drinking.

My first meeting was fun—everyone seemed so nice. By the third meeting I figured I must also be an alcoholic since I enjoyed drinking and *normal* people did not. After hearing stories about the *disease* and its progression, I became terrified. I immediately threw myself into the program, desperate to find the *character defects* that made me drink. After six months, I was more miserable than I had ever been in my life.

Any thought or emotion I had seemed to have some slogan to answer it. The result was this: I showed up at AA happy, energetic, and confident in myself, and ended up a broken-down, terrified shell of a person, suffering from extreme anxiety attacks, unable to work—in other words, a total mess!

Why didn't I get out right away? Because for well over a year I believed the people in AA when they said I was now dealing with the real things I had been afraid of. Somewhere deep down I didn't believe that, but I couldn't trust my beliefs because I had a disease that wanted me dead. No wonder I suffered anxiety attacks. How can you live thinking you have, living inside you, a disease that wants to kill you? It all seemed like a nightmare—it was so hard to believe that I was right and all these other people could be wrong.

What really woke me up was when I went back to Maine, after two years, to visit my old friends (something I was advised never to do). I started to tell them what I'd been seeing in the program—that every thought or feeling I expressed was immediately answered by a standard AA reply.

Example: *I don't want to go to meetings anymore, but they tell me if I don't I'll drink and then I'll die.*

But they tell me, but *they* tell me; that's all I could say—I think or feel this, *but they tell me . . .* When I heard myself talk like this, I realized, *Oh my God, this sounds just like a cult!* My friends were so worried about me that they didn't want me to go back to Delaware. They could not believe the terrible changes in my confidence and self-esteem.

I had to go into therapy to recover from this program. And I am very lucky to have my therapist. When she first told me she knew of people who had left AA and were doing well, I was afraid. My program *friends* promptly told me to get another therapist. It was so hard to believe that I was right and all these other people were wrong. The whole experience has been devastating to me.

I also watched my boyfriend go through the same thing. He'd been a young, beautiful person, who was full of life and enthusiasm (at three months sober). Soon, he became unemployed and rarely left his bedroom. He finally ended his involvement with AA by getting drunk. I once said I could understand why people relapsed, because it was the only way to get out of the program.

I am happy to say that we are both feeling 100% better since we made the decision to leave AA. For me, it was the hardest thing I had to do; I was terrified that I was suffering from the *terminal uniqueness* I'd been warned about, and that *my disease* had progressed and would kill me if I left. But I knew I could not spend the rest of my life with the immense fear, guilt, and negativity AA engenders. It breaks my heart to say that. It also breaks my heart that I put myself through two years of hell tearing myself to pieces looking for my defects. I am reluctant to totally dismiss AA for other people—but it's not for me.

I recently heard through the grapevine (no pun intended)[*] that a friend of mine in the program really went down the tubes. After seven years of sobriety in AA, he went straight to crack cocaine, which he had never done before. They found him down by the railroad tracks, where he had fallen and split his skull open. Currently, he is in ICU in a vegetative state. I knew this man for two years. He was quiet, shy, and very lonely. He was not happy during those seven years of sobriety. But is this his reward for working his program? I understand it was his choice, but I believe it shows that a different approach is needed. This is not an unfamiliar story. In AA, of course, it will be used as further "proof" of what happens if you don't work your program.

---

[*] *The Grapevine* is an AA periodical.

12 ▲ Tom

My AA Cult Experience

It's funny how it happened—I overdosed on heroin. By some miracle I woke up, but I was paralyzed from the waist down, and I was handed my arrest papers while strapped to a backboard. I stayed in the hospital rather than jail. Paramedics thought I had broken my neck, though the doctors never did find out exactly what caused the paralysis. They think it might have been a small stroke, but I've never heard of anyone having a stroke from heroin. Eventually, slowly, I regained the use of my legs. I walk perfectly now.

But it was three months before I could make it to my arraignment. I could walk again by then, but with a limp. I was charged with felony possession of narcotics which, in my state, is a class C felony carrying a 7-15 year sentence. I would have been grateful for any way out of jail time. But in my state, the only way to escape jail sentences for drug-related crimes is to go to a state-run 12-step treatment program. My family had no insurance to pay for that. So it looked like jail for me.

But my lawyer intervened. He asked for a six-month continuance, which the DA agreed to. This would allow me to try a program my father knew about, at a place I will call Serenity Ridge. He knew the folks there because he had done some work helping them sell a recovery magazine they used to print. We called Serenity Ridge, and they said, *Yes, bring him on up.*

Serenity Ridge is in the middle of a rural area in the northeastern U.S., and spans several parcels that members' families own, property that covers the top of a small mountain. As you drive up the mountain you pass various houses, which at first I did not realize were inhabited by these member-families. Near the top of the ridge is the main house, which is called the Upper House, and where all the activities take place. It doubles as a guest house. About 500 feet away is a small trailer park, which is where I lived during most of my time there.

The Serenity Ridge Group was founded in the late 1960s by Tim T., as an AA group. Quickly, the group turned into a recovery center populated by hippies. As time went on, most of the hippies left, and Tim T. picked up more members during his travels through the southern U.S. These new members packed up their families and moved north to join Tim's group. Hence, many of the members in the group are now third generation—their grandparents are the ones who joined. They themselves, and their parents, were born into the group.

This, of course, means that probably 60%–70% of the group never had a problem with any sort of addiction. Imagine an AA meeting with ages ranging from 80 down to 12, and all of those in attendance under age 40 never having had any addiction problem. They just inherited their membership in the fellowship from their parents! Also, keep in mind that the group lives together, and everyone donates a portion of their income to the group as a tithe.

Serenity Ridge used to promote itself as a state-approved treatment center. Sometime in the past they had been told they could not do that because they had no medical staff and no one with any formal psychiatric or psychological background worked there. And, apparently, many things had happened there no one wanted to discuss. By the time I arrived, the group had switched to being a religion, one where all male members are considered ministers who can perform the Eucharist. As such, they charged my family $30 a day.

It took only a few days for me to realize that Serenity Ridge was weird. That was when they informed me that twice a week I would have to drink a quarter cup of castor oil and follow it up four hours later with a one-quart enema. And once a week I would have to get up and drink a cup of lobelia tea—an emetic that is poisonous in large quantities. I was to follow that up with a quart of water, then force myself to vomit. This was supposed to cleanse my system. Of course, these were only *suggestions*. But a lot of force was put behind them. My protestations resulted in two senior group members taking my inventory for about two hours straight.

The rules the group lives by are fanatical. They seem to put almost as much belief into the old Oxford Group stuff as the Big Book stuff. Ebby Thatcher is held in higher esteem than Bill W. (Tim claims to have known both of them.) The old Oxford Group "Four Absolutes" are still highly touted. [The "Absolutes" are purity, honesty, love, and unselfishness. —ed.]

The "Four Absolutes" include, prominently, *Absolute Purity*—sexual "purity." No sex is allowed outside of marriage. None. Nada. No masturbation, no birth control, period. Even marital sex relations are controlled. While I was there, married couples slept in separate rooms, and Tim decided who was to be married.

In fact, Tim's *suggestions* had the force of law. Most books and literature that people in the group read were approved by Tim first. We were totally cloistered. No newspapers, no television, no radios. No one was allowed to eat meat. Toothpaste with fluoride was not to be used by members either. And no "normal" allopathic medicines were allowed at all.

I could go to a doctor if I got sick, but I was not allowed to take *anything* he prescribed for me. On one occasion, they took me to a doctor for asthma. He prescribed an inhaler for me. They sat and listened while he gave me the inhaler and explained how to use it. As soon as we got outside, they confiscated it. I also suffered through a couple of major sinus infections with no real medical help. The only medical help allowed at Serenity Ridge was the castor oil, lobelia with vomiting, enemas, and homeopathic remedies diluted with Everclear, which is nearly pure ethyl alcohol. The folks at Serenity Ridge purchased and diluted these remedies themselves. (More about that, soon!)

Children in the group were raised communally, with little outside contact with the rest of the world. They have rarely been exposed to other ideas. To me, that is a real tragedy. These kids know of no other way of life but the 12 steps taken to an extreme. Members' children do not go to public school—the group runs its own school. Parents were expected and *required* to use corporal punishment if a child misbehaved. Child Protective Services has, in the past, been called in to remove children (including Tim's) from the community. At one point, Tim's oldest daughter and the daughter of another member called Child Protective Services and had the place investigated. CPS came and put both of the kids into foster care. There were allegations of sexual abuse, but these were unproven. I never saw any sexual abuse go on there. Since then, the case has gone to court. Both girls have done very poorly away from the group. Tim's daughter wound up coming back. The other girl was in and out of institutions the last I heard.

The worst treatment at Serenity Ridge is the constant emotional abuse. *Hot seat* sessions are common. They also call these sessions *haircuts,* a term which is also used at treatment centers. One member will have his inventory belligerently taken by four or five other group members for an hour or so. They often videotape these tongue lashing sessions and play them back. This is supposed to point out how the person was arrogant when they were *correcting* him, of how he didn't want to surrender his will, or how he was a perfect example of *self will run riot*. These sessions are classic cult-style ego busting. I've seen them do it to adults, I've seen them do it to children. The decisions as to who would be hot seated were arbitrary, although there seemed to be scapegoats.

There was one guy named Rudy, for instance. At a meeting, someone would accuse him of not paying attention (although it was clear to me that he was paying attention). Then everyone would start yelling at him, saying they were trying to help him, he was resenting them for it, and he needed to do a fourth step right then and there. Another time, there was a neighbor kid in the trailer park who got hot seated by four adults, all male. They surrounded him and began telling him he was arrogant, he needed to get humble, and he needed to start working the program better. This happened a 12-year-old kid who was born there.

Meetings were held three or so times a week. These were supposed to be AA meetings, but most had little to do with recovery. The topics included The End Times, the importance of the Oxford Groups' Absolute Purity, in the sexual sense, the Mythology of the Holy Grail, Edgar Cayce, and Homeopathic Medicine vs. Regular Medicine. They also did what they called "Big Ten," which was, basically, a hot seat meeting that would go on for as long as 24 hours straight in order to crush any mental barriers one might be able to put up.

This sounds like just another nutball fringe group. But this guy, Tim T., claims to be running his group the way Bill Wilson intended AA to be run. That's not too far-fetched a claim, if you look at the Oxford Group, from whence AA came.

According to Tim. T, drug guru Timothy Leary not only tried, but succeeded, in contacting Bill Wilson. Tim T. once told me that he, Wilson, and Leary drank Morning Glory seed tea, a hallucinogen, together on at least one occasion. Tim also claims to have co-authored *12 Steps and 12 Traditions* with Bill W. Tim *has* written several books published in his own name, and I'm sure a linguist could figure out whether he did write some of the *12 & 12* as well.

I know that some of the history Tim told me is true. For instance, Tim did know Bill Wilson, and in all likelihood Bill was his sponsor. I've seen in Tim's library his copy of the first edition Big Book, with

Bill and Bob's signatures inside. I have seen pictures of Tim and Bill together at the Serenity Ridge Community. I have seen a copy of a short note written to Tim by Bill giving the Serenity Ridge group and community his blessing and approval.

In retrospect, I think Tim T. was drunk most of the time. He was always carrying around these little squeeze bottles of the various homeopathic remedies diluted in Everclear. All day long he would squirt these remedies into his mouth.

To the credit of mainstream AA, most of the surrounding AA groups thought the folks at Serenity Ridge were absolutely nuts. Very seldom did any of the group members go to outside AA meetings anymore, although on occasion Tim's son would attend meetings nearby. His father no longer was even invited to speak at speaker meetings, but that could be because he was getting senile and the other group members didn't want to let him out.

Tim was 83 years old when I knew him. He was divorced and had remarried a 50-year-old second wife. He had a 50-year-old son from his first marriage, and three daughters from his second marriage, aged 19, 17, and nine. All except his first wife were members of his group.

Do not think that I have come to bring peace on earth. I have not come to bring peace, but a sword. For I have come to set a man against his father, and a daughter against her mother in law, and a man's foes will be those of his own household.

—Ascribed to Jesus in *Matthew 10:34-36*

This is the exact quote thrown at me by one of my sponsors at Serenity Ridge when I pointed out to him that a close relative of mine, who had been in AA for 10 years, did not agree that I needed to do all the things my sponsor insisted on—abstain from sex, take enemas, make myself throw up, stick to an organic vegetarian diet, and pray one hour to Jesus daily. It was suggested to me that I cut off all ties with my family if they did not buy into and support my following these rules, which I had no interest in doing.

My sex sponsor was 30 at the time he sponsored me. The folks at Serenity Ridge thought he would be a good sex sponsor since he had masturbated as an adolescent. They thought that was an extremely serious problem, and declared that one was not even supposed to think about sex. Any sex thoughts that popped into my mind were supposed to be taken care of immediately by confessing them to my sex sponsor. But I spoke to him as little as possible on the subject, and I was lucky, became they didn't press it. During the first couple of months, they did ask me if I was having any sexual thoughts while I was there, or if I had masturbated, but I just answered no across the board whether it was true or not. After that, the issue kind of died.

I always kept myself out of the indoctrination process, a skill I have, which is lucky for me. I knew all this was kind of wacky, so I was able to protect myself psychologically. A lot of people don't manage that. The evidence for that is the entire families who have been at Serenity Ridge for generations.

Finally, I started objecting to the vomiting as medically dangerous. I have spent time at the hospital with bulimic girls, and I've seen what forced vomiting does to the system if you do it repeatedly—abscesses on the tonsils, enamel chewed off teeth, etc. One of the head honchos at Serenity Ridge said *Oh. Well what are you? A doctor?* I replied, *No, but you aren't either, and I've seen what vomiting does.* They kept being arrogant about it, so I told them I was leaving. They said, *That's fine, you can leave, but don't expect any family support.*

When I finally escaped from Serenity Ridge, I entered one of the hard-core "therapeutic" communities, the kind of place where they hang signs on you and scream at you. It was still a blessing after Serenity Ridge. There were rigid, structured rules, but at least you knew what you could get in trouble for. At Serenity Ridge I constantly waited for the hammer to drop, because what they could nail you for was totally arbitrary.

The latest news about Serenity Ridge is that Tim T. has been telling folks that since wine used in the Eucharist is not really wine, but the blood of Christ, and since all male members of his group are ordained in his church and can perform the Eucharist whenever or wherever they want, they can, basically, drink as much wine as they want so long as it is consecrated wine. *And* he has been recommending drinking large quantities of consecrated wine as a remedy for stress.

Can you believe that?

13 ▲ Michelle

Screwed by Drug /Alcohol Therapist

I went to residential treatment and then aftercare in the Midwest at a place I'll call The Happy Destiny Pines Rehab. Naturally, I was taught that AA is the only way, and that I would have to attend meetings for the rest of my life.

Things became difficult for me in AA after my outpatient counselor and his girlfriend gave me a ride home from an AA meeting one night. I believe that she and two other AA women became very jealous of me, and as a result I was completely ignored by all of the women in the group for a period of several months. One after another of the men "hit" on me, trying to get me to visit them at home and things like that.

It was a very difficult time for me, because at aftercare I was being told to get a sponsor, but at the meetings no women would speak to me—only men. One man in particular kept offering to be my sponsor. I later found out that he had sex with every female that he sponsored.

I couldn't understand what was wrong with me. I finally rebelled and refused to attend any AA meetings at all. Aftercare at the treatment center was the only place that I could get any decent support, the only place where I was not treated like a pariah.

But after a year of aftercare, and then another year of outpatient treatment, my outpatient counselor asked me if I wanted to have sex. I'd had a crush on him for a very long time, and I agreed. We went to his house where he lived with his girlfriend—she was at work—and we had sex. As we were putting our clothes back on, he said, "Hey, I can't be your therapist anymore." And, of course, he swore me to secrecy.

We had sex several more times after that, again at his house, in the outpatient building, in the group room—on the floor—and once in the parking lot in his car. In February I stopped going to outpatient treatment.

I am still paying the bill for getting screwed by my therapist.

14 ▲ Little Wing
Betrayal in AA Put Me in a Psych Ward

I got clean from crank addiction at 19 years old, after seven years as an IV user. I did not go into AA because I simply could not take all of the religion in the rooms and instead went to NA. The NA group I went to was the only one in town, and none of the regular members had more than one year clean time. In fact, the group had been around for only two months. My sponsor had also been a crank addict; she had only three more months clean than I had.

This is not the horror story—this, in fact, was the closest I have ever felt to a bunch of addicts in my life. But at 18 months clean, a problem developed. I finished my fourth step before my sponsor did, and she promptly fired me. I said I would wait until she finished hers, but she refused. She said she was following the rules.

I looked around for someone to do my fifth step with, and—to be honest—I wanted to impress her in a big way, so in an act of sheer bravado I asked an AA member who came to our meetings occasionally to sponsor me. This person is nationally famous in AA circles, and a Catholic priest to boot. It took a lot of courage for me to ask him, but as soon as he said "yes," I started to feel like there was something wrong.

At our initial meeting, he let me know what he expected, starting with Christmas and birthday presents—which he would by no means reciprocate—and ending with perfect punctuality. Then—I am Comanche—he went on to explain what is wrong with Native Americans. Then he began to harp on problems with blacks. (My husband is racially mixed).

When I objected, he said he was just being "realistic" and proceeded to explain how I was "emasculating" my husband by cutting up his credit cards when he spent us into debts we had no hope of repaying. He added that I was in denial when I disagreed with his statement that Indians' problems all stemmed from the "fact" that *Indian women psychically castrate their husbands.*

Against my better judgment, I continued with him. I just didn't want to admit what a mistake I had made. He was universally idolized and, with rare exceptions, still is in our area. I put off actually doing the fifth step with him as long as possible. But finally, after more than a month of stalling, I agreed to do it.

I had barely begun, and had reached the part I had written about being sexually abused by my stepfather when I was a child. My priest-sponsor stopped me right there and told me that this sexual abuse had no place in my fourth step. I said it had shaped my using behavior, preparing me to trade sex for drugs, and to devalue my sexuality. The silence sort of roared between us for a few minutes. Then, he repeated, *what you have written is not a fourth step.*

I shut down. He told me to call him when I had written a *real fourth step.* He then gave me a fourth step guide he had written. In closing he said, *You aren't nearly as intelligent as you think you are.*

I could have argued, but I left. When I got home, I looked at this fourth step guide—all 1500 or so questions—and found that most of it was just insane. A good number of the questions were totally irrelevant things about whether or not you masturbated, and if you did whether or not you used a vibrator. Suddenly my choice was clear—I might end up totally ostracized, but I had to dump him.

I called him right then and told him I needed a female sponsor. He seemed surprised. I thought the ordeal was over. Little did I know that he would want revenge.

I proceeded with my life. I did the fifth step with a former prescription drug addict, and received little solace as she was totally overwhelmed by my story. But at least she didn't belittle me.

Meanwhile, my husband was having sponsor problems of his own, and he relapsed. I was trying to hold my marriage together, keep my sanity, and not use drugs or alcohol.

But when I went to my fellow sufferers for help, I discovered I had been sabotaged. This man, this priest, this paragon of sobriety, had gotten even with me the best way he knew how—he lied about me. He went into the rooms of both NA and AA and lied about me. He went to the trouble of personally contacting my former sponsor I loved so much and telling her I had lied to him and he had fired me for it. *In fact,* he said, *she's probably been lying to you all along. I couldn't even say for sure that she's really clean.*

I had followed the 12-step edict to stay away from old friends, so when I suddenly found myself a pariah within the 12-step community, I was totally isolated. Against all odds, I did not use drugs or alcohol. However, I did become suicidal to the point that my husband committed me for a brief stay on a locked psychiatric ward.

It took two years before I returned to an NA meeting. I have stayed totally clear of AA. Still, even today, it is impossible for me to feel completely at ease at a meeting, even with almost ten years clean.

15 ▲ Jesse
I learned Dysfunction in 12-Step School

My name is Jesse. I'm an 18 year old from Nashville, TN. On December 4th, 1998 I was sent to a therapeutic boarding school by my mother for reasons including drugs, violence, family difficulties, and failing in school. While I was there, I was forcibly subjected to almost all aspects of the 12 steps. The school was based on intense, year-round use of 12-step and Gestalt therapy. People were rewarded for following the 12 steps with privileges, better housing, more freedom, more respect, and, best of all, more power to control their peers. I could go on forever about their policy, but it would take too long to type. Lets just say I truly understand the pain of a condescending, *It's OK, you're right where you should be; it's all part of your process.*

The day before I was to leave for the 12-step boarding school, I broke my hand. The lady from admissions told me that I would be able to see a doctor later that day for it. My mother offered to take me to the doctor and bring me back if necessary, but they assured her that everything would be all right and I would be taken care of. After she left, they told me that the nurse was out and I would be able to see her after the weekend was over. I was taken into a bathroom and strip searched. All my possessions were searched, my money was taken from me, and I was taken back to the group.

I asked another kid if it would be possible if I could go to the doctor that day. If it wasn't possible for the school to take me that day, my mom could come back and take me. My hand was swollen, twisted, and it hurt horribly. He responded with a laugh, as if I had just asked to borrow a thousand dollars.

That night I slept in a very small room with six other kids, two in bunk beds, one on a single, and me and three others crammed on the floor. I slept shoved under the single bed with only a single cotton sheet in the mountain chill. The small mattress had a vinyl coating that made it absolutely frigid to sleep on. It was three days and three cold nights before I got my comforters and a change of clothes.

After two weeks of repeated run-around, I was finally allowed to see the nurse. The nurse scheduled me for an appointment at the hospital a week later. So a full three weeks after my arrival at the school with a broken hand, I was finally taken to the doctor. The doctor said I had a fracture in my hand and gave me a cast and a prescription for the pain. The prescription was supposed to be for two weeks, but was halved after two days, and the school staff refused me any additional pain pills after the fourth day. No doctor was ever consulted on this change.

The lack of medical care of the students was probably the worst thing that went on at that school. Once I was on a work crew (physical labor punishment) to destroy the inside of a barn with sledge-hammers and crowbars. Two other students and I were in a very small room in the barn. We had to knock down walls and beams, and tear out the fiberglass insulation with our only protection being the work suits we wore every day. Fiberglass was everywhere, on the floor in piles, being ripped out, in everyone's suits, and in the air in a thick pink cloud. After we finished and went back to the dorm, all of us complained of itching on our skin. I had once heard from my father, a health and safety inspector, that if you get fiberglass imbedded in your skin that you should take a hot shower immediately to get it out or infection might occur. We were not allowed to take showers and had to endure constant itching. A few days later all three of us complained of stabbing pains in our chests and asked if we could see a doctor. We were not even allowed to see the nurse. But later on, when I got very sick and started throwing up pink vomit, the nurse was called. She said I would be fine. Two days later, because the vomiting persisted, I was allowed to go to bed.

Once a student got a horrible bloody nose. He was filling up garbage pails with blood from his nose over the course of about a week. He grew pale and weak, so much so that he could not even sit up in a chair, which was his punishment at the time. He would frequently have to take breaks to lie down. No doctor was ever called, nor was the nurse ever informed.

That school is currently being sued by parents who had a daughter who went there. The daughter was taking lithium, a salt. She developed a bladder infection and had to go to the bathroom quite frequently during the day and in the middle of the night. When one person has to go to the bathroom, they have to take the whole group, so it soon became a problem. The staff came to the conclusion that this behavior must have been some way of getting attention, and her water intake was limited to two glasses a meal. This caused dehydration and the lithium levels rose in her brain. This quickly resulted in several physical symptoms, such as energy loss. She was so tired that she fell asleep in class all the time. It got so bad that she couldn't even feed herself. My girlfriend had to change her tampon for her. This was all attributed to her wanting attention, and no nurse or doctor was informed. This continued on until she started vomiting bile for several days. She was finally taken to a doctor, who quickly identified it as lithium overdose. She was put on kidney dialysis, but by then she had suffered irreparable brain damage.

The story doesn't end there. When the state decided to press charges, the 12-step school got the kids to plead the fifth. They told the students that the state might want to send them to jail and the school was going to do everything necessary to protect *them*. Most of the students had already been involved with the law and were scared, so they agreed to be quiet.

The group therapy sessions were horrible. An actual therapist was present at group therapy only once a week. Our only *therapy* was a session involving no one but other troubled teenagers, each with their own agendas, problems, and manipulations. People were forced to tell their innermost secrets in front of everybody, or else be chastised by the group for being dishonest. If someone didn't agree with another's opinion, they were confronted for not *taking it in*. Teenagers with severe emotional problems were given as much authority as licensed therapists.

If a student ran away from school, the dorm that they ran from was punished. I saw a student forced by staff to stand with his face in a doorway corner and not turn around for an hour. I have been *silenced*—not allowed to talk—for two days, or else face other punishment. One time the whole dorm was forced to hold hands for two days straight in the same room while an angered student held us hostage by refusing to cooperate.

One of the worst things done at that school is the prevention of legal adults from leaving. This is kidnapping, plain and simple. A 22 year old who enrolled himself, but later wanted to leave, was forced to sit in a room for a week until he "decided" to stay. An 18 year old who went to the main office to withdraw was instead sent to the punishment unit.

After I turned 18, I saw what I had never seen before—the school for what it really was. It was a system of lies to make the headmaster money. So, I decided to leave with my girlfriend. We had to sneak away at two in the morning and leave all of our possessions behind. Later, the school gave our stuff to Goodwill.

The first night we had to hitchhike along the interstate, but were not picked up and had to sleep during the day in the woods. We got a ride to a garage in town, where they gave us water and some cookies. They were worried that the sheriff would drive by and see us. They told us that he wouldn't care that we were 18 and would take us back regardless. A man there gave us a ride to a truck stop, and from there we made it to friends in Pennsylvania. From then on, we were safe.

Four months later, the school is still not out of our lives. There is a policy at the school to convince parents that if their child runs away, they are not to talk to their child at all. My mother would not help me at all for weeks, but I moved in with my father, who had nothing to do with the school, and with whom I had not been allowed to have contact while there. My girlfriend was not so lucky. Her parents still do not speak to her, so she must live with a friend's mother. She called her father to let him know she was alright and with friends, and he hung up on her. Just getting her identification was hard. The school has refused to send her transcripts to her, although she's following all legal procedures. My mother, although she will speak to me, still refuses to support me. I fear that she has been brainwashed.

Even now, as I am living with my father, the school still haunts me. I am free of the drug problems, emotional problems, and violence problems that used to control my life. But the school refuses to let go. My mother recently paid for another year of enrollment. So, the school refuses, with no reason, to give my transcripts to my new high school. I fear that I will never be allowed to leave the school, and they will prevent me from graduating from high school.

All I want to do is live and move on with my life. But I am not allowed to put this period behind me. Every day, certain words or images bring up memories of my school programming. I constantly fight the absurd things taught to me, forcibly shoved into my thought processes by the school's therapy sessions. I am glad, at least, to have the support of my girlfriend, whom I love dearly, and who shares my experiences at the school. She can relate to me. Without her support I know I would not have made it through this ordeal.

16 ▲ Ginger
Big Book Cult

I think "soul rape" is a good way to describe it. During my voluntary participation in the steps, I felt the effects of maybe not "forceable soul rape," but perhaps "soul statutory rape," or "soul brutalization" in a fanatical Big Book cult, the head sponsor being an AA member named Miguel.

Members of our intense little group spent many self-centered conversations tracing our spiritual lineage back to Miguel and his sponsor, an ex-Jesuit priest and homosexual, Dodd T. Whenever either one of them was in town, they would stay in their sponsee's homes, room and board free. Sponsees grateful to Miguel for their sobriety also contributed cash for his expenses. The most spiritual way to contribute cash was to send it anonymously. But then Miguel would not know of your good deed. I didn't care. It put joy in my heart to secretly send Miguel money. He would mention sometimes that "money from God" came in the mail, and I would feel like I had a connection with God, who was using me along with others to take care of Miguel.

The Big Book cults flourishing on the West Coast are based on an invention of Miguel's—the "Big Book study." The Big Book study usually takes place in someone's home. Newcomers who come to AA or NA meetings are invited. The Book study cultists do not recognize a separation between AA and NA members. As far as they are concerned, addiction to drugs and alcohol are the same "malady." We were told that Jimmy K., the first NA member, got clean from taking the AA Big Book, crossing out the word "alcohol," and substituting "heroin." Then he just followed the rest of the directions.

The study is given in a series, so that a newcomer can work the steps along with the book study. This type of book study, unlike a regular meeting, is taught by one person. The teacher/sponsor takes the group through the book, line by line. Using this method, it takes about 12 weekly three-hour meetings to go through the first six chapters of the Big Book. Later chapters are taught separately, and only to those who have done their fifth steps. These book studies spread from Sacramento to surrounding areas. Miguel also had a fairly large cult going near Albuquerque, New Mexico, and many, many of his sponsees moved to other towns and started Book studies. The woman who heard my second fifth step (I was told I had not done it correctly the first time) conducted her own studies, and moved to Pennsylvania, starting the Book studies there.

The attitude of the rest of the fellowship toward Big Book studies is usually one of disapproval. That's because quite often those who get sober via the Big Book study will go to regular meetings and tell everyone there they aren't truly sober because they didn't work the steps according to the instructions in the Big Book. However, sometimes the Big Book studies become so popular that the voice of the local fellowship will change, and become much more fundamentalist. This can happen very quickly, since Big Book cultists are much more likely than average AA members to accept secretaryships, and secretaries are the ones who pick the speakers for the meetings. When I was a secretary, I picked mainly other Big Book cultists to speak. Often, the meetings become battlegrounds between this Big Book mafia and the more liberal members of AA.

I once asked Miguel how he got the idea for Big Book studies. He told me that he listened once to Joe and Charlie, AA speakers who go to conventions and explicate the Book. (Joe-and-Charlie tapes can be ordered from online AA groups.) He said his Book study grew from theirs. I've heard the Joe-and-Charlie tapes. Miguel's study is much more intensive and detailed.

In the Book studies, newcomers are taught, as per "The Doctor's Opinion" foreword in the Big Book, that real alcoholics and addicts are allergic to alcohol, and to use even a little on the skin in perfumes, deodorants, makeup, cleaning products, etc, is to tempt the "phenomenon of craving" that results from contact with alcohol. Miguel also claimed that middle-of-the-road AA is not working the program as intended; its members are not doing thorough fifth steps, daily tenth steps, or working with others as God via Bill W. intended. This reasoning appealed to the resentments of many of us who had been ignored by the AA elite, and who had trouble getting sponsors. In the Big Book cults, one never wanted for a sponsor, as having many sponsees is a desirable status symbol in this cult.

In the Big Book study groups, the 12 steps are practiced by strictly adhering to the Big Book instructions. Third steps are to take place saying the exact prayer on page 63 aloud, with someone else. Moral inventories are enormous analyses of past "selfishness" that fill entire notebooks, and fifth steps take at least entire weekends.

Those who get the most approval and are considered to be the most *spiritual* are those who spend all their free time in 12-step work. It is even justifiable to stay on welfare or SSI in order to preach at AA meetings, give Big Book studies, listen to fifth steps or tenth steps, allow newcomers to detox in homes, and all the other activities approved by this particular culture, or by Miguel.

The goal of the steps is to have a *spiritual experience.* Yes—*conscious contact with God* was the desired and *expected* result. If you haven't had a momentous spiritual experience, you must have left something out. One woman, Kay, who is still conducting Big Book studies in Buena, California, told of being lifted from her bed and levitated by God.

The only valid experiences are those had by newcomers part way through the ninth step, just as promised in the Big Book. Sponsees who come in still drinking or freshly detoxed but claiming spiritual experiences are discounted. *It wasn't enough to get you sober, was it?,* I remember saying to one sponsee, whom I had considered to be pitifully deluded. It was only those who did the work who got the results, according to Miguel.

Thinking that one has a direct line to God because of one's own hard work can cause a lot of problems. So can feeling pressed to confess every little incident one feels guilty about in order to maintain that contact. If one did not practice these confessions, or tenth steps, on a regular basis, the channel to God would get clogged up. The recovered alcoholic would lose his *conscious contact,* drink again, and maybe die. These confessions would sometimes become ridiculously embarrassing. A couple of men in the Big Book cult confessed to me that they were coming over to be *worked with* because they had a crush on me. Another man admitted that while making two sandwiches, one for himself and another for me, that he put the biggest piece of ham in his own sandwich.

The most inane tenth steps were confessed lies. I would have an interaction with someone, then go back home and think about what was said. Sometimes it would come up in my mind that I had *lied* about a motive, a reason for doing something, or how I did it. I once confessed to my sponsor, John, that I'd lied about a dream I'd had about him. Later, when I thought more about it, I realized I had not lied at all. Then I was confronted with this ridiculous question: should I tell him I had not lied at all, or should I just let it rest? Sometimes we'd call each other back and forth all day with silliness like that. To us it was very serious. All character defects and wrongs—selfishness, dishonesty, self-seeking, and fear, had to be admitted to another human being as per step ten. Any lies had to be "amended"— admitting to the one lied to that you lied. I once confessed a lie to a store clerk, whom I had told I didn't want some socks. I went back and told her I had wanted them, but could not afford to pay for them.

Sometimes making amends could make a situation much worse. One type of amends that can be very destructive is described on page 77 of the Big Book, at the end of paragraph two:

> The question of how to approach the man we hated will arise. It may be he has done more harm than we have done him and, though we may have acquired a better attitude toward him, we are still not too keen about admitting our faults. Nevertheless, with a person we dislike, we take the bit in our teeth. It is harder to go to an enemy than to a friend, but we find it much more beneficial to us. We go to him in a helpful and forgiving spirit, confessing our former ill feeling and expressing our regret.

The problem here is that the person you think you hated probably does not want to hear about it—I certainly didn't. Yet I have had two people in this cult come up to me out of the blue and admit, *I've had ill feelings about you and I regret them.* I would get such a terrible, sinking feeling, knowing I had been secretly hated. There was one woman, a former sponsee, who particularly hurt me with this amends. Toward the end of my sojourn in the Big Book cult, I began to speak out against their ways, saying I thought some of the stuff was unhealthy. Verna, who had been my sponsee, asked me about the "hate" amends. I told her the point of amends is to repair damage, that there was no reason to make amends to someone you had not hurt, and that she didn't have to go around making amends to people just because she disliked or hated them. I also told her other things that I thought were wrong with the cult. Then I didn't see her for awhile.

Apparently she'd been sticking with the cult and going to the Big Book gurus for spiritual advice. I would call her from time to time and ask how she was doing, thinking everything was fine between us. Then one Christmas she came over with a nice card and a little present. She gave me a hug and told me, *There's something I have to tell you. I've had ill feelings about you, and I regret them.* I felt like I'd been slugged in the stomach. I was depressed anyway, due to untreated, clinical depression that was slowly getting worse, thanks to the programming I have been describing.

A lot of women fell in love with Miguel. I had fallen in love with him too, and for awhile that really kept me going. "Love" raises the endorphins and gets people to do the most amazingly foolish things. Miguel was always available to talk, and a woman would get the feeling that he could stare into her soul and know her fully. As assertive top dog in any Book study, and having that charismatic *I know what I'm talking about* aura, he would naturally attract women. He could also be emotionally abusive. He would make offhand comments in the groups that showed who had won his approval and who hadn't. I remember an aging woman friend of mine (who I know secretly loved Miguel) making an innocent comment at one of Miguel's book studies. Miguel looked at her coldly. *That's either honest, or it's not,* he said, thereby calling into question her honesty. To Miguel, spirituality had a direct relation to "rigorous honesty." Funny thing about spirituality—it was usually the youngest, prettiest women who were often approved of as "the most honest" and so forth.

Many men loved Miguel too, and many of them as well as some women began to act and sound just like him. While giving their own Big Book studies, they'd take on many of his mannerisms and voice inflections. I told my weekend-long fifth step to a woman who not only sounded like Miguel, but also looked somewhat like him—a smaller, feminine version of Miguel. She confessed to me that she loved Miguel too. The "love" women, and men, would feel for Miguel was obvious but never widely spoken of except in the cloistered arena of a fifth step or tenth step. And though I too was wholly in love with Miguel for awhile, I was afraid of him, of saying something that might show I was *spiritually unfit* in some way. Although I'd loved Miguel, I'd never spent any time alone with him, except on the phone. I really believed I had a spiritual link with him, and that I could tell, with my step 11-promised *sixth sense* (Big Book, page 85), when he was coming to town and what he would need.

It's funny how you can think you love someone and yet fear him deeply at the same time. I was terrified of Miguel's disapproval. I felt that I could sense his every little nuance of attitude toward me or someone else. I could barely even talk to him, for fear of his disapproval of some inept thing I might say to expose myself as unspiritual.

There was a certain way the *spiritually fit* had to talk. If you said "I" too much, or talked about your life, that was self-centered. If you complained about something, you were angry and in need of a moral inventory and a confession. Talking about something you liked was "ego." The only time it was okay to complain was if you were complaining about your own defects. If you talked about what others were doing, that was gossip. The only really safe topic was to talk about how to be of service, or to ask questions, or give advice about the spiritual needs of sponsees. Sometimes when Miguel was in a room full of people, I would sense tension and fear so thick it felt like you could cut it with scissors. The presence of my own sponsor, John, who in turn was a sponsee of Miguel's, would make that even worse, since John was quite verbally abusive. No one could relax until he left the room. Yet in between spurts of loving Miguel, I loved John with all my heart too, in spite of the fact that he once told me I was selfish, dishonest, self-seeking, and frightened, and had been that way since the day I was born. He also, in a meeting, called me a small-town slut. He treated all his sponsees that way, though, so I felt *part of the family.* *He's tough, but he's a good sponsor,* people would say. Anyway, most of the time, I was quite willing to find and admit my own defects.

After making a habit of finding defects, it was easy to realize that nearly everything one does is based in selfishness or fear. In fact, one of the most celebrated lieutenants in this Big Book cult, a man privileged to be one of Miguel's first sponsees, wrote a list of things people might find themselves doing or saying that showed their defects. He would pass it around to sponsees as a daily 10th-step check. Here are a few examples from the chart: "Resentment, dishonesty, selfishness, fear, arguments/discussions, melodrama, worry, 'don't like' something, lies, anxiety, self-concern, annoyed, crocodile tears, asserting 'rights,' speeding, retaliating, feigned interest, trips, criticizing, restless, sugar-coating, TV, unresolved 'issues,' boredom," etc. The list went on and on. After looking at even part of it, it is fairly easy to see how totally defective one is. You can hardly draw a breath without being selfish!

One of the worst aspect of the Big Book cults is the disapproval of psychiatric and pain medications. Big Book thumpers routinely went off meds or bravely refused codeine after trips to the dentist. One woman I know went off her Stellazine (a medication to control the hallucinations of schizophrenia). She had been told by Miguel that her visions were from God and that she could learn to live with them.

She tried, but some of them were so scary she ended up shunned by most of the group for being unhappy all the time. She eventually ended up drunk. While a member of the Big Book cult, I should have been treated for depression, which would have helped a lot of the obsessive thoughts and resentments I was having, resentments that I was foolishly treating with continued confessions and amends. This type of repressed anger and self-humiliation became a vicious cycle. By the time I left the Big Book cult, I was suicidal.

Throughout most of my three years with the Big Book Cult, I had made little progress toward having a regular life. I'd taken cleaning jobs to barely support myself, and rented rooms where I held, of course, Big Book studies. I was praised widely among the Big Book crowd for my spirituality, my willingness to work with anybody, my lack of materialism. I would spend entire afternoons and weekends listening to fifth steps. I had many sponsees, but no car. I rode my bike around town. Unfortunately, I could not easily get to out-of-town meetings by bike. At the same time, I slowly began to notice that those who preached Big Book recovery were not always working the program themselves. Once I learned that a young man John and I co-sponsored was going to speak at a speaker's meeting out of town. I asked John if I and my new sponsee could ride along with him to the meeting. He was supposed to call and let me know. He never did. Finally, at the last minute, a sponsee of his, with this ugly job thrust upon him, called. There was no room in the car for me. Some of the younger women, who had nice clothes and their own cars, and who could afford trips to the beauty parlor because they worked full-time, were being taken. There was no room for my chubby sponsee and I.

I also noticed these other prettier but less spiritual women were getting laid, and I wasn't, not in the Big Book cult anyway. Of course, I had a good dating life among the much less spiritual guys who liked to talk about themselves and who had other blatant character defects. Being a good listener, quiet and undemanding, acting happy all the time, and more than willing to cook for them, the less spiritual guys thought I was the greatest! But really, I was mainly dating them to lure them into the cult. Yes, I was willing to get laid for God! How I wanted a Big Book guru—one of those guys who was completely *recovered* and knew what he was talking about! I wanted to be a Big Book mistress —perhaps have Miguel himself move in (or if not Miguel, my own sponsor, John, would do) and together we would construct a Big Book study empire—just like the house Bill W. describes in the chapter, *A Vision for You.* I would be the eternal Big Book goddess —cooking food and dispensing spiritual pearls for the pitiful newcomers who came our way. But in spite of having many friends and men to date, I was lonely. It seemed like all the Big Book dons were going after young, voluptuous women or more mature women with nice homes, jobs, cars, workout clubs, and clothes. And some of them were dating several of these women at once, which occasionally caused a "Big Book scandal."

In one such scandal, one of the Big Book lieutenants—the same one who wrote the tenth-step guide, above—was found to be 13th-stepping about three women at once, all of whom knew each other. One was a newcomer with less than three months, who was a beautiful but very emotionally disturbed 19 year old. The news got around after she did a confession of her part—*she wanted love*—and a flock of angry women showed up at the "sex inventory" section of his Big Book study and just sat and stared at him.

As a result of this mass criticism, the whole group was castigated for "gossip" by Miguel. It seems he had found himself in a similar situation in Albuquerque, and so he empathized with his spiritual son. Gossip was the problem. If it hadn't been for gossip, no one would have known the fox was grabbing the most delectable morsels from the henhouse.

On another occasion, Miguel's sponsor, Dodd T., came to town. I invited him to dinner a couple of times and introduced him to my friends, some of whom he would *work with.* Once I walked into my living room, and there was Dodd, with a gay friend of mine, Petey, sitting on his lap. *He's my spiritual grandpa,* Petey said. It soon became apparent that the people Dodd wanted most to *work with* were the younger, better-looking males. He seemed not to have much patience with women. In fact, I think he hated women. He once said that spirituality is passed from men to women, because men, being more honest, were more spiritual.

One day my friend Andy came over brooding after having spent the day with Dodd T. Andy seemed to have a lot of problems. He had been sober for six years, but was often disturbed, depressed, or just quiet. I asked what he thought of Dodd T. Did he think Dodd could help him. He said, *No, he didn't help me. I think he wanted to suck my cock.* I don't know why I was shocked, but I was. Later, after Dodd T. left town, some other members of the Big Book mafia attempted to help my friend, Andy.

I had been close to Andy since coming into AA. We had both been English majors and we hung out together a lot. For awhile, I had quite a crush on him because he was a kind, good looking man who played the guitar very well, and he was nice to me. Eventually, though, he went off to France. Meantime, I got caught up with the Big Book mafia. When Andy came back from France, he got involved with a woman he'd met out of town. He fell in love. She got pregnant, then dumped him. He was heartbroken. He became more and more depressed. He also confided to me that he was deeply disturbed by a scene in the movie, *Misery*, where Kathy Bates bashes the feet of a helpless captive male so he can't get away from her "loving care." Andy'd had obsessions about that scene ever since he'd watched the movie. *I should never have watched that scene*, he would mutter, with his hands to his forehead. Now, of course, I realize that Andy was beyond the help of AA, and that he needed a therapist and possibly psychiatric care. I doubt a single AA member recommended that to him, though. He would go to daily meetings and talk about how he felt, but that didn't seem to help him.

One night Andy and I were out biking, as we often did, having coffee downtown and going on small-town adventures. For the first time, Andy took me back to the house where he rented a room, and we had sex. I cared for Andy in a more friendly, settled-down way by then, and I hoped that this new path in our relationship would help snap him out of the depression over the woman who had rejected him. I would be disappointed. After that, Andy avoided me for a few days. I was a little disturbed, so I confessed *my part* of the incident to my male Big Book mafia sponsor, John. Later, I made amends to Andy by letting him off the hook. I ran into him downtown and said, *Hey, don't worry about the other night. Let's just be friends like we always have been.* Andy seemed quite relieved. He was still very much in love with his old girlfriend, and I think he'd hoped sex with me would help.

Later, Andy called me and was all upset about his old girlfriend. He'd called her on the phone, and she'd hung up on him. He told me he thought she started hating him when she found out he had genital herpes. *And he was having an outbreak now.* When Andy told me this, my stomach sunk. We'd had unprotected sex only a little over two weeks before. Was this Andy's way of telling me I was exposed? I thought that was pretty lame, but I knew it would be unspiritual to be angry. I just looked at my part. I'd had unprotected sex hoping to help someone. Hmmm, not good enough. I'd had unprotected sex because I was lazy and wanted a man. There, that sounded more selfish and would be good enough for John. I called my sponsor and told him my inventory. (The real truth was quite innocent. I hadn't had sex for awhile, I cared about Andy, and as far as protection went, I trusted God. Foolish maybe, but not selfish or defective!) I also confessed fear that I might have herpes.

John gave me the number of a medical hotline. I called and learned that if I was going to break out with genital herpes, I would have already had symptoms. Oh, the relief I felt! I swore off unprotected sex. But by then, because of my tenth-step inventories, my sponsor, John, knew all about what was going on with Andy.

Since Andy hung around at my house a lot, another Big Book guru, Dirk, started preaching to him and driving him around town in his Jeep Explorer. Andy by this time was nearly helpless with despair, and willing to try anything. Dirk told Andy he was unhappy because he'd never "worked the program." He told him he might as well go out and drink. Dirk and some of the other thumpers, my sponsor John included, hammered at him about his faults. They told him he was selfish, dishonest, and frightened. They would take him to breakfast and tell him that. They told him he had to turn his will and his life over to the care of God and work an *honest inventory*, or he would drink and die.

Finally, Andy started drinking. After he started, Dirk actually took him to a bar, bought him a drink, and said, *Go ahead, drink. Notice you are powerless to stop. Notice the phenomenon of craving. When you come back, if you live, you must turn your life and will over to the care of God.*

Most sane people know, of course, that my friend should have fled AA, sought real mental health care, and, of course, not drank. But I think Andy was too far gone emotionally to have any idea of what he needed, or what options he had. I now believe this is a case where Big Book thumpers literally drove someone to drink.

Andy was soon drinking around the clock with another AA member who was drinking. My sponsor, John, laughed when he found out: *What did I tell you,* he gloated, *he never did his sex inventory, and now he's drinking!* John actually believed Andy was drinking because he'd had sex with me without telling me he had herpes! Eventually, Andy came over to my house wanting to stay and detox. He sobered up, then took off in his car. I heard he went up to the town where his pregnant ex-girlfriend was. Later I heard he was sober there, and that she was letting him visit his baby.

There are so many more true tales of folks spiritually abused in this group that it's difficult to know which to share.

One of my sponsees, Shelly, had been separated from her husband. She was half nuts from a serious detox, terribly lonely, and vulnerable—like many newcomers to AA and NA. She became mesmerized by Dirk, the same Big Book thumper who drove Andy to drink. Dirk took Shelly under his wing. He would call her, give her spiritual advice, and drive her places. I warned her not to take his attentions seriously, that he took many newcomers out in his brand new Jeep Explorer, but she was mesmerized. She ended up giving him a blow job in the Jeep during one of their excursions, parked near a tomato field. He told her not to tell anyone. Afterward, he stopped calling her, and he began to ignore her at meetings.

Later, I could tell something was wrong with her. Shelly had been thrilled with sobriety, and now she was glum. It was easy to get the story out of her. When I called to confront Dirk, he blithely said they *didn't go all the way*.

This woman probably weighed less than 100 pounds. I don't think she held him at knife point and made him unzip his breeches. He accepted oral sex, told her to keep it a secret, and trashed her like an expired credit card. It's one thing to make a mistake, another to clean it up properly, which he didn't do and never has. He's still driving newcomer women around, showering them with attention, and they are still, vulnerable and lonely as they are, falling in love with him. People in the know gossip about it, but I am the only one who ever came close to calling him on it. Anyway, the consensus of the group was that she was a hot little number who couldn't keep her meathooks out of men's pants, and that there's nothing in the Big Book saying newcomers can't have sex with old-timers.

Anyway, turned off to AA, she's now out drinking again. Dirk is now bringing guru-type spiritual conventions to hotels in the wine country and the Sierras, charging money and preaching. Last I heard, he still has women from miles around coming to see him for his spiritual wisdom. A former sponsee of mine drives a couple hundred miles every week or so to spend an hour in the glow of his spirituality.

Wouldn't it have been nice if Shelly had been safe with the men of AA? And then, if she were determined to get laid and maybe be hurt, let a bar-room pickup do it? What kind of liability would there be if a therapist had sent her to AA for this kind of treatment?

From five years in AA, this is only one of the many cases I know about. Multiply it by the tens of thousands of meetings, most of which have at least one predator-in-residence. Such scandals are not unusual, but rather regular occurrences, and have been for at least 60 years of AA's existence—and everyone in AA knows it!

Once I realized how many people whose love and approval I longed for were breaking the same rules I was stringently keeping, I began to feel really screwed. I began to feel the amazing anger you sometimes see in people who feel they got spiritually raped in AA. At the time, I did not understand the strength and the righteousness of this rage. I kept taking inventory, finding my fault. Every time I did this, I transferred emotional investments into the sponsor or group. Of course some of it *was* my fault. I wanted love, approval, a group to belong to. But I also really believed I needed to take those actions, follow those directions to stay sober. For years, counselors had continually sent me to AA. Nevertheless, I had periodically become depressed, then drunk. When the capos of this Big Book mafia came along, paid attention to me, took me through the book and told me I had kept drinking because I hadn't "done it right," I believed them. What else could I think? No one in AA had any other answer, and the counselors kept sending me back to AA.

Anyway, my depression deepened, and as I began pointing out the hypocrisy of the Big Book mafia, I began to be shunned. I tried to get another sponsor from the less rigid part of the fellowship, but she turned out to be crazy. Still sober, but disgusted, I left AA altogether, after five years that had resulted in a sobriety filled with anger and despair.

Eventually, I had to get drunk to avoid sitting in front of a train on the railroad tracks out back of the old hotel I lived in. Actually, this turned out to be one of the best choices (of those I was capable of) that I could have made. Because if one thing will cut off your associations with AA members, drinking will. As far as many AA members are concerned, if you drank you "didn't try hard enough" or "left something out." One woman I'd been friends with for years, when she heard I drank, asked me, *What did you leave out?*

Thank goodness for information encouraging self-recovery. Without access to it, I don't know what might have happened to me. Fortunately, a friend of mine who had deprogrammed himself from the same Big Book group in the same way as I would, loaned me a copy of Jack Trimpey's *The Small Book.* Oh, how we laughed at the blasphemies therein! I spent three days of detox, that should have been miserable, pissing myself laughing. Everything that I needed to know about what had happened to me, and about what I needed to do, was right there.

I have now been sober on my own for three years. Its great to be sober *and* free!

17 ▲ Sarah
My Moment of Clarity

The day I knew I would never go back to AA again was when, after five years in the program, I realized my life was worse, much worse than I ever imagined it could be. I was poor, I was depressed, and I was living in the same house as my sponsor, who had gone totally nuts.

By that time I did not really need a sponsor at all. But everyone I knew had a sponsor, and I really thought I needed one too. My last sponsor had dumped me for questioning his treatment of me at a meeting. But when I asked Minnie to be my sponsor, I had no idea she was a closet lunatic. I should have picked up a hint when she always wanted to meet at my house and never at hers. But I thought maybe she just had good boundaries.

Then I learned that she had been staying several days at another sponsee's, Linda's, house. The reason was supposed to be that Minnie's landlord had found rats in her house. Minnie wanted to stay elsewhere until the rats were exterminated, because she was afraid. Later, there was a grapevine rumor about some kind of big fight between Minnie and Linda. Apparently, Minnie called Linda's boyfriend and got confrontive because she thought Linda was at his house when she was five minutes late meeting Minnie.

I didn't know very much about those problems. I just figured, like most folks in AA figure, that it was probably the sponsee's fault. I asked Minnie to be my sponsor. Later, I let my daughter, a new mother, and her boyfriend take over our apartment. My plan was to rent a room somewhere to live in.

Minnie asked me to share a house with her, since she had to move out of the rat-infested house. Having nowhere else to go, I agreed. Minnie had eight years of sobriety, had a good job, looked good, offered good shares in meetings, and was a good listener. I did not foresee any problems. The trouble started when Minnie had to move out of her old house and needed help. That's when I learned why she had rats. I have rarely seen a house so dirty. There was mildew on the living room walls where Minnie's furniture had been. The corners hung with cobwebs, the bathroom was a nightmare of mold, hard-water stains, and soap scum. The bathroom faucets, which should have been star shaped, were rounded with soap scum, from about five years of turning the faucet on and off with soapy hands and never cleaning it. Minnie said she would pay me to clean the house before her landlord came in to inspect. I felt sorry for her and accepted.

I spent about 12 hours in that house cleaning. I couldn't bear to charge her for all that, so I only charged her for six hours. She kept forgetting to pay me. When, needing the money, I finally asked, she paid me, but she acted angry about it. Then we had some trouble because I'd had sex with a man I'd begun to date (at *his* house), and I had not mentioned it until a week later. After I told her about it, she acted angry. I couldn't understand why, so later I asked her why she was angry. She admitted it was because I had engaged in sex with Ralph and had not confided in her immediately. I simply did not agree that sex was a big deal, with both the guy, Ralph, and I being divorced and free to date each other. I didn't think it was a big enough deal to tell her about it. It was certainly no threat to my sobriety. It was then that I realized sex *was* a big deal with Minnie.

But I had already moved in with her. Real trouble started when I stopped going to the Baptist church she'd wanted me to attend with her, and kept seeing some of my AA friends she didn't approve of. She didn't like what I call their *AA politics*. Some of my friends were less conservative AA members, believing in goddesses or no god at all, and following the AA program somewhat differently than Minnie did.

Then Minnie was horrified when I started going to a Mormon church with a family I worked for taking care of their mother, an Alzheimer's patient. I had no plans to become a Mormon; I just wanted to see what they were like. But this was a big deal to Minnie. She seemed fearful of anything or anyone unusual.

She also wanted me to go to way more AA meetings than I wanted to go to, and she hinted constantly that such-and-such a meeting was at this time or that time, although I knew very well what time the meetings were held. Also, I felt totally unaccepted by her in many different ways. She seemed angry at me all the time, and eventually I would just come home and stay in my room.

The shit hit the fan when she wanted me to pay a utility bill I thought I had already paid. I was simply trying to get her to remember that I paid it, but she went bonkers. She seemed to have trouble communicating about money, or talking in a matter-of-fact way about it. I think she might have been ashamed that she had forgotten to pay the bill, and we had a two-week notice. She ended up screaming at me in the kitchen, and she pushed me into a corner. Later, she barged her way into the home of the people I worked for to tell me the next time my homeless friend Bob came to the door for a cup of coffee, she was going to call the police.

I waited a day or two until everything had calmed down, and then told her, in a nice way, that I was going to move out. She looked shocked. She asked if I was going to be *responsible*. I said I would give her two weeks notice, but she said she needed at least next month's rent, so I gave her six weeks. I then ran a newspaper ad soliciting a room for rent.

I should have been able to stay another six weeks, but as soon as I gave Minnie the rent money, she began to drive me out early. She was absolutely enraged with me. I still do not understand the levels of her rage. Her fury seemed all out of proportion to anything I could have said or done.

I knew I had to move right away, instead of waiting until my ads panned out, when I came home from my job in the afternoon and saw that she had left piles of notes for me, one after the other, in stacks in the kitchen: *Sarah be sure you close and lock the door tightly. Sarah turn the volume down on your message recorder. Sarah please don't bring Betty* (the Alzheimer's patient) *over here. Sarah, take your clothes out of the washing machine. Sarah, fold the white quilt neatly and put it on the couch. Sarah, make sure the screen door is closed tightly. Sarah please put all my books back in the bookshelves.* She also called my phone number while I was gone, again and again, and filled up my message recorder tape with long, insane messages. She began to stalk me, showing up at a meeting she knew I loved and sitting right behind me until I would feel prickles go up my back. I learned later that she had to see her therapist on an emergency basis every evening during this period. Apparently, she had worse problems than alcoholism, for she had gone almost completely psycho.

I was scared to death of her. I needed more time to find a place to move, though I was calling around for apartments. The ad wouldn't work, for I could now not even depend on being able to get my messages. Naturally, being a good AA, I knew I must need spiritual help, and, of course my sponsor Minnie could no longer be turned to for this. So I called another AA woman, a doctor's wife who had many years of sobriety, and seemed very sane and well liked, a good speaker in meetings. I needed help, advice, validation. I started to tell her what was going on, but she wouldn't even let me talk. Immediately, she started harping on her experience with God curing her breast disease. She nattered on and on about *Saved by the Lights*, and angels, and crystals, visions, rainbows, and whatever. I sat and listened to this crap for 45 minutes, slowly realizing I was totally on my own. I doubted that any of what had been taught to me in AA was true— God was not managing my life, or, if He was, then being on the streets was His will. The steps were not helpful to me in true times of need; AA sponsors were not helpful; and meetings were not helpful. I had to help myself.

It was an enlightening moment. It was the last time I ever expected another human being, or God, to help me solve problems that adults solve every day on their own. I was a capable adult; I had not had a drink in five years, and I was probably more together than the assholes I was looking up to for advice and solutions just because they had been *sober* longer than I had and *sounded good at meetings.*

A girlfriend who also had to move let me stay with her during her own last three weeks at her house. We went into the house and moved out my things while Minnie was at work. My dear Mormon friends let me store my things at their house. I left a bed that Minnie pushed me to buy at her house, because I never had wanted it. She was beside herself calling and calling, coming to where I worked to try to get me to pick up the bed. But I never did go get the bed, and I'm glad.

It was such a relief to get away from Minnie. For the first time in months I felt like I could just relax and be myself. Later I found a tiny apartment in an old motor hotel. It was small and I had very little furniture, so I slept on a mat on the floor. It was warm, though, and it was mine.

I stopped going to meetings as well, and started therapy. It took a few months, but I began to feel much better about myself and my ability to make my own decisions. I started doing many of the things I'd always wanted to do, such as taking art classes and going to poetry readings. These were thing I had avoided because I thought I needed meetings and step work. How I loved lapping up all the good things I had been missing. How free I finally felt! I have now been sober many years without AA.

18 ▲ Joshua
Betrayal

I am a recovering IV drug user. Right now I have 16 months of clean and sober time.

A few years ago, I tested positive for HIV. I was informed that getting clean and sober would improve my chances of survival. I went to AA meetings looking for the right group. After much research, I picked a home group, where I saw a potential sponsor. I asked people what they thought of this man, and they told me that he was good natured and had over eight years of "quality" sobriety. So I asked him to be my sponsor, and he accepted.

About a month later, we were at a meeting where a former drug user was chairing. After the meeting, my sponsor asked me if I had even done hard drugs. I said yes. He asked if I'd been tested for HIV. I said yes. He then asked what the results were, and I told him the truth.

The guy freaked out, and he dropped me as a sponsee. Soon after, he spread the word about my HIV+ status. At one point I was threatened with physical violence if I did not leave that group.

I left the group and relapsed. It took a year and a half to get clean again. I still go to meetings far away and have had to seek professional help (therapy). Word has spread about my HIV+ status from meeting to meeting, so I cannot attend meetings in my own community. I go to an NA meeting several cities away and that's about it.

19 ▲ Dora

They Should Have Taken Me to the Emergency Room!

I was at a well-known East Coast recovery house, which I will call Hope Lodge, from November 6, 1996 until February 12, 1997, under the direction of an old-timer AA member, who says she was personal friends with Bill Wilson and Dr. Bob Smith.

Since then, I have read a few of the books about alternatives to 12-step recovery, and also material on Moderation Management. This information has helped me a lot. I am now in therapy and am feeling somewhat better than I did when I left the recovery house, although it took my grandmother many days to deprogram me. Yet I doubt I will ever be the same.

My story has nothing to do with heroin or cocaine—I have never used them in my life. Nor have I ever been a drinker. It all began when I was having migraines along with other health problems, which included depression and anxiety. I was taking prescriptions for these problems. Although I always took the medication as prescribed, within four or five days after starting the new migraine medication, I had a bad drug interaction, with very severe symptoms. I had been visiting my parents when this happened. I now feel my mother's decision—to send me to rehab—was an extreme overreaction. They should have just taken me to the emergency room. Instead of calling an ambulance, they waited a few hours for me to wake up. The medicine had put me in a deep sleep, and if they really thought I was in danger, they should have gotten me to a hospital.

A few months earlier, my mother had stopped drinking cold turkey, after having drunk daily and heavily during my formative years. She never did call herself an *alcoholic*, although she still carries on and on about AA stuff. I really think I ended up at Hope Lodge because one of my parents' friends lives AA day in day out, or so he says. I think he's just a con man, but he told them he went to Hope

Lodge himself, and thought it was fine. Because of my experiences there, my father is no longer friends with him and does not keep in contact with him. My father now fully supports my point of view and helped me get the excellent medical care that I now have.

I first went to a detox house for 15 days before being transferred to Hope Lodge. I hadn't been eating very well for months; I'd been on a protein powder diet. The powder had all the necessary vitamins and minerals in it, but I had dropped to 110 pounds. I am 5' 7" and had always weighed around 135. So when I first got to the recovery house, I thought I was going to a place that addressed eating disorders. However, at this detox, I had nothing to detox from. I was allowed to keep the antidepressant and anti-anxiety medication—Zoloft and Xanax—prescribed me.

Later, when I was transferred to Hope Lodge, they told me that no one ends up there by accident. I heard a lot of that kind of *God's will* stuff. But even the head nurse asked me at the intake if I really thought I should be there.

Before signing in to Hope Lodge, you are not told that they will take all your credit cards, money, and I.D. They tell you there is a phone at Hope Lodge—but there are no phones for clients. I read over the papers they gave me upon admission, but they were so vague I had no idea what I was in for. So, yes, I signed myself in, but I will never sign anything so ambiguous again.

My parents told me they would come every Sunday to visit, but we were lucky if Hope let them visit once a month. The location of Hope Lodge was remote, and leaving was discouraged, if not made an overwhelming task. And at Hope Lodge you don't even have to relapse to get back in. When one of the clients was simply *fearful* of a relapse, they told her to come back for a few weeks. She was still there four months later.

Upon arrival, I was subjected to a standard search of my things and me. Then I was introduced to my *buddy*. At such 30-day recovery places, the buddy is supposed to be just another client appointed to hang out with you for a few days to make sure you get to where you are supposed to be. But in actual practice, having a buddy means having to spend two weeks with that person no further than six feet away, ever. If one of you wants to stand, the other must. And all the while you are constantly being observed by staff, who note how you react to this very unnatural situation.

The routine at Hope Lodge was regimented. We had a strict

schedule of when we got up, ate, went to meetings and groups, wrote in our journals, and did step work. We were run ragged—it was like a miliary regimen. All day we were inundated with a constant barrage of AA stuff. They held *hotseat,* where the counselor and other clients would all gang up on one person to break him or her down emotionally. This was especially done to clients who said the wrong thing, or disagreed with some aspect of the program. I was in so much fear I would hardly say ten words; I just went along with everything I thought I was supposed to say and do.

And, within hours of admission to Hope Lodge, the harassment started about the Zoloft, the antidepressant I had been taking for quite some time, and the Xanax, which I needed to quell severe panic attacks. I was persuaded to go off my prescribed medication. No doctor oversaw this procedure, and the doctor who diagnosed my depression and anxiety was not consulted. They were fanatics about other medication as well, even over-the-counter stuff like aspirin and antihistamines. When I threw away mine, the result was disaster. I still have not regained the progress I had made while I'd been taking the antidepressants and anti-anxiety medication.

Although they took any reading material clients had, much of the daily regimen included writing, so they had a dictionary available to clients. I was so hungry for something besides "recovery" to occupy my mind, I took to reading the dictionary, just reading the lists of words and their meanings. I never let anyone see that's what I was doing; had they known, they would have taken it away from me. This dictionary-reading was something of my own, a part of myself I didn't relinquish and that kept me going.

It took me 95 days before I could get over the horror and shock enough to write to tell my oldest and dearest friend where I was. We have been best friends for 28 years. I was so embarrassed. She is married and has a family, and I was afraid she would want to come and get me. She had been calling my family and couldn't get an answer as to where I was. She knew something was terribly wrong.

One of the biggest effects on my personality from the abandonment of my medication, and the AA brainwashing that took its place, is fear. While in the recovery house, I developed a fear of many things. I now feel like I am missing out on so much. There are now parts of life—traveling, shopping, visiting—that I should not be afraid of, nor had I ever been afraid of before. I will never be able to forget when those little things that many people don't think about were not available to me then, and because of my fear, seem out of reach now. My friends are always asking me to go here and there with them. They already know I won't go, but at least they still call and keep asking me to get out of the house. I feel like I have turned into a little old lady overnight.

Fear. Yes, but next month is a new month so maybe I will then think about going places again. I might not, but at least I have the freedom to make those decisions.

At Hope Lodge the only "decision" we were allowed to make was that *we are powerless,* which I am not. They told us that we had to relinquish our wills. Hope Lodge was wrong again; I hung on to my will. That's how I survived at all—my will. They are very good at breaking you down, but they didn't break me down all the way.

The only extra reading we had at Hope Lodge was the daily newspaper, the national edition of the *New York Daily News,* and a local paper, the *Day Ledger.* They were not put in the lounge until after three o'clock, which was also the same time as mail call. We had until 5:45 to be seated for dinner. Women had to wear dresses every night, and had to sit at the table, six to a table, until 7:00 p.m. All the while, the staff sat there and watched us to make sure we were interacting. It was such a strange feeling to have these weird people watching us. The evening brainwashing session started at 7:15 and lasted until 9:00 p.m. Then we could watch television until 10:00 p.m. They had a terribly old television with an antenna that only received the four main stations, and whoever got to the TV first decided what we watched. I never got to see the evening news, since the earliest news was at 10:00. But the newspapers were still out to read. I could take leave of the dictionary and read the news, which I did, hungrily, if I got to one of the papers first.

If you insist on leaving, you have to put in a 96-hour notice, and then the staff will dump you at a bus stop in the nearest town. But what would you do with no I.D., no money, no credit cards? I had been physically weak for years, and after the ordeal at Hope, I didn't feel I would be able to make the 60-some mile trek on foot to my grandmother's. After three months of being off needed medication, along with the verbal and emotional abuse, being treated like a child, having no freedom, and being subjected to nearly continuous brainwashing, I was a basket case. I started crying, and I couldn't stop.

They finally called my father, and allowed me to ask him to take me home. Once he picked up on how emotionally unstable I was, and how clients were *really* treated if they didn't like the multitude of rules and regulations, he came right away. Before that, my parents had simply accepted what they wanted to hear. The day that I signed out, I was so glad to be leaving that it didn't bother me to sign a form absolving the lodge of responsibility for my condition. I was not allowed to say goodbye to the friends I'd made.

Once my parents picked me up, they agreed to take me to my grandmother. As soon as my grandmother saw me, she said—*Dora's not leaving this house.* My grandmother was born in 1914, well before recovery centers sprang up all over. She had watched the recovery movement over a period of time, and never liked any of it. While I was with her, sometimes I'd spout AA cliches as I was programmed to do, and she would remind me that was not how the world worked. For example, I'd say *Let go and let God,* and she would remind me that this was quite possibly crap, a way to avoid problems, and that everything that happened to me was *not* God's will. The leader and others at the center had told me what they *thought* God's will was, and my grandmother would tell me, *How do they know what God's will is? They don't know that.*

Update

Thanks to continued good psychiatric care, a good therapist, being able to tell my story, and having someone *listen to me and believe me,* I am getting better. Lately, I've been able to leave the house to go pick up my elderly aunt and drive her to go shopping. I have been able to work in the family business as well. I have survived—although if something like this were ever to happen to me again, I doubt I could stand going through it.

20 ▲ Georgia
The 13th Step

I was an active AA member for over five years. During that time I saw it all: abuse, attacks, assaults (both verbal and physical), vicious gossiping, deceit, and betrayal. I finally found the courage to leave the cult in March of this year.

When I was 26 and had been sober for over two years, I was 13th-stepped by a man with over five years. I trusted him because he was a sober member of the program. I had not been sleeping around with anyone else, and we discussed our HIV status (both negative). However, after our second sexual encounter I discovered that he had given me herpes. Needless to say, I was devastated. I didn't understand how he could do that to me, and if I was living this great spiritual program, why would God allow this to happen?

I found my sponsor and told her what had happened. She was less than sympathetic; in fact she was judgmental, as always. When I told her that I was angry about the situation, her response was to yell at me, *Well I'm sure you didn't ask God if it was his will before you jumped into bed with him, did you?*

It was hardly comforting. She made me believe that this happened to me due to *self-will run riot*. It was my own fault, not the fault of the man who deceived me. Her counsel did nothing to help me through this difficult experience—in fact, it made it worse. It took me a few years even to be able to discuss this with anyone. I eventually found out from other women in AA that herpes is rampant in AA here (a large city in the south). Many of my friends had it, and they all contracted it from men in the program. *Oh well, as long as those guys aren't drinking today . . .* is the consensus.

I dread to think what will happen when someone with HIV introduces that virus into ever-incestuous AA. A couple of years ago, a man with over 10 years sobriety committed suicide. He had been extremely promiscuous within AA, and there were rumors that he was HIV-positive. Maybe the time bomb is already ticking.

The last few months have been difficult for me. I am ultimately happy to be free of AA, but I almost feel like I need to be de-programmed. There is a lot of freedom in being critical of the program. Up until a couple of months ago, I could not do it. When asked by friends and family why I had left the program, I would only tell them that AA just wasn't for me. I was still thinking that AA was the only way, and that by being critical of the program I might doom another suffering alcoholic to death, insanity, etc. Today I would be happy to dissuade someone from joining AA. Finding a group of people who have been hurt in AA, and making friendships with people outside AA, is helping me a lot.

21 ▲ Captain Bill
Soul Rape

I am a former U.S. Coast Guard helicopter pilot who asked for help. Instead of help I received torture. U.S. Navy alcohol treatment was abusive beyond my wildest imagination. I lost my career for resisting it and later sued (without a lawyer) on the grounds that all three religion clauses in the Constitution were violated. I actually won an appeal in the U.S. Court of Appeals for the Fourth Circuit. Here is what happened to me.

In November 1985, I was an officer and helicopter pilot with the U. S. Coast Guard with eight years of active duty. My fitness reports reflected a history of being a good officer and an excellent pilot.

Upon arrival at my new duty station, the U. S. Coast Guard Air Station at Elizabeth City, North Carolina, I confessed to a drinking problem and asked my commanding officer for help with it. He scheduled me to attend inpatient alcohol rehabilitation at the U.S. Naval Hospital in Tennessee. I was scheduled to go into treatment on December 23, 1985, and was supposed to stay 30 days.

But I then learned that the acting executive officer had conversed freely with civilians about my treatment plans. I felt the privacy of my medical information was compromised, so I requested not to go to the military inpatient alcohol rehabilitation treatment program and asked instead to see a civilian counselor on my own.

I was then sent by the command to be evaluated by a Navy psychiatrist at the U.S. Naval Hospital in Portsmouth, Virginia, who reported back that I was normal, fit for flying, and likely to have a bad reaction to inpatient treatment. In spite of this evaluation, the command sent me involuntarily to inpatient treatment.

I spent Christmas week 1985 at that treatment center, observing and being subjected to intense, humiliating, and intimidating verbal abuse. Counselors insisted that I *believe* in Alcoholics Anonymous' *spiritual* principles and that I *believe* that I had the "disease" of alcoholism. These intimidating sessions took place in a room where a large poster with numerous references to God hung conspicuously on the wall. I was subjected to mandatory Alcoholics Anonymous meetings that opened with the Serenity Prayer and closed with the Lord's Prayer, with all present holding hands.

The treatment was based on coerced spirituality and beliefs in religious principles that were inconsistent with the my own religious views, especially the torturous lifelong stigmatization of self and others, which is contrary to the teachings of my own God. About the sixth day of treatment, I told one of the staff members that I did not believe I had the disease of alcoholism and that I wanted out of the program.

On December 31, I was called into a staff office. There, the entire five-person staff surrounded me in a semicircle, slammed books on a desk, yelled at me, and told me that my deceased father, who did not drink, was a *dry alcoholic*. In an intensely coercive setting, they demanded that I profess belief that I had the disease of alcoholism. I refused.

I stated that if religion was the basis of the treatment, I would be better off placing myself in an environment of my own religion, as I had done while attending graduate school at a university sponsored by my religion. Staff members responded to this by shouting more abuse at me. One staff member stated that she had tried that, and it did not work for her. Hence, their *spiritual* program was the only way to solve my problem.

This interrogation session was really an inquisition of my beliefs rather than my actions. I had already confessed to periodic abuse of alcohol. But when I was discharged from treatment early, on December 31, 1985, the follow-up reports stated that I had failed to cooperate in treatment.

Shortly after my return to duty, I had a conference with the district alcohol and drug abuse representative, a senior chief petty officer. This conference was also attended by a civilian co-worker of the senior chief. I stated that I did not want to attend Alcoholics Anonymous meetings. The senior chief and the civilian became quite indignant. In the following session, the senior chief stated that these religious activities would be mandatory. He said that he knew from personal experience—being a member of Alcoholics Anonymous —that his program was the only way to solve my problem.

I was ordered to attend three Alcoholics Anonymous meetings per week, where religious dogma and prescribed prayer were part of the program. As proof of attendance at these religious meetings, I was required to submit to the command slips of paper signed by Alcoholics "Anonymous" members of the civilian community, thus compromising their own religious privacy.

Mandatory attendance at these religious meetings was torturous, especially since my duty station was in Elizabeth City, North Carolina, the town in which I had grown from infancy to adulthood. It was the place where my parents had introduced me to my own God, and where we worshiped God in our own way, and in our own place of worship.

During the nine-month period between my discharge from treatment and discharge from the Coast Guard, all of my operational capacitations, including flight status, security clearance, and operational watches, were terminated. Finally, I was discharged from active duty in the United States Coast Guard for not completing inpatient treatment.

I still feel, even now, that I was ruthlessly stigmatized and kicked out of my position for not submitting to tyranny by the religiously aligned AA members in government.

22 ▲ Jerry
Shunned and Slandered

My story's not that bad compared to what I've heard and seen in my time, but professionals may not realize that it's not just the clients who can get into trouble with AA.

I was four-and-a-half years clean and sober before I walked into my first 12-step meeting. I only went because I started volunteering to help set up and run a much needed detox, and my new co-workers (funny how it turned out they were *all* AAs) were on my ass to go, to support our clients and avoid relapse myself. I felt fine without the meetings and had known for years that I would never use again, but I wanted to know more about AA.

AA is very seductive. At first they had me fooled, and I was spouting the party line even though I didn't believe I was powerless, diseased, or that there was such a thing as a higher power. *Not for me, for you,* I'd say to clients. But that just didn't sit right with me. I didn't fight my way back to a good life just to act like a junkie again.

After a time I realized why most of our clients (by this time I was involved in other addiction recovery projects and training to be a counselor) continued to fail to stay clean and sober. They seemed to be taking the ideas of powerlessness, disease, and higher powers and twisting them to where they were now an excuse for why they didn't have to go through the discomfort of quitting forever.

I decided to look for something else. I found out about Rational Recovery and opened a small RR office and an "open all day" meeting room next to the office.

I made the mistake of getting some publicity for the place, and I expected all of my friends and contacts to refer clients to it. My real business pretty much ran itself, and I was free to hang out and volunteer in the RR meeting room most of the day.

That's when the trouble started. Almost everyone from the recovery community turned on me. First my so-called AA friends were giving me the cold shoulder, and then my contacts at Social Services,

Salvation Army, treatment centers, shelters, etc. also turned their backs on me.

I was disappointed and a little hurt, but figured it was better to find out what they were like before getting in any deeper with them. Surprisingly, some AA people secretly supported me and helped me through the whole thing, by letting me know, for instance, what was being said and done about me. But even those who supported me privately refused to do so publicly.

Despite everything, the RR meeting room had at least some success. A lot of AA and NA failures joined RR and did quite well. And lots joined and failed at RR too.

The strange phone calls (most only wanting to "save" me, but there was abuse from a few angry nuts) coming to my home at all hours of the night and day started to scare my wife and teenaged (at that time) daughters. We had to change our home numbers to unlisted ones, and we ended up changing those one more time. Attacks on my reputation (at the time I owned several small businesses) followed, and then a reporter started doing surveillance on my house. He had been told that my wife, who appears about 10 years younger than me, and my two daughters were hookers who were living and working out of my house. I got a lawyer and managed to get the story stopped before it went in the paper. The guy didn't even want to meet my wife, he was so sure the story was true. He just wanted me to quick-quick deny it so he could print it.

The most disturbing incident was a break-in at my RR office. They (I have no real proof who) pried open a file cabinet and took all the files, but left a new lap-top computer (sitting open on my desk with all attachments packed and ready to go in the computer bag sitting next to it) as well as other valuable office equipment that I'd put in there. The only thing missing were files.

It's about five or six years down the road now and my name is still not too good in the local recovery community. I keep my head down now and do my little addiction recovery counseling thing very low profile. I try to go out of town to the clients whenever possible, and I still do volunteer work, but I try to do it out of town. I've got too much to lose. How do you fight someone who's on welfare trashing your name? My lawyer says you can't get blood from a stone, and I'll just look like the bad guy if we sue.

I think it's harder on 12-steppers when they see you walk away dissatisfied than it is for them to see you walk away a failure.

And here I was, speaking out that I didn't believe in a higher power, didn't think I was powerless or diseased, and didn't need to go to meetings. I talked about being "recovered" and respectfully rejected their assertions that I was in denial. But I also made sure they knew I respected what they were doing if it made them happy.

And they had *always* accepted me as I was—until I walked away and started doing something else. My fall from grace was swift and absolute. Lois Trimpey (of Rational Recovery) called it "the gift of rejection" and I guess I have to agree.

23 ▲ Dr. Jeffrey A. Schaler
An AA Inquisition

Since 1982, I have been very active in writing about public policy issues in addiction care, and doing public service in addiction care, mainly in Montgomery County, Maryland. I was on the Montgomery County Drug Abuse Advisory Council from 1982-1988 where I was appointed by the county to be a representative for the mental health profession. In addition, I did my doctoral dissertation on controversial issues regarding the disease model of addiction, and what I call the "free will" model of addiction. I have authored several books on addiction and on mental illness.

My wife and I moved to the Philadelphia area about two years ago. The Chairman of the Graduate Psychology Department at Chestnut Hill College, about two miles from our new home, called and asked me to come and teach there. He'd seen my name around and respected my expertise. I was interviewed in the summer of 1997, and he asked me to teach a course called "The Spirituality of the 12 Steps" in the fall 1997 semester. I was not sure that he was aware of my position on the subject, but I gave him all my materials, and he was quite excited about my coming on board. One can teach such a course from several different angles, and I decided my class would examine the 12-step philosophy from an interdisciplinary perspective —where it's looked at from an historical, anthropological, psychological, and scientific point of view. This was a course in a graduate program in psychology; people were getting licensed to practice as psychologists, and I decided it was important to teach from this standpoint.

The professor who had taught this course in the past did not wish to release his syllabus. I thought this was peculiar, but I created my own syllabus and taught the course. It proved to be a very interesting fall semester. There were a couple of people in the class who had been and still are in AA. But when it became clear, in class, that many of the things taught in AA are not scientifically valid, and that AA is, in many ways, a religious program, one woman in particular got upset. She seemed intent on maintaining what she had been taught by AA about alcoholism and addiction as the truth. I said, very patiently, that there was no scientific evidence to support AA's ideas and that, in fact, there is plenty of evidence that shows AA's ideas are not true.

She then became very emotionally upset. I found out later that she complained to the chairman of the department, and to others, about me. Additionally, she wrote in the class evaluation that I was a dangerous person. My point to her was—and I told her this on several occasions—that if AA was helpful to her, I supported her. However, I also reminded her that she was in a graduate program and that it is important to look at the truthfulness of, and the origin of, AA's ideas. If she couldn't handle this, she probably didn't belong in a graduate program.

Another student in the class was very much in agreement with me. He was concerned about the issue of people being coerced into AA programs by the state. He was quite vocal about this, and as a result there was a marked polarization in the class between these two people and their points of view. Again, I tried to mediate so that no one was offended personally.

Anyway, the semester came to an end, and everything was fine except for the one woman who had complained so vigorously. I was asked to teach a second course in the spring 1998 semester. The class would be called "The Foundations of Addictive Behavior." I looked forward to teaching this, because I had taught related courses at Johns Hopkins University and American University.

In the course, I used some of the works of Thomas Szasz, Herbert Fingarette, and Stanton Peele. We had a great class. However, we got to a point in the class where we began to look at the similarities between the drug experience and the religious experience. I pointed out how many of our current attitudes about drug users are similar to the scapegoating attitudes of religious persecutors in past centuries.

In other words, throughout history certain people have been assigned scapegoat status and blamed for different social problems. Christians, Jews, homosexuals, and blacks have fallen victim to this, and today, of course, drug users are scapegoated and blamed for any number of problems. That part of the course really wasn't very controversial. The part that stirred things up was the comparison of the drug experience to the religious experience.

There is a tendency for people who are religious to say, *Oh, I know that Jesus is talking to me.* When you ask, *How do you know that?*, the answer is usually, *Well, I just know it.* There's no real evidence; it's simply an unsupported self-report. Many people who are on drugs believe what they imagine in a similar way. When I began to talk about this, it really seemed to upset one or two people in the class. I equated some of the drug experience with the experience of Holy Communion, where one believes one is eating the body and blood of Christ, where the metaphor is literalized. One student, a Jewish woman, said in class, *But Dr. Schaler, when people take communion they know they aren't eating the literal blood and body of Christ, but that they're consuming the metaphorical blood and body of Christ.* One woman shot back, exploding: *I beg your pardon, I most certainly do believe I'm eating the literal body and blood of Christ!*

As an example, let's take people who use LSD—their imagination of the world, what they "see" under the influence of LSD, is believed as literally true. That verges on what we in psychology and psychiatry label as *psychosis.* A person who can't, or won't, is incapable of, or somehow fails to differentiate what they imagine about the world from what is literally true, is said to be experiencing psychosis. In religious experience, something similar happens. If I say, *God is speaking to me,* that's something I imagine, and that I assert is true. However, because that's a socially acceptable delusion, I'm not going to get into much trouble. If I say, *Martians are walking around on the ceiling,* I will be labeled as psychotic because that's a socially unacceptable delusion. Qualitatively, there's not much difference; it's a matter of which delusion is more popular. So, we could say that people who have religious delusions are psychotic, or we could say that people we label as psychotic are, basically, having religious experiences.

In a graduate program, it should be completely acceptable to talk about this type of thing. In my opinion, individuals in graduate programs should be developed enough to be able, at least, to talk about these ideas without becoming too upset. In my class, one or two students became extremely upset about discussing this. One of them said, *The religious experience is not in any way similar to a drug experience.* In other words, a religious experience was superior, and, somehow, a drug experience was inferior, according to their way of thinking. This was ironic in that on the one hand these same persons said they wanted to protect the welfare of drug users, that they cared for them a great deal, and on the other hand, they assert the view that the drug experience is an inferior experience, thereby stigmatizing drug users.

Discussing these sorts of issues in class seemed to get me in a great deal of trouble. Despite strong objections from a few students, after that course—and I'd received very good evaluations by the majority of students in the class—I was asked to teach yet another course in psychology during the summer. This would be another graduate course, an introduction to graduate topics in psychology. It was not a particularly controversial course; however, I did use some books by authors who did not believe in the disease theory of addiction. It is important to note that there is a faction of strong intellectual writers in the field of psychiatry and psychology who do not believe there is any such thing as "mental illness." This does not mean that some people do not do things that seem peculiar, but that these behaviors don't fit the scientific criteria for "illness."

During that time, I was getting better acquainted with other faculty members of Chestnut Hill College. While on the worldwide web, I found that one of the faculty members, a tenured professor, had a home page which had a "suggest-a-link" section, where a visitor could add a link to different psychology pages. I did not know this professor personally, and I had no idea of his orientation. I had recently created the Thomas Szasz Cybercenter for Liberty and Responsibility (http://www.szasz.com). I did not expect him to agree with me, and I did write introducing myself. I told him I was teaching at Chestnut Hill College, and asked him if he wanted to connect.

At this same time, I had contacted the webmaster at Chestnut Hill College, and told her that she could connect the college web page outline of summer courses to my syllabus, which I had up on a separate page inside the Thomas Szasz site. The webmaster said, "fine."

Meanwhile, the professor with the links page wrote back to me and said he was deeply offended by my political orientation, that given my political orientation any connection with Chestnut Hill College was unacceptable, that I had not asked permission to "do this," and that if I had asked permission, I would be denied. I had absolutely no idea what he was talking about.

After I investigated, I discovered that the Szasz site had changed hosts. The site used to be at St. John's University in New York; however, the professor of psychology there who had asked me if they could host my site for free, was moving to another location and he asked if he could take my site with him. I consented. Unknown to me at the time, he had set up a referring page so that when people went to my syllabus via the Chestnut Hill College web site, they ended up at the home page of the Szasz site. This was not intentional on my part. I figured that this is what had upset the professor at Chestnut Hill College. I apologized and explained that the whole thing was quite unintentional. I told him that to avoid further confusion I would simply ask the webmaster at Chestnut Hill College to eliminate the link. I thought that was reasonable. But then, I wasn't asked to teach again.

I kept calling the chairman of the Graduate Psychology Department, but he refused to return my calls. Finally I reached him and told him that I didn't understand what was going on. We had a meeting. I told him that I was concerned that he might not want me back because of the misunderstanding I'd had with that particular professor over the web site. I thought everything had been straightened out, but I worried that my not being invited to teach had something to do with his dislike for me and for what I was teaching.

The inquisition then began. The chairman asked me what I thought of Alcoholics Anonymous. I told him that I taught my courses from an objective point of view. He asked, *What do you think of AA, personally?* I said, *Personally, I don't think it's a very good program. I think it goes against what we know to be true in contemporary psychological research. I think it's very destructive in what it teaches people. For example, if you teach people that they don't have the power to choose, they will believe it.*

He asked, *Do you think it's a cult?* I replied, *I do, and I've given evidence to support my position. I'm not demanding that my students agree with this, but I am asking them to look at the evidence.* He then said, *Well, you can't teach here.* I said, *Are you telling me I can't use peer-reviewed articles from sociological journals and similar academic materials in a graduate course in psychology? Are you telling me I have to toe the line according to Alcoholics Anonymous?* He replied, *That's exactly what I'm telling you.*

Then he asked me what I believed about mental illness. I told him I was a friend of Thomas Szasz, and that I believed that much of what passes for "mental illness" does not meet the criteria for disease. I also assured him that I teach about mental illness from many different points of view, rather than only from my personal understanding. I also told him that I didn't understand how my personal opinions were relevant to my teaching abilities.

The chairman then told me, *Well,* (the tenured professor) *told me that I must not have your name on any college literature from now on.* When I told him I did not understand this, the chairman replied, *Please bear with me; I don't want to upset him. Maybe I can sneak you in to teach a course on psychological theory without having your name on any of the college schedules. I will be in touch.*

While leaving, I picked up a schedule of classes for the fall, and I saw that all the courses I had taught were being taught by other adjunct faculty members. Apparently, the chairman had been dishonest with me. It had already been decided that I would not teach at Chestnut Hill, most likely because of my views on Alcoholics Anonymous. The reason he did not get back in touch with me for so long is that he'd already picked others to teach my courses.

I wrote a letter to him saying that he'd been dishonest with me, and that it looked as if the college policy was that peer-reviewed articles are not acceptable, and that the AA line must be followed in order to teach psychology there. I thought that was an outrageous and cowardly abridgement of academic freedom. I sent a copy of the letter to the president of the college. Then the shit really hit the fan.

The chairman called me up and said, *You might as well have hauled off and hit me in the face.* I replied that he had been cowardly and deserved it. I wanted to bring this out in the open.

The president of the college assigned the matter to the vice president of academic affairs, who was also the dean of faculty. He wrote me a letter and asked for a meeting. The three of us—the dean of faculty, the chairman of the Graduate Psychology Department, and myself—had a meeting in June or July of 1998. During that meeting I recounted everything that had gone on. The dean of faculty was able to witness my interaction with the chairman of the department. I also repeated that my dismissal was a blatant infringement on the principles of academic freedom, and that I was going to have the AAUP— the American Association of University Professors—investigate this matter.

(The AAUP is an organization which, in the 1940s, coined the term "academic freedom," which means that professors must be free to talk about controversial issues, and that a college shouldn't endorse [or suppress] any point of view. Academic excellence is based on this principle, and, generally speaking, academicians feel very strongly about this. Academic freedom must be protected at any cost. Any college that tries to limit academic freedom risks being censured by the AAUP.)

After going over all the material, the dean of faculty decided that my academic freedom had been infringed upon. He said, *I come from a background of history and political science. This case is similar to that of a department that was primarily Marxist excluding someone who represented a free-market capitalist point of view. That's unacceptable. We don't have to agree, but you should have the right to present your point of view, and you have been excluded precisely because of your point of view, and that is unacceptable.* I said that I appreciated his decision. He asked me what I would like.

I told him I wanted a guarantee that I would not be discriminated against on the basis of my political orientation or point of view. His response was a gracious apology, and an assurance that I was considered a member of the faculty. I stated that I appreciated this, that I wished, as well, to put the problem behind us, and that I looked forward to teaching there.

During that time I had asked the AAUP to investigate, so I wrote a letter to them stating that there was no need for an investigation because the matter had been resolved. That was a year ago. Since then, I asked the chairman of the department for the student evaluations of my teaching from my last course. He wouldn't send them. Finally, in February, I did receive them after many letters. They were all outstanding evaluations of the course and my teaching.

I wasn't hired for the fall of 1998; I wasn't hired for the following spring; I wasn't hired for the summer; and I wasn't hired for the fall. In July, I wrote a letter to the dean again and summarized the situation, stating that it had been a year since he had apologized and had assured me that my academic freedom would not be further infringed upon. Nevertheless, despite his assurances, I had not been given classes to teach. I had called off the AAUP investigation because I'd trusted him, and now he'd apparently betrayed me.

I heard nothing from the dean in response. I then decided to place the situation in the court of public opinion. I posted all correspondence about this situation on my web site, and titled it "Todschweigen [a German word meaning "death by silence"] at Chestnut Hill College." It's a way of shunning people by just not responding to them.

A few weeks later, I got a call from a senior writer at the *Philadephia City Paper*, and he did a big article on the situation. Soon after this, American University, which has always been very protective of academic freedom, did a major story on me in their faculty newspaper. They mentioned the inquisition at Chestnut Hill in the story, and also discussed one of my books on addiction. The story was also picked up by *The Chronicle for Higher Education,* a very prestigious academic newspaper. They did an entire story on academic freedom, and mentioned several instances of controversial topics being squelched in colleges around the country. Some colleges do this by hiring adjunct faculty—untenured instructors—semester by semester, as a way to control course content. That way, colleges and universities don't need to fire someone if they don't like their views. If the adjunct professors' ideas are impolitic, they are simply not rehired.

Since then, I've written once more to the AAUP and requested a formal investigation. In their most recent letter to Chestnut Hill College, the AAUP strongly requested an explanation as to why I was not rehired.

That's where the matter stands. I feel satisfied that others are publicizing the issue, because there's not much else I can do. I can't sue, because any private university has the legal right to make decisions like this. But I can make the problem public: *You say that you subscribe to the principles of academic freedom, but, in fact, you do not, and the world should know about it.*

Notes:

My web site is at
http://www.enabling.org/ia/szasz/schaler

The "Todschweigen" article is at
http://www.enabling.org/ia/szasz/schaler/todschweigen.html

The book discussed in the *Philadelphia City Paper* is *Addiction Is a Choice,* by Jeffrey A. Schaler, Ph.D. Chicago: Open Court, 1999.

24 ▲ Dolores

Cult Peyton Place

First let me give you a little history. I have been "sober" for 18 years. My first nine years were in AA. My recovery *from* AA has been quite difficult for me even after all these years.

My first horror story happened when I was about four years into the program. I became ill and was diagnosed with lymphoma. Some so-called friends from AA came to see me in the hospital to cheer me up. The way they cheered me up was to tell me that I was responsible for my illness. One woman said: *You know you have no one to blame but yourself, you brought this on.*

One would think I would have wised up then and gotten out of AA. But I stayed active in the program for another five years. The incident that made me finally leave was the realization that my group was attempting to define immoral behavior as moral and acceptable.

My husband and I were friends with another couple in recovery. He was in AA, and she was in Al-Anon. The man often spoke badly of his wife at AA meetings when she wasn't there. So most of the AA group had pretty strong preconceptions about her that, from my perspective, were unfair and untrue. And I knew her better than anyone else in the group. His behavior disgusted me, but since he was my husband's friend I tried to be tolerant of him. He was an airline pilot, so they could live anywhere in the country they chose. She was unhappy in Texas and wanted to move back to her home, California. He agreed to the move, but decided he would still fly out of Texas. So, he would need a place to stay in Texas.

He rented a room from a woman in our AA group. It didn't take long before this man and woman were having an affair. My husband and I were suddenly in the middle, with all three people in this love triangle contacting us and wanting information about the others. When I brought up my distress to other members of our AA group, they all said that this couple was doing nothing wrong, that his wife was a *bitch who couldn't control her temper,* and *who could blame him?* As for the other woman, well, *she had 15 years of sobriety,* making her beyond reproach.

By the way, their child was deeply hurt by these events, and the wife called many times in tears, asking me how could this have happened. Our group had the some of the longest "sobriety" in the city, and it was supposed to be one of the "healthiest" groups. Well, I knew I had to separate myself from these people. I no longer had any respect for them. I knew if they could justify adultery on the basis of who was part of the group and who was not, then they could justify all sorts of immoral behavior.

This is when I realized that AA is a cult. How else can you explain an entire group of decent people no longer able to distinguish right from wrong?

25 ▲ Derek
Caught in the Step Machine

I grew up in a stereotypical Irish Catholic community with many conservative cops around me, including my father. He developed a serious drinking problem and often became violent. This resulted in my mother's divorcing him after being seriously injured during a fight. My mother was given custody of me, but her back problems were severe, and I was unofficially adopted by my grandparents, who raised me from age 7 until I was 18.

In my early years, I was the ideal child, excelling in school and sports, yet somehow I was full of insecurities and was often unhappy. After attending Catholic school, I was given a scholarship to a private high school just about the time puberty struck. After having been indoctrinated at school and home about the evils of sexuality and having received a steady dose of authoritarianism, parochialism, and other forms of narrow-mindedness, this transitional period was too much for me to handle. At age 13 I started smoking marijuana and quickly dropped out of my family's surreal world. I became a discipline problem, stopped playing sports, and my grades plummeted. To cope with this situation, I resorted to other pharmaceutical remedies, including a lot of LSD. Tuning out made much more sense to me than my family did. However, after getting away with my delinquent behavior for a year or so, I was finally caught when my diary was discovered.

My father—the distant disciplinarian who was never really involved with me—re-entered my life. As an alcoholic and former cop, he knew how to handle lawbreakers. I got off easily. He only hit me —unlike my mother—once. Besides grounding, and being forbidden to see certain people, my record collection and guitar were taken away (since rock and roll was partly to blame) and I went away to live with him for the summer. I was to learn how hard work was necessary to instill discipline. I worked as a short-order cook in a bar he owned, and needless to say I found more role models in the bar.

I soon started drinking and also continued getting high, which was actually easier to get away with around an inebriated dad than it had been around my mom.

I went back to living with my grandparents during the school year and my life continued to consist of evading my family and myself. I managed to make it through high school, despite being very depressed and wanting to drop out very badly. During this time, a few significant things happened. I was sexually molested by a former teacher who was then a clergy member (and probably still is). I was also in an alcohol-related car accident after I sped away from a police officer who tried to pull me over. It was a miracle that I survived crashing through a wall, but I didn't feel very lucky at the time and expressed my thoughts about it to my family. They blamed my problems on not praying enough, rock music, and a bad crowd. To think that my upbringing was dysfunctional was inconceivable.

After high school, I moved back and forth between family members for a year or so. A romantic relationship I was involved in ended. At the time, I thought it was the only thing to live for. I managed to get through this period and decided to go to college, but I continued to drink and was arrested for a DUI. After going to court for this, I encountered the treatment industry for the first time. I had to go to classes for six weeks, after which I would get a certificate stating I completed the program and my DUI would be expunged from my record. This didn't go quite according to plan.

By answering several questionnaires about my drinking and drug use honestly, I had incriminated myself. Apparently, unbeknownst to me, the program directors had the authority to determine whether or not someone needed more treatment, although this wasn't stated in my sentencing. I was singled out with a few others from a class of about 50 as needing further rehabilitation. Besides the lack of due process, what was ironic about the situation was that I had gone into "remission." Somehow, beginning to use my intellect critically in college had changed the way I thought about the world and myself. I had drastically cut back on drinking and wasn't using any other drugs. I was selected for "treatment" because of my past history and for having a family history of "alcoholism."

Conceivably, this could have been a learning experience for me if it had been done properly. However, I had to pay for this extra treatment—about $800, which was difficult. I was working at a low-paying job and had just moved out on my own. Also, I got three different counselors during the six months that I went to treatment. I was scheduled to go for 15 weeks once a week, but two counselors quit and hadn't kept records, so I was forced to go to about 25 meetings because I paid cash and so couldn't prove my attendance.

I stood out in the group a little. I was the only one under 40 (I was 19 at the time) and one of the few with a high school diploma. I couldn't relate to beating my wife, losing job after job, and drinking shots upon waking. So, I didn't feel quite at home in treatment. Also, these "regulars" were all AA veterans who had been going to 12-step programs for a long time. The group meetings essentially consisted of these people "witnessing" for the program with an official moderator there to make sure everybody participated, I felt like I had been delivered back into the environment—the world of tradition, authority, conformity, and self-hatred—which I had sought to escape from when I drank and got high.

I continued on with college, but I still drank, sometimes out of the frustration of that treatment experience and, sometimes, because I didn't know how else to relate to others. Along the way, my father killed himself driving drunk. I didn't handle it very well. I started drinking again much more heavily and began to romanticize my father's life. I thought to myself, "He went to bars all the time and he was very popular. I think I'll do the same." I tried to outdo him by using illegal drugs which I could share with others.

I gained popularity but realized that I needed to fund my habits, and what better way to share the wealth is there than to buy larger quantities of drugs at a lower price? Why bother doing favors for people by running to purchase things for them? I could just keep them on hand and I could make a little profit for myself. This strategy wasn't as clearly thought out as I'm portraying it, but another event happened which made it seem the best option.

While I was walking with a girlfriend of mine, someone tried to steal my father's chain from my neck. After a brief struggle, he was unable to wrest it from me. I thought the ordeal was over, but when he turned to run, he pulled a gun out of his pants and shot my girlfriend in the chest.

I spent a lot of the next month in the hospital with her. My boss was unhappy that I was taking so much time off, so I fought with him and decided to quit in protest. To make ends meet, I dealt drugs. I freely admit that my behavior was harmful to myself and others, but I couldn't see any other choices at the time.

Anyway, the next three or four years are kind of blurry, marked by major drinking and snorting binges which usually ended up with me passing out for a day at a time. I had not finished school, I was not working, and I was not happy, but I sure had a lot of friends. The money wasn't bad and other people envied me, so at least there were some things going for this lifestyle. Then, one day, while trying to get backstage at a concert (I was now supplying touring musicians who were in town), I was confronted by a group of police officers who ignored my right to be free from unwarranted searches.

I was arrested and charged with possession with intent to distribute cocaine. I pled guilty and was sentenced to four months in prison because I had a great lawyer, I was white, I was a first-time offender, and while awaiting sentencing I went to treatment to prove I was an addict and an alcoholic. Others are not as lucky with the criminal justice system and end up spending years in prison for what I did.

Allow me to return to my pre-sentencing treatment for a moment. The counselor I'd gone to was an avid supporter of 12-step programs and insisted they were the only method that works. I'd tried discussing a few points concerning alcohol and other drugs upon which I disagreed with her, to no avail. I also explained that I had studied philosophy in college and did lots of reading, and I was very familiar with "spiritual" questions and my right to be free from religion. Predictably, I was told this was another symptom of *denial* and that I needed to stop "intellectualizing" things so much. I evaluated the situation and decided that it was in my best interest to keep my mouth shut because my fate in court was partly dependent upon this counselor's opinion of my potential for "rehabilitation." So, I played this game, only occasionally mouthing what was really on my mind.

During that time, my main concern was dealing with the fear I had about prison. My counselor told me that the most important thing was to become clean and sober. I said I couldn't think about prison without becoming completely distressed and that was why I was drinking and using so heavily. This tug of war between us heightened my fears, and they continued to get worse as my sentencing date approached. Her tack was to probe into my early childhood experiences to see why I had such a problem with authority. When I reported that I was really unable to recall much, her demeanor changed and she reacted to me in a different way. She started asking questions about my sexual behavior and my experiences with the Christian Brother in high school, while concentrating on my memory lapses from childhood. The net effect of this treatment was to make me suspicious that something traumatic happened to me when I was very young, and that I had repressed this for years.

As many know from experience, 12-step indoctrination attacks your confidence in your own judgment. You are told it is your best thinking that got you to where you are and that you need to surrender to a Higher Power in order to improve. The Big Book states: "The first requirement is that we be convinced that any life run on self-will can hardly be a success," and, "We hope you are convinced now that God can remove whatever self-will has blocked you off from Him," etc. This attack on rationality and the self is rampant throughout the entire Big Book and 12-step philosophy. As an individual who was extremely vulnerable and not employing his intellect very effectively, I started to think that "self-centeredness" really was my problem. I had often thought that being alienated from my true self was the problem, but now I had a simple explanation and the seeds of doubt had been planted in my mind.

After entering prison, I suffered severe withdrawal symptoms that went untreated. I had been drinking the equivalent of about a fifth a day for about the previous year and snorted lots of cocaine and used other things, especially Valium and Xanax, to come down from being too wired. My withdrawal consisted of lots of sweating, involuntary muscular contractions, mild hallucinations, severe trembling, and not sleeping for about a week. Then I started to adjust as well as one can to one's first prison experience. I became friendly with some of the other inmates and was scheduled to go to the "work release" area.

I also began taking this business of recovery seriously, which I had been reluctant to do before. I thought that just maybe it really was my thinking that was crooked, and I immersed myself in reading about the "disease" of addiction and all its manifestations. I tried to maintain a critical stance, but with the pressures of confinement (which were many) and my body still trying to reestablish equilibrium, this only stressed me out more. At the same time, I started obsessing over the supposed lapse in my memory which the counselor seemed to think was very significant to my understanding of myself. I experienced my first-ever panic attack when I started getting images of being sexually abused as a child.

The veracity of these "memories" seems highly doubtful, but what happened after this panic attack still seems unbelievable to me. I asked to talk to the prison psychologist about these disturbing thoughts I was having. His solution was to remove me from the relatively comfortable work-release environment I was in and have me attend encounter groups with convicted sexual offenders to discuss the problem of sexual abuse!

Within a short time I was in shackles and being transported to a new location. I had another panic attack and woke up in an unfamiliar cell with someone else. Shortly thereafter, I started having thought disturbances and was very confused and afraid. I was taken into another room by myself where I stayed for the next seven weeks. I spent most of that time naked, lying on a cement floor with no pillow, blanket, mattress, toilet paper, mail, or anything else in the cell except roaches, a toilet, and a sink. When I wasn't sleeping, I was having horrible delusions and was scared out of my mind. Many of the details of this experience are still quite vivid and I don't think I will ever forget them. The proverbial "living nightmare" is a literal description of what I experienced. The physical deprivation was nothing compared to the mental torture I endured, which still haunts me in nightmares on occasion.

Through the relentless efforts of my mother and girlfriend, I was released to a hospital after they finally reached a human being with pull in the prison bureaucracy who cared about my plight. Upon arrival at the hospital, I was fairly disheveled, suicidal, and acutely psychotic. After about three weeks, I could finally sleep in a bed. Previously, I had curled up in a corner in a fetal position, too afraid to sleep. I was discharged after about a month and a half into a partial-hospitalization rehabilitation program.

The partial-hospitalization program was heavily into the 12 steps. In this dual-diagnosis treatment center, I complied with the program because that was part of my probation requirements. At least this program was free, but again my individual needs were ignored. I sat through a Bible class, a hygiene class explaining why showering and brushing your teeth are important, and the group's rendition of "Kumbayah." Part of morning stretching included doing the "Hokey Pokey" which I refused to do; I was verbally reprimanded for my bad attitude. This wasn't particularly funny at the time. I was in the unenviable position of trying to prove I was "mentally competent" and complying with "treatment" by engaging in these ludicrous activities.

In the 12-Step groups run by the center staff, I was repeatedly lectured for not working the steps or going to outside meetings when I wasn't at the center. Other activities I enjoyed which I consider healthy were discouraged. I was told not to spend so much time reading or playing guitar at home since these were forms of isolating and/or intellectualizing my problems. I was also warned against anger and resentment, which only created more of it.

Watching television was encouraged and so was going to church, even though I professed to be an atheist. Again, I was alleged to be "in denial." They said that I should go to church to be exposed to "spirituality," just like I should "fake it until I make it." After about two months of trying to politely explain that I was in a program which was on a lower level than I was and that I was getting nowhere, I got a little more assertive and pled my case to the program's doctor, who agreed that I was fully functional. He couldn't do anything though, since he wasn't my caseworker; but he was a sort of unofficial insurance policy in case I got in trouble with my probation officer. I asked my caseworker for help finding another program. She totally refused. I pleaded, but she told me that I wasn't meeting the requirements of the current program, despite perfect attendance and talking within groups, etc.

Finally, with an incredible amount of restraint (consider what would have happened if I started screaming at this person), I said, "I disagree with your evaluation and I don't think you are helping me." A few minutes later, after reminding me that I might go to court or prison again over this, she slapped an official release down in front of me to sign stating that I "refused treatment in direct violation of the terms of my probation." She then proudly signed the statement with another witness from the program snickering at me. This just seemed to me to be another outgrowth of a program that is supposed to work by attraction rather than promotion. Essentially, this attitude amounts to saying you're going to hell if you don't follow our path.

Fortunately, after I explained the situation, the probation officer wasn't concerned. He helped me find another 12-step-oriented rehabilitation program which was on a higher functioning level. I ended up with a better counselor, who was exceptional simply because she didn't force the steps on me and let me talk about what I felt was bothering me. She wasn't a great therapist, but she was the first in my "recovery" experience who actually listened to me.

Eventually, I was released from the hospital. After about six months, I found an alternative to the 12 steps. I had managed to stay completely abstinent on my own. Since getting involved with secular recovery methods, I've rediscovered reason, sanity, and respect for individuality. I've re-enrolled in school, adding a psychology major to my previous philosophy major. I have four more classes before I graduate, and I intend on going to graduate school. I've been coordinating meetings for about a year now, and I'm tentatively planning on becoming a drug and alcohol counselor.

26 ▲ Lynnelle
My Life Got Worse

My name is Lynnelle, and I was at one time what you would call a "functioning alcoholic": professional, educated, kids, middle class, but with more than my fair share of husband problems. Many of these problems I treated with alcohol. My real problems went unrecognized because the professionals I went to, immediately upon hearing about my drinking, sent me to AA.

My story of mistreatment and subsequent withdrawal from the AA program began in late 1992 when I was attempting to finish MBA school while also holding the dam back on my looming divorce—living in denial of my emotionally abusive husband's drug, money/taxes, and womanizing problems. In addition, I worked in a high-stress managerial position, and was commuting a total of three hours each working day. I was also trying to raise three kids. Heck, who had time to devote to *recovery*? Anyway, I still tried to find the time to attend AA meetings twice a week, on the way home from night school —about 11pm—instead of having a quick drink at the bar.

Well, the long and short of it is that at about three months into the program, with me pretty much *dry*—and who can say that *dry* is different from sober?—some son of a bitch followed me out of the meeting and began to lecture me all the way to the parking lot, and for about an hour kept leaning on my car door so I couldn't close it. Then he followed me home. He parked in my driveway, somehow talked his way into my home—I kept thinking he was just trying to help, or maybe having a hard time himself. But he must have had some kind of sixth sense that my then-husband was away on a business trip and my nanny couldn't care less. Because, while pontificating about spiritual matters, he kept trying to get closer and closer physically. Finally, I'd had enough. I'd never really wanted him there in the first place. When he started touching me, I slapped him and threw him—literally—out of the house. Thank heaven he was a wizened old cirrhotic fart who probably weighed less than 100 lbs!

You would think recovery might go better after that bit of assertiveness, but as far as AA goes, there was just one bummer after the other. The whole AA concept seems engineered for the satisfaction of the male ego, and the manipulation of females. The best example is the 13-stepping that begins during meetings and goes on after—and if you, a female, don't like it: *go find another meeting.*

To top things off, my then-husband, probably because I told him about the wannabe 13th-stepper I'd thrown out, started accusing me of having affairs whenever I was gone for meetings.

Perhaps my story will help other women, because women still routinely blame themselves for every aspect of their own behavior—even for their own toxic defense mechanisms, that is, drinking over the pain of abusive relationships and crawling into a hole. I finally found an online abuse survivors' site that mentioned how little professionals who treat addicts understand women who are both abused and addicted. Too often, these professionals ignore the abuse and treat only the addiction. That's a recipe for failure.

27 ▲ Barney
Yes, I Am in Jail

People need to know about the corruption of our legal system. From where I sit, in jail, it is obvious. It seems that almost no one from the drug court program goes to jail unless they get new charges. All the addicts want drug court; they all know that drug court is very tolerant of drug use. Ask anyone here: *How do drug courts reduce recidivism?* The prisoners will probably tell you: *Because if you say you are powerless, they won't violate you for a dirty urine analysis.*

These guys really do *fake it 'til they make it.* They all think that they are getting one over on the system by conning their way through treatment. But it is still damned obvious that 12-step treatment is having its intended effect—the addicts *keep coming back,* and everyone else keeps getting paid.

Don't let attorneys and judges bullshit you. They all know AA is crap and that it is keeping people addicted. Those assholes in alt.recovery.aa—who do they think they are fooling? They get on the net and try to act like all is well. All the while the local membership is a revolving relapse club.

Meanwhile, my P.O. is asking that I serve an unheard-of six months, in spite of the fact that I am clean and sober, and was clean and sober well before they sent me to jail (on a marijuana charge). That doesn't matter though. What matters is that while I faithfully attended treatment and consistently turned in "clean" urine samples, I refused to work the 12 steps. Others with similar charges who say what the counselors want them to say stay free, even though they turn in "dirty" urine samples; the counselors don't turn them in because they're supposedly *trying* to "work a good program." Even though I'm clean and sober, I resisted the "program" and I'm sitting in jail—on the recommendation of my counselor.

Yes, I could have gone along with 12-step treatment and got a reduced sentence, probably with no jail time at all. But if my next probation officer wanted me to, I would have had to attend AA meetings afterwards, probably for years. This is a really sick nightmare. I am sitting in a drug-infested jail, in the middle of a drug-infested state.

The folks here are interested in alternative methods of recovery. I have a copy here of *Rational Recovery: The New Cure for Substance Addiction.* There is a waiting list of guys who want to read it. To these guys, 12-step treatment is only a way to get out of jail. Most of these people do not know anyone who has kicked an addiction using the 12 steps. The sad part is that many are under what I call *the AA spell—they believe they are helpless over their addictions, and this becomes a self-fulfilling prophecy.* They really do *keep coming back.*

28 ▲ Faye
Sponsors

I spent over five years in AA, and many of my worst memories involve my former sponsors. Here are three of them:

Vivian: There used to be a female AA member I'll call Vivian, who, I heard, had about 42 years sober. She was a member of one of the first fellowships I went to, and she was my first sponsor. She disturbed me deeply and seemed to want to bore through boundaries by alluding to very personal matters whenever I was stuck trying to talk with her. When I first started going to meetings, I talked with Vivian, because she seemed to always be there, ready to help newcomers. With her, however, I always had the feeling that it was not okay to say I was "fine."

But I did feel fine; I usually felt good during the first few sober weeks after a bad bender. But Vivian would act like I was not being honest if I said I felt fine. She would call me, too, which perhaps I should have been grateful for since in many groups newcomers are ignored. When we talked, I always felt pressured by her to go to a meeting, or I would feel like I had to act a certain way, or that I was not asking the right questions. Vivian personified AA in that way. To her, I was not acceptable as I was.

The suggestion to attend 90 meetings in 90 days bothered me. My family needed my time and attention, and I wished to make up for neglecting them during benders. And I didn't understand what they were talking about at meetings. Also, I don't like to talk in public, but felt pressured to do that at meetings. It seemed that many in AA, especially Vivian, did not approve of me, though others were nice.

But, I needed to work. I began to take in typing assignments at home. One night, I had an emergency assignment from a student who had to get his final exam in. Vivian called. *You're coming to the meeting, aren't you,* she asked in her gravelly voice, like coals on the grate. *No, I've got a typing assignment, and the man is depending on me.*

There was a moment of silence on the other end of the line. This moment was filling rapidly with my guilt over disappointing Vivian. *Well,* she said, *make lots of money then.* Her emphasis was not entirely lost on me. I knew then that to the AA way of looking at things it was not okay to think about money, and that I should be thinking of something else; but what that might be remained a mystery for quite some time. What I had wanted was sobriety. And I was sober, so what was the big deal? No one would ever explain that to me, especially Vivian. All I heard was *90 in 90, keep coming back,* and *stick with the winners.* Also, *it works if you work it.* And *read the Big Book.*

I'd read some of it, and I didn't like the steps. I believed in God; that wasn't the problem. But admit to someone all my wrongs in a confession? Who would listen to it? The people in AA? I didn't know them well enough. And what were you supposed to admit? Your deepest secrets? No way! I wasn't ready for that. But when I told Vivian I was going to stay sober without working the steps, she assured me that was *impossible.* Somewhere, somehow, someday, I would drink again. *Alcoholics work the steps or die.* Maybe I hadn't had *enough,* she said.

I heard later that she had groups of newcomers over to her house for special AA meetings, where she would put them on the "hot seat" and tear into them, trampling their boundaries. She was scary, but everyone seemed to respect her because she'd been sober since the days of Bill W. And I eventually found that she was typical—nearly every group has its stock, abusive old-timer. Everyone shrugs their shoulders, for rarely is an old-timer challenged. Old-timers are icons in the AA subculture; time sober is held in awe.

The whole deal confused me. I wasn't with that fellowship long, though I did come back to it from time to time, and Vivian was always there, giving abusive shares.

When she died, the usual four-star AA funeral was held, with weeping AAs giving powerful and loving tributes to Vivian's "tough love." Amen.

Yesterday, while talking to my sister on the phone, I found out that several years ago she cleaned house for Vivian. Vivian told her never to go in one room. Barb went in anyway and found an enormous stash of booze bottles. Some were old, many were fresh. Hearing this years later, I was shocked.

You just never know.

But the end of Vivian was by no means the end of sponsors for me, unfortunately. I was not yet finished with "tough love" in AA.

During these naive days when I thought dying drunk was the only alternative to AA, I went through a couple more totally inept sponsors. By the late summer of 1991, I had drunk myself out my life in the San Fernando Valley. The realty company sent a letter advising that my lease on a downtown house would not be renewed. I didn't blame them. My noisy lover and his family had frightened the owners of the beauty parlor next door. Our electricity had been turned off, and at night we'd been lighting the house with candles.

Druggie acquaintances would show up at the door evenings and knock. I'd hide in the back rooms and wait for them to go away. Sometimes, I'd find haven in the nightly AA meetings at the nearby courthouse. No one paid attention to me there. I could be swallowed up in the sea of the court-coerced attendees with their papers to be signed. One day, especially anxious and desperate, I approached some of the women for their phone numbers. But during that time, one of the women in AA had been found murdered, and everyone was going to the funeral. One woman told me, *Okay, here's my number, but don't call for about a week. I'm still upset about Liz* (the dead woman). Others said I could call, but when I called, no one was ever home. Often I'd walk to the phone booth, put my last quarter in the slot, and lose it when the message machine came on.

I decided to move with my children, now teenagers, and start over in the nearby university town where I had studied foreign languages. One day I ran into an AA member, Cecelia, who laughingly called such a move *the geographical cure*, and predicted failure with the warning, *Wherever you go, you take you along!*

I had buzzed all over trying to find housing, but no one in town wanted to rent to me, because by that time I was on welfare. Although I did have a housing voucher to offer and had always paid my rent, my bad credit report sent prospective landlords fleeing. A friend I'd met in community college, who was also an AA member, helped me find an apartment. She herself would not be staying much longer—she'd been accepted at Wellesley and would be moving to the East Coast. She was a winner, and being happy for her soothed my own despair at being a loser. I had three friends left who cared for me, and at least one of them was a winner.

From the very first day I dealt with the people in this wonderful little city, I felt at home! The first apartment complex I applied at welcomed my family. I found that PG&E wanted a $1000 deposit, so my son, now 18, opened up a utilities account in his name. The apartment complex was beautifully kept, quiet. How wonderful it was to have a refrigerator that buzzed! How fine it was to come to a well-lit home at night, and cook on an electric stove. I felt like one long marooned in icy lands now come home to warmth. We were safe here, I thought.

Also, though I was now sober and determined to remain so, it was clear that I had not been successful at that in the past. How long would it be this time? Two months? Six months? I really could not think of anything I could do but go to AA. And, if nothing else, people at the meetings would know more about the job market in town than I did. Shortly after I started going to meetings in my new town, I met my next sponsor.

Hilda: Few who meet Hilda ever forget her. At the time her attempts to tutor me in the AA way of life began, she was ensconced at the front table of the Friday Noon Acceptance Group, the oldest group in town. This group was, somewhat against the traditions, run by a rapidly dwindling core of old timers, six folks who had known one another for years. They chose the secretaries of the meetings.

Hilda would settle her 300-pound bulk into her chair, spread her skirts about, and surround herself with knitting and tatting projects taken from a sewing bag beside her. Then, she would knit or tat throughout the meeting, putting aside her handiwork only to speak, filling a full 20-minute segment of the 90-minute meeting with her praise of the Clancy group from Pacifica, where she had found sobriety, and also, more and more often, her rage emerged, directed at the fellowship members whom, she assured us, often neglected, slighted, and insulted her!

It was true. Often others of the little core of old-timers really would treat Hilda badly. Occasionally they would plot ways to exclude her from lunches and gatherings. She had no car, and might not have been able to fit behind a wheel anyway, so she depended on others for rides to meetings and other social gatherings among the fellowship. Sometimes she would be snubbed, or even tricked.

For instance, once Hilda was told she was getting a ride to a tea. But the person "forgot" to pick her up. Then it was too late for Hilda to find another ride. We had to listen to her rant and rave about this petty trickery for weeks thereafter. But Hilda, and anyone else who complained about other AA members at the meetings, was careful to not name the guilty parties directly, making reference to *this person*, or *a member of the fellowship*. But we all knew who was being talked about, although we did not always know exactly what the person did, because gossip in the fellowship was so wild and repeated so inaccurately that often, by the time the tales got to the last ears, an incident would be changed so completely as to be unrecognizable.

Anyway, Hilda said she would help me. The rules were, I had to call her every day at 9 a.m., and go to a meeting every day. I said, *Meetings really don't help me*. But Hilda asked me who was sober 10 years—me or her? So I agreed to go to the meetings. And I started calling Hilda every day at 9 a.m. She'd ask me if I'd had anything to eat. When I said *no*, she'd say, *Well, fix a peanut butter sandwich and go to a meeting*. She insisted I go to meetings every day. Once when I wanted to go to a poetry workshop instead, she said, *Fine. When you get drunk, call your poetry teacher*.

After awhile, my ties to Hilda became burdensome. She needed a lot of help with shopping and cleaning. I'd drive her shopping and about town in the 100-degree heat in my big old black station wagon. She would be very nervous, and quite often she'd lose her temper and scream: *You shouldn't be driving. At two months sober, you can't even see yet!*

Also, it was hard for her to move around because of her arthritis, and so her apartment would become filthy, with several days of dirty dishes piled high; there were so many of them they wouldn't all fit in the sink. So, I had to move them onto the stove and on top of the fridge in order to get started with the hour-long job of washing the dishes. They smelled so bad I would gag while trying to clean them.

She paid me for cleaning, but after awhile I did not want to venture near her house. I dreaded talking to her, because you never knew what would set her off. If I called her, she would briefly ask how I was doing; then she would rant and rave about the latest slights and rudeness that came her way from other members of the fellowship.

Most of the time, I felt that I was helping her more than she was helping me. I didn't mind that I guess, but I had been told I needed a sponsor, not that a sponsor needed me. Come to think of it though, in meetings I would sometimes hear someone say: *I need my sponsees as much as they need me!* I just hadn't realized that meant as a taxi, cleaning, and listening service.

Billie: When another woman, Billie, who had 28 years of sobriety, offered to help me so I could get away from Hilda, I gladly accepted. Hilda was hurt, and there was a terrible fight about it. It seems these two were enemies. Billie, my new sponsor, now started to get up and go outside for a smoke whenever Hilda started to speak at the Friday noon meeting. I thought that was rude, but how can you tell your sponsor she is being rude and just making your former sponsor more angry? Billie would not go to lunch afterwards if Hilda was coming, and both of them would try to get the other women to go with them.

It turned out Billie also wanted to run my life, but in a different way. She was a rich widow, and did not understand what it's like to be a single mother. She wanted me to open all of my old bills and pay them. I was barely off welfare by then, and had no money to pay old bills with. I did not think this was a big deal, but apparently she did, because later, after the joy of getting a sponsee away from her enemy wore off, this woman dumped me for having "too many problems." One of my problems was that I had discovered I was pregnant via my old boyfriend. Billie wanted me to immediately make an appointment for an abortion. I was not ready to do that yet. I had never had an abortion, and I didn't want one until I'd had some time to think. I thought maybe I wanted to have the baby, although I knew there was no way I could ever afford it. So she dumped me.

I went through a couple of other sponsors. It seems that whomever I asked to help me had some agenda. I did finally decide to have an abortion. Everyone in AA who had sponsored me couldn't help that day, so another newcomer, someone who was scorned by everyone else because she talked too long during her "shares" at the meetings, drove me down to the Planned Parenthood clinic. That was the worst day of my life. Somehow I got through it sober.

Eventually, I became more and more depressed in spite of AA meetings, sponsors and steps. I drank again. If there's one thing that will separate you from your AA associates very rapidly, it's drinking. But I sobered up again and, fortunately, I found a doctor who would prescribe an antidepressant for me. It turns out depression, not alcoholism, had been my problem all along. Now I am five years free of drinking, depression—and AA and its sponsors.

29 ▲ Jack Levine
A Gambler's Horror

Fifteen or so years ago, I quit a very heavy and very dangerous methamphetamine and marijuana addiction. It had gotten way out of hand, and I made the decision to never do it again. I ignored that whiny voice in my head that screamed at me to go get high again. It eventually stopped, and I wasn't an addict anymore!

Fifteen or so years later, I was astounded to discover—first through Rational Recovery and later through www.aadeprogramming.com—that when I quit being a drug addict, I hadn't invented anything. I had merely self-recovered, as so many others had before me.

Getting to that same place with a gambling problem, though, almost killed me. Twelve years ago, I had the misfortune to stumble into a Gamblers Anonymous meeting because of a very expensive weekend after having moved to Las Vegas. I can trace my eventual bankruptcy, several near suicides, a nearly failed relationship, and many other hardships to that meeting.

In truth, I was ready to quit gambling just as I had quit drugs. I was 95% there before I walked into the first meeting. All I wanted was some encouragement for a week or two. Instead, they scared me with their horror stories. No one warned me! Where was Ann Landers when I needed her? Ann, Abby and others had suggested that GA was the place to go if I thought I had a problem with gambling. It seemed like good advice.

Little did I know!

Many of the GA groupers I met were doing 14 or more meetings a week between GA, NA, AA, ACOA, etc. They told me that I had to essentially waive all of my common sense and humanity, to stop trying to tell them that this is a religion and that I was an atheist. I had to work the steps, which were incomprehensible to me. They said *I had to give up control of my life.* They said *I was powerless.* I quickly came to believe that I was. They said *my best thinking got me there.* I stopped believing in myself.

When I gambled some more, they said, *See—we told you so.* They said I could not trust my intellect, or my human nature, or my common sense. They convinced me that I had a *disease.* They did everything they could to undermine my having, on my own, quit drugs. They refused to believe in me or my resolve. *Who are you kidding,* they said. *We're the experts on addiction. We know people who abstained for 20 years or more and went back out there. Everyone falls off eventually. Be extra careful after each recognition chip—that's when most people relapse. Relapse is normal. Quitting isn't an option for addicts like us. Quitting on your own is an oxymoron. You must know you're like us, or you wouldn't be here.*

And an inner voice screamed, *Well, if you can't quit, then let's go gambling! Relapse is normal, why wait for an anniversary? You still have one credit card that isn't maxed, GA will still be there if you lose, but you might win, and then you won't need to come back. You're bound to have a winning streak, it's your turn, just a 20, just a hundred, just another thousand . . . blah blah blah . . .*

And guess what, I continued to gamble away my life's income and savings, and I ran up a hundred thousand in credit card debt that had to be bankrupted away. Unlike drugs, with gambling I did everything except quit—12 years in and out of the rooms, 14 different 30-day chips, five different 90-day chips, one for a year and a day. (Hey, it was my fault; they had warned me! I should have worked my program harder!) How many useless hours did I spend trying to find the childhood trauma that caused my illness in the first place? No 12-stepper ever told me that I could quit! Unbelievable! There I was in the belly of the beast surrounded by all the people who were trying anything they could to avoid finally and resolutely quitting for good gambling/drinking/using. They told me to keep coming back if I wanted what they had. *And by the way,* they said, *you didn't quit using drugs, you just found a high that you liked better than drugs.*

Fortunately, somewhere around a year and a half ago, I found *The Real AA* book by Ken Ragge. Finally I was sane again. I finally had the clue that I needed, and from there I found Rational Recovery, and voila! Within a month the self-destructive inner voice was gone. Now my finances are stable and improving quickly, depression and suicidal thoughts no longer control my life, and I will never, ever, ever attend another 12-step meeting.

I now know that I am the best authority on addiction that I have ever met. I have introduced a dozen or so others to this way of thinking. All I had to do was give them the clues, and they solved the puzzle for themselves. We didn't even have a meeting. All anyone needs is a clue as to where to get started. I believe that 12-step programs are destructive. And I believe that most people sitting in the 12-step rooms right this minute are thinking some of these same thoughts, but are still too terrified to voice them.

—Jack LeVine (I will never be anonymous again)

30 ▲ Brenton
AA vs. Cult AA

It's as if 12-steppers want to deny that there is a natural emotion called anger, a natural emotion that is a perfectly normal response to injustice. I recently heard a woman whose house had been ripped off by newcomers she let stay there say, *I had to look at my part.* Aaargh! What a crock. Of course, after blaming herself, she didn't go to the police, because she saw that she *trusted too much.* When my wife got into recovery, she was told to forgive her stepfather for sexually abusing her. She said, *Fuck that!* Of course, she was labeled as *not willing to recover,* but I think that it was a big healing step for her to realize that she was entitled to feel angry about the harm done to her.

Many 12-steppers seem unwilling to look at any recovery method that doesn't jibe with the Big Book. I've seen people shamed and criticized for taking antidepressants, being told that if they only "worked the steps" correctly their depression would magically go away. I know of one extreme case where a woman took her own life after taking "medical" advice from an AA member. Was that her fault, or the result of AA pressure?

One of the hallmarks of cults is that the individual is expected to accept the tenets of the cult without question. When I attended AA and wondered about how certain aspects of the program worked, some crusty old-timer hollered at me that I needed to *stop thinking about it and do it.* I also refused to shave off my goatee just because the Clancy clones don't believe in facial hair. More criticism. When I refused to go to a men's Big Book weekend campout and leave my 36-week-pregnant wife at home alone, my sponsor told me, *you'd better go,* whereupon I fired him. I was later criticized for doing it. When I see people in the program blindly follow gurus like Clancy and also see that they are miserable, I have a problem with that.

By the way, AA did work for me. I have over five years of sobriety. I've just modified the way I work the program so that I'm not one of the 12-step zombies whose whole lives revolve around AA or NA.

31 ▲ Toni

Some Are Sicker than Others

First of all, I want to say this isn't really a horror story. However, I believe it has value in demonstrating an important fact about the people who comprise 12-step recovery groups. I believe that many of us, when we first join a recovery group, are extremely vulnerable. Some of us are easily seduced into believing that anyone with "time" —a long period sober in the program—has achieved sainthood. In our desire to find easy answers we once again find ourselves looking in all the wrong places—AA, for instance—for love, approval, and/or a "spiritual" way of life.

In my case, I failed to realize that some of the people I met in recovery had brought just as much, if not more, baggage into recovery than I had. While someone with a year of sobriety is sure to look and sound more stable than someone who walked in the door a day ago, and while this may look exceptionally appealing to a sanity-starved, shaky newcomer, the fact is that no one is likely to find a lot of sound, stable, well-balanced, unselfish, healthy souls in a room full of recovering addicts and alcoholics. Just because a person is in recovery and talks about the steps and a spiritual way of life does not mean that he or she has forsaken all personal agendas and become godlike.

But many newcomers fall under the sway of 12-step gurus, and I have seen this become a stumbling block in the recovery process. As a case in point, I would like to share a personal experience. I had been sober for approximately a year when I became involved with a non-profit group that served free meals to needy people in a small, West Coast city. They were talking about opening a homeless shelter.

I thought volunteer work there would be a wonderful way to be of service to practicing alcoholics and addicts. Although the work started on a volunteer basis, I eventually found myself on staff, managing the shelter, and working 14-hour days, seven days a week—and getting high on it.

During this time I met Terry, who, like me, was a member of Narcotics Anonymous. He came into the program about six months after I had. Terry was a perfect example of the "90-day wonder" syndrome. He became a key volunteer at the shelter, formed a couple of clean-and-sober group homes, and landed a job with the local mental health clinic, an organization serving the county's homeless or poor mentally ill and addicted population—some of the same population the shelter served.

We became friends, working together. Terry had recently married a woman who was a mental health counselor and recovered addict, a woman who had also worked with me at the shelter and was a friend of mine. About a year later when they were divorcing, I offered her a room to rent in my home, and she accepted gratefully. But she decided at the last minute to get an apartment, and Terry, who had nowhere to move, asked if he could take the room. I said, "sure."

That was the beginning of a four-year relationship. It took only about three months for us to get into bed together. Meantime, Terry worked tirelessly on behalf of his clients, as did I. We worked together and got much accomplished. Our shared work was the ground upon which we had met, and on which we lived and prospered.

We enrolled in school together so we could become certified drug and alcohol counselors. In fact, we shared many dreams and goals. I felt I had met my almost perfect match. There were a couple of glitches, but they seemed minor. After all, we shared so much, what did it matter that some of my needs were going unmet? In order to be in this relationship, which seemed perfect to all my NA and AA friends, I could certainly sacrifice some of my wants and needs.

School gave me the opportunity to realize I had some "old stuff" moldering in the recesses of my psyche, so I got into therapy. In recovery one hears over and over that *some are sicker than others,* and I took that to mean that sometimes professional help should be sought. It was a good move on my part, perhaps the best thing I have done for myself.

Terry and I finished school, and each of us found more promising jobs counseling others with addictions. Terry loved his new job working with mentally ill substance abusers, and his fellow counselors and supervisors seemed to love him.

But then Terry got fired for having sex with a client. He denied it and, of course, I believed him. The incident was unfortunate, but we felt we would survive. And he was immediately hired somewhere else—it seemed that everyone loved Terry. With his wonder-boy reputation and winning smile, he seemed to inspire confidence wherever he went.

In no time, he became chairman of the local mental health board. I loved and trusted him. I only vaguely missed having a satisfying sex life, and it was easy enough to put sex aside—we were both so busy.

Then the unthinkable happened. I made an accidental discovery as I was looking through the history files on our computer for a web site I'd forgotten to bookmark. I stumbled upon something I can only describe as shattering. Terry had been meeting people for sex, women he'd found on the Internet. He'd been having *cyber-sex* also. Oh my God!

Shortly thereafter, I learned that he'd had a year-long affair with a mentally ill client/co-worker. Thank God I was in therapy. It soon became clear that Terry was a practicing sex addict. I had been totally deceived by someone whom nearly everyone believed to be a "to-gether" recovering person. Well, everyone, especially me, was wrong.

All along, Terry was just a fucked up unit who got off drugs and alcohol and into something else.

I have heard of other such nightmares happening in 12-step culture, and I guess my point is that 12-step groups are jam packed with folks who have more than just substance abuse problems. Those who are too vulnerable and not careful enough can get hurt there as easily as they can get hurt anywhere else. No matter where you are you must beware. AA and NA are not peopled by the most well and recovered humans in the world. Listen when they say, *some of us are sicker than others*. They speak the truth.

32 ▲ Martin

Trouble with the Spiritual Path

I have had a total of about 12 years experience with AA, and I also work in a youth treatment center. I am beginning to fear for my health and safety. Not from the clients, but from the staff, and the AA way of life.

My first bad experience was when a girl I knew had gone out to dinner on her AA birthday and someone had seen her use wine vinegar on her salad. When she went to the meeting to get her sobriety chip, this asshole showed up and filibustered the meeting until nearly the whole group had come down on her and she had to leave in shame. (There is no alcohol in wine vinegar.) Two days later, when members of the group went to save her from her evil ways and bring her back into the fold, she was found dead: suicide.

Another time we had a 16-year-old girl in treatment who was "having trouble" getting the *spiritual* part of treatment. (The treatment center has a way of shunning kids who aren't *getting it* by giving them very little time with counselors. This shunning goes on despite the fact that the state requires two hours of one-on-one counseling per week with a certified counselor.)

The neglect of this particular girl went on for about three weeks, and she was becoming acutely depressed. I went to her counselor and asked what was going on. She told me that the reason the young girl was not getting any time was that she was so much healthier than others and didn't need so much time.

But after a couple of more weeks, when she still hadn't *cracked in group*, they decided that the only thing that could possibly be keeping her from breaking down was that there was something in her past that was so bad that she must be burying it deep enough to go catatonic when these things were brought up. Of course, none of this was the problem—the girl was depressed, uncomfortable in group, and not getting any one-on-one help.

Two weeks later her saviors decided she was just being stubborn.

They decided to use a very strange form of psychology. They thought if they called her probation officer and told him she had confessed to a *murder*, that she would finally break down and talk about her *real* problems.

When she found out about this, the poor girl decided she'd had enough. She escaped from "treatment," and through the help of a good lawyer is now safe and doing well.

(PLEASE DON'T USE MY E-MAIL OR NAME. The treatment center I work for gives all their employees free Internet access. But we've found out that everything we do on the net is being saved at the main office *for the employee's convenience in case they lose something*. Right.)

33 ▲ Sarah
Stupid Therapists

If the malpractice hadn't happened so long ago, I would sue the Big Books right off the shelves of three different therapists who sent me to AA.

For 18 years I suffered periodic depression that was highly treatable. But because I drank to self-medicate the depression, the therapists that I went to sent me to AA, instead of treating me for the real problem.

Of course, if I had known what was wrong with me before I sought help, I could have avoided wasting 18 years trying to find help in an organization that could not help me. I would have simply have found a 12-step-free psychiatrist, described my symptoms, and been treated. As the AA cliche goes, simple but not easy!

The first professional I went to was a psychologist, Dr. M., whom I went to in 1978. He had been recommended as a *good psychologist for alcoholics*. When I came to him for help with a drinking problem I was already sober, but I wanted to stay that way. I had found that I could stay sober for long periods of time on my own, but that eventually I would start feeling really bad, and drink.

Yet at our first visit, he suggested I go to AA. I told him I had been to several meetings the year before, but that I didn't understand what the people were talking about. AA had seemed like some kind of religious group, one which I did not particularly care for.

Dr. M. would not take *no* for an answer. He encouraged me to go to a different meeting. *If you don't like the AA meetings in your neighborhood, then try some out-of-town meetings.* He gave me a meeting schedule from his desk. I agreed to go to meetings, and to see Dr. M. once a week.

At the meetings I went to, I often saw Dr. M. and his wife. Apparently, she was the alcoholic, and he was an Al-Anon member who went to open AA meetings with her. They were staunch and ardent steppers. I did not mind this AA group particularly. They didn't scare me like one group I had gone to; actually, a few members talked to me very nicely and offered phone numbers. That was fine with me. I never volunteered to share, and was not called on anyway. One thing I did notice, however, was that the focus on drinking made me want to drink. I would be feeling perfectly fine, having forgotten about drinking, but would leave meetings wanting the taste of a nice cold beer.

But I went anyway, and didn't drink. I went back to Dr. M. every week for several weeks. We would talk about what I was doing and how I felt. Having never been to a psychologist before, I had no idea what we were supposed to talk about. I just answered Dr. M's questions, and followed his lead.

Apparently I had other symptoms, because by my third session he had diagnosed depression. I wondered what that meant. I knew my mother had problems with depression that were controlled with medication, and I assumed he would treat me for depression because that was what I was there for. But he never discussed treatment for depression, never prescribed anything, or even recommended that I seek anyone who would. He just wanted to make sure I went to AA meetings.

Meantime, in AA, I kept hearing that I had a disease. Some of the speakers would say sober people shouldn't take any drugs, including doctor's prescriptions, and I began to feel guilty about wanting medication. I also heard that my symptoms—crying often, resting much of the day, and feeling sad—were *pity pot* and *stinkin' thinkin'.* I felt that I should never complain, and that I should pretend to be *happy—fake it until you make it.* But according to others in AA, for a newcomer to act happy was *dishonest.* I needed to *get real.* It seemed that no matter what I did or how I acted, someone in AA told me it was wrong. Nobody seemed to think I was okay as I was.

Finally, I stopped seeing Dr. M. All we did was sit and talk about how I felt and about AA. This wasn't helping me, and I kept feeling worse and worse, like nothing was any use. I quit going to AA because I began to feel very uncomfortable around the people at meetings. Yet while I was there, I would smile and pretend to be happy. I still did not understand how sitting in a group of people talking about past drinking and how happy or unhappy life was today could make a difference. Although by this time I believed I had a disease I was powerless over, I had no idea how going to AA would help.

Now that I've been sober several years, I think that believing I had an incurable disease, alcoholism, hurt rather than helped me, because once I began to drink again, which was within weeks, I didn't even try to control it. My drinking turned into a very serious binge pattern. I'd drink around the clock, even waking up in the middle of the night and drinking myself back to sleep. I began to end up in hospitals and detoxes—just as had been predicted at the AA meetings.

The second professional I saw, several years later, was a drug-alcohol counselor whom I'll call "L." He worked in a county alcohol program in central California. I went to him in desperation after having wound up with a case of severe withdrawal syndrome during detox. I was still shaking when I came to his office.

L. asked me questions about my life, and alcohol and drug use. I answered the questions honestly. Then he read off an evaluation of me, based on the answers to my questions. It sounded something like this:

> *Sarah is a 32-year-old woman who has been married twice and has two children. She did not graduate from high school. She has been using alcohol, her drug of choice, since she was 13. She prefers beer and wine, but if those are not available she will drink other forms of alcohol. She currently uses marijuana four times a week. She has used LSD, crank, cocaine, and barbiturates. She has exhibited symptoms of stage-4 alcoholism, has been to the county detox twice, and been hospitalized twice due to drinking. She has had alcoholic hepatitis.*

This evaluation sounded like everything worth saying about me had to do with drinking and using. Actually, I had grown up in the late '60s and early '70s, and had experimented with drugs in ways similar to those of others in my social group. I had never been addicted to drugs. At the time I saw L., I'd been attending community college and was on the dean's list. I had a job as an English tutor, and I was getting poetry published. I had written for the local paper analyzing the way the prison staff handled visitors to the state prison in our town. In addition, I worked part time as a bookkeeper for a real estate company, and was much liked and needed at my job. My children and I lived in a clean apartment, and they were happy and healthy, although my week-long benders, which occurred about three or four times a year, always upset them. But in between benders I teetotaled.

L. told me I had a "disease" that was terminal—alcoholism—and that I had a 97% chance of dying of this disease unless I submitted to treatment for three years. Treatment consisted of going to 90 AA meetings in 90 days, then at least one meeting a week thereafter. Plus, I was to do something fun once a week.

I told him I was already doing fun things more than once a week, and that AA meetings made me want to drink. I said that I'd rather be treated with one-on-one therapy. I told him I would give up the marijuana (I did) and that I could stay sober on my own, but I was having trouble staying sober longer than six months at a time, because I would start to feel so bad that I wanted to die. Then I would simply drink, and stay drunk for a week or so.

He cut me off. He did not like *pity pots*. He said to go to AA anyway. Again I went, determined to make the 90 in 90. I began to attend meetings at Serenity Lunchers, a daily noon meeting held in an Alano Club room in a small Bay Area town. Propped in the back of the meeting room was an old toilet seat, lined with fur, above which a sign blazed: *Pity Pot.*

At the third meeting I attended there, I was surprised to see L. at the front table chairing the meeting. He told a standard tale of past drinking woes, turned to happiness thanks to AA. But then he said something that made me feel terrible. *I hear newcomers say*—he used a whiny little voice for this—*But meetings make me want to drink!* Then he proceeded to bawl out at anyone so foolish and ungrateful as to say such a thing. My heart sank. I had said just that in his office a few days before. I got his point.

I kept going to meetings. I got a sponsor, a big, kind-hearted, mothering woman of Italian heritage. "Stella" called herself a former "party girl," and used to talk about how she had gone low enough to "turn tricks" in between her many marriages. She had 15 years of sobriety at the time I met her. I still think she is a fine person. But unfortunately she was not a professional, and had little experience with those who needed professional help. As far as she was concerned, AA was good enough for most folks. I called her often, and I also hung out with a very interesting older man who was very kind to me. Harv would take me out to coffee, and he called often to see how I was doing. He called me his "adopted daughter." He was a fairly well-known wire sculptor, and gave me a beautiful sculpted tree on a platform of marble. He had a wondrous tale, a true AA rags-to-spiritual-riches story that struck the hearts of all. I loved hearing him at meetings.

Stella seemed suspicious of all the time I spent with Harv. There was much gossip about Harv and the "adopted daughters" he took under his wing. But in spite of the gossip, Harv was innocent of trying to 13th-step me.

I kept going to meetings, and kept calling my sponsor. I worked the steps up to the third, where I turned my life and will over to the care of God. I was starting my fourth step, the moral inventory. I kept going to meetings. By the 89th day, I had been severely depressed for about a week. My symptoms were exhaustion, crying, sadness, and sleeplessness. I couldn't stay interested in schoolwork. I craved bad food like chocolate and salty fried food. I became very sensitive and would feel angry and sad over small slights or rudeness, and I would stay angry. Later, I found out that these kinds of unreasonable resentments are really symptoms of deeper problems. I was severely depressed and just didn't realize it. By this time, my sponsor, Stella, had labeled my symptoms *pity pot* and *stinkin' thinkin'*. And I, full of ignorant guilt, agreed!

So there I was at the meeting, which was full of the usual testimonials, interspersed with arguments between members over whether or not the verification papers of folks sent by the court should be signed before or after the meeting. I felt sorry for the poor schmucks, just sitting there feeling stupid while sparks flew all over the place about how to handle them.

As for the testimonials, I believed in God and tried praying, but He was not fixing whatever was wrong with me, nor did He do anything to interfere with what I was about to do. I left the meeting slightly early and, on the way home, got a big supply of booze and stayed roaring drunk for a week. I ended up in the county detox, sweating and shaking.

When, after a a few days in detox, I went back to AA, one member told me I shouldn't have left the meeting early. Another told me I should have been doing steps one, two, and three every day. Another told me I didn't really want to quit. Stella thought I drank because I hadn't done a fifth step yet. So I finished the fourth-step moral inventory and told her my fifth step—confessed everything I could remember that I ever did wrong, from squishing moths or sucking my thumb as a child, to errant sexual flings and mean thoughts. It was all terribly demeaning, and I didn't feel any better after doing it. I felt ashamed, as if I had vomited on the floor and left it there.

Again, I got drunk. That particular bender resulted in a week-long detox in a mental ward. I had attempted suicide while drinking. It was there that I was put in contact with Dr. R.V.

Dr. R.V. was a psychiatrist who worked out of an office in the small town I lived in, and also spent time treating prisoners at the nearby state prison. When I told him about my pattern of benders, the first thing he did was prescribe lithium. I asked him why lithium, for I was not bipolar. No one in my family history was either.

Dr. R.V. said that he was "experimenting" with "alcoholics" who he called "periodics." I started taking this lithium. It made me fat, and I had to go and get blood tests regularly. Worse, I did not feel better. It made me feel "flat" emotionally. But I kept taking the lithium and kept seeing Dr. R.V.

I had told him during the first visit that I wasn't going to any AA meetings. I was busy with school and work, and AA had never done anything but make me feel like a failure.

After about eight visits, I was feeling good. I'd been admitted to a prestigious university, and I had been able to rent a very lovely, large house. My children loved the house, and they were happy. More of my poetry was being published as well. But the lithium made me feel logy, fat, and flat much of the time. I wished I wasn't taking it. Couldn't we try something else? Dr. R.V. didn't answer. Instead, he asked me how AA was going.

I looked at him, surprised. *You know I'm not going to AA,* I said. Dr. R.V. went bonkers. He started yelling at me, saying I was trying to con him. I left the place in tears.

Later, my sister called him to ask what was wrong with him and demand an apology. She didn't want me to give up on getting the help I needed. He told her it was all a big misunderstanding. When I got up the gumption to go to another appointment, Dr. R.V. acted like nothing had happened, as though I had misunderstood his *concern.* I saw Dr. R.V. a couple more times after that, but I didn't trust him anymore. Eventually, after a continuing spiral of depression (the lithium didn't seem to make a dent in it) I drank again.

Incidentally, the reason I can't sue him is because he's dead. A doctor I was dating knew him, and told me Dr. R.V. had died of a narcotic overdose.

As far as AA goes, do these therapists and doctors have any idea what goes on in and around meetings? Here are some of the things I have seen, heard about, and experienced during several years in AA:

I know of many deaths, including that of one man I knew personally. Rami died believing he was powerless; he died in spite of step work he had done precisely as outlined in the Big Book.

He was of East Indian descent, had a heavy accent, and was not sought out much by the AAers here in California. His accent was such that it was real work to talk to and listen to Rami. As a result, he never got into the social aspect of AA, which is really what motivates newcomers to stay sober, in spite of what the program says about God keeping alcoholics sober. The fringe, cultist groups in AA *will* socialize with newcomers, though. They sponsor newcomers, ask them to coffee, movies, and lunch. One of the Big Book gurus I knew would wait by the phone for newcomers to call. This is who Rami fell in with. How could he resist them? Alcoholics tend to be lonely, and the cultists take advantage of that. He really believed what they told him, that God would remove the desire and even the ability to drink alcohol if he worked the steps properly and experienced a "spiritual awakening." He never had one. His sponsor dumped him when he started drinking again, saying he must have left something out of his fifth step. Rami died a year or two later of alcoholic pancreatitis.

Countless others are enduring depression because they think taking antidepressants means you haven't had a spiritual experience and that you'll get drunk and die. One woman in the group was told she had to get off her antidepressants or she would never have a true spiritual experience. She tried. One day she called me up, crying, paralyzed. I told her it was wrong for her sponsor to persuade her to go off her medication. I told her she should go back to her doctor and take whatever he prescribed. She did. Thank God AA is not responsible for her suicide. I know an old-timer woman who doesn't tell sponsees to get off their medication anymore; years ago, she had a sponsee who obeyed and ended up committing suicide. Now she just says, "Go to a doctor." Too bad she had to learn through some-one else's death.

Another woman I buddied with had such bad panic attacks that she couldn't even drive a car. She was told when she *got honest* and did a thorough fifth step that she'd stop panicking. She never could stay sober long enough to do a fifth step, though. She said her panic would get so bad she'd have to have a drink just to calm down. She was told that was just an excuse. No one would go out of their way to help her until she *became willing*. We didn't see her for a while. Later, I ran into her downtown. She had been sober for two years. How? She'd gone to a doctor and gotten on a medication to control her panic. She was healthy, happy, and able to drive a car. But she was through with AA.

Eventually, I found a doctor and therapist who would help me, but only because I was lucky enough to have found information on depression and drinking. Apparently—something I should have known after 18 years of seeking and failing to solve my alcohol problem—people who drink to relieve depression rarely make it in AA, or in any program, until their depression is adequately treated. To find the right doctor was no problem—I just stayed away from doctors who were recommended for *alcoholics*. I found an Asian psychiatrist who had nothing to do with substance abuse programs of any kind, and told him my symptoms. By that time I was suicidal. He asked about family history. I told him about my mother's lifelong depression that had by that time lifted, thanks to Prozac. This is what he prescribed. I also began seeing a therapist.

They say it takes a month to feel the full effects of Prozac. I started feeling better the second day. I began to feel normal. I began to feel hope. Suddenly, doing things and being outside during the day seemed wonderful. The gnawing anger and despair slowly faded. At the end of the first month after I started taking it, I realized I had not cried for three weeks. The therapist I'd begun to see noticed, too, that I could sit through a session without breaking into tears.

The difficult part of my treatment was *finding* a therapist who wouldn't try driving me into AA. I knew I was having many problems in my relationships with men, and it was clear by this time—I was 39 and had been through two husbands and three or four live-in boyfriends—that I had underlying emotional problems that had not been helped by AA any more than my drinking problem had. Through the local clinic, I found an MSW who was willing to donate time to me.

But the first thing she wanted me to do was to go to AA meetings. I had to insist that I would never again go to another meeting. I told her I had seen too many people victimized and abused in AA, and that their dogmas were destructive to my well-being. She said I should go to meetings out of town. I assured her I had been to plenty of different meetings—I knew what was there; it wasn't for me, and the thought of attending another meeting made me literally sick to my stomach.

She agreed to see me anyway. She was not an alcoholic, addict, or 12-stepper of any kind herself. This was lucky, because by that time I was willing to risk dying before going to another meeting or working a single step ever again. Still, she warned me that if I got drunk it would spoil all the work we were doing. At last, after several months, she realized I was committed to sobriety, and was not lying about my ability to stay sober. I would thank God for this woman, but I had to work and fight to get her help, too. How many other deeply depressed people have the gumption to go after what they need? It was my anger that saved me—the anger so maligned and despised in AA.

My life took off. I have accomplished more in the past three years than I did in the prior 18 years floating from therapists to meetings and back again. Not one, but three separate therapists—a psychologist, a psychiatrist, and a drug/alcohol counselor—failed to treat me for my real problem. To them, I was an *alcoholic,* which automatically meant I needed to go to AA.

Like others who are victims of this type of malpractice, I went to professionals because I didn't know what was wrong with me. They should have treated me for my depression. Instead, blinded by their own indoctrination, they thrust me into AA. Dr. M. used me as a paying AA sponsee. To L., I was just another pity-pot alcoholic to be treated no differently than other alcoholics. I was not worth listening to; AA meetings were good enough for me. And Dr. R.V. used me as a guinea pig.

What therapists need to be doing is warning clients *against* AA. I hope clients treated the way I was start suing the therapists who fob them off on 12-step groups.

34 ▲ Darlene
Rebel Incognito

I've been sober six-and-one-half years and, like many others, I went to AA for my drinking problem. Four years ago, I married Fred, a man whom I had met in AA. At the time we married, we bought a house, and I became an instant mother to Fred's child who, much as I love him, was a spoiled brat.

Then I was laid off from my job. After a lot of thought, we decided that, rather than my going out and finding another job, we would try to run Fred's mom-and-pop shop ourselves.

I became too tired to go to four or five AA meetings a week. And my doubts about AA had already begun. I got tired of being greeted with, *Haven't seen you at meetings in a while,* instead of genuine interest in me. I got tired of being made to feel that I'd better offer a damn good explanation. And I became more discerning about what I heard people say in AA meetings, compared with how I saw them act.

So, with all my new and quite different responsibilities, my meeting attendance dropped and dropped. Call it resentment or whatever, but when I go to a meeting and people are chilly to me because I've got a life and can't get to meetings, I feel angry at them. I'm frustrated because my husband can't let go of them, and I feel paranoid that he goes to meetings and thinks that our private life together should be sorted out in front of people who will take sides with him because he's at the meeting and I'm not. I used to spill my guts at the meetings and swallowed the crap that all my problems should, no matter who it concerned, be their business. I don't want to live like that anymore. I'd like some things between my husband and me or my stepson and me to stay private, between us and us only.

If I go to meetings now, it's only to be with Fred. We don't have much time left over for "dates." Well, I went with him today. The topic was the Serenity Prayer and acceptance. My turn came.

I couldn't talk *AA-speak.* I said I was having a tough time with acceptance. Two friends died this weekend—one was Fred's boyhood friend, who blew his head off with a shotgun. Money's slow in coming from those who owe us. Income taxes are right around the bend and we owe and don't know where it'll come from. We are behind in bills. I haven't had a chance to visit my dad since last summer, and he's crying out to see me. He's 79, won't be around forever, and he needs some help. Then my father-in-law got ugly with me Wednesday and backed his truck into our fence. When I went to help him, he started cussing at me—fuckin' this, fuckin' that—then he started raving about what a piece of shit property we had. The caring AAers then took turns sharing their drunkalogs, and one suggested I not take stuff so seriously.

No one (including me, I'm ashamed to say) gave the person who brought up the *acceptance* topic any suggestions on how to be more accepting. Every sentence uttered started with *"I." I used to have trouble with acceptance, but now . . . with the help of this program and you wonderful people. . . .* It gets so saccharine I could gag. I refuse to discuss AA with Fred anymore—I'm afraid people in the group will suggest he divorce me. It's not a joke.

Anyhow, consider me a spy! Here's a quote from a recent meeting: *You can't get sober without AA.* Since I've reduced meetings, gotten a life, and met more people in different organizations, I've talked with many who made a decision on their own to stop drinking. And despite the claim that one cannot get sober at church, I've met quite a few who did. Oops, I forgot, *they weren't **real** alcoholics.*

It seems that whenever a person or organization constantly talks about how wonderful, good, faultless, and near perfection he, she or it is, then that overused word *denial* is truly in existence in that person or organization. I want to gag whenever I witness the never-ending pats on the back of AA members to the organization and each other. To hear it is to realize these people truly believe that, as members of this group, they are extra special and superior to the rest of the world, which they believe hasn't a clue.

My main focus in life now is to do my part for me, my family, and the community I live in so we don't all become one more whiny burden on society. That doesn't give me much time anymore to sit hour after hour and talk about myself. Thank God!

35 ▲ Lisa
AA Made Me Worse

Let me start by saying that AA provides a useful framework for many, many people, and I always encourage new members of the alternative recovery group I now use to give AA a shot and at least check out a few different meetings. I also encourage participation in other alternatives to AA, because I think it's important that individuals explore anything that might be helpful to them. I believe that recovery is an intensely personal journey, and every person must find his or her own mix of recovery-supporting activities and beliefs. I also believe that a coercive and close-minded approach to sobriety does a terrible disservice to people in great need of help.

My experience in AA was not a good one. For about two years, I tried earnestly and desperately to "make it" in AA, and to stick with and be one of the *winners*—with an alarming lack of success. This was a very dangerous and self-destructive time in my life, and one in which I was repeatedly told that AA was my only option, my only chance for salvation and survival.

I got involved in AA after years of dependence on alcohol and after a number of serious incidents, which eventually made it clear to me and to the people closest to me that I was in serious trouble. Initially, I wasn't convinced that I wanted or needed help, but attempts to control my drinking resulted in disastrous lapses, and I began a long string of hospital treatments. A few weeks of outpatient treatment was followed by a week of inpatient treatment, which was followed by two weeks of inpatient treatment, and eventually a 28-day stay at an inpatient treatment center. During every one of these treatment stints, there were mandatory daily AA meetings. AA was presented as the only means of achieving sobriety; no mention was ever made of any other program, philosophy, or possible way to get sober. Indeed, it was frequently stated that there was no other way, and anyone who believed there was, was fooling himself or herself. Lack of enthusiasm for any aspect of AA was deemed resistance to treatment.

So, desperate to get help, I threw myself wholeheartedly into AA. My drinking had, in fact, been life threatening, and I took a medical leave from work to attend AA twice daily. I got a sponsor, I collected and used phone numbers, and I spoke at meetings. I asked for help. I tried to do everything that other people told me to do, since I was told that my own judgment was of very little value.

But every time I had questions or issues, I got platitudes for answers, or my concerns were discounted. Instructions like *leave your brain at the door* and *just don't drink* were not helpful. Nor was the emphasis on humbling myself and discounting my own needs and intuition—both of these were tendencies that I already had, and that I actually needed to counter in order to get sober. In spite of very active participation in the program, I spiraled into deeper and deeper depression, with periodic bouts of drinking and suicidal behavior, which only served to demonstrate that I clearly *wasn't working the program,* or that I *didn't want to get better.* Such thinking led me to hate myself even more, and believe in myself even less.

After a third DUI, which ultimately resulted in a mandatory minimum prison sentence, I finally decided that I didn't really care anymore what other people thought. My family and my husband had about given up on me. They no longer cared how hard I was working and how many meetings I was going to. There was no longer any reason to try to prove myself to other people. Things were bad enough that I was really and truly alone with myself and my problems. And I knew that I was going to have to find something that worked for me—screw what everybody else thought. I was going to have to start taking care of myself, believing in myself, trusting in myself, and doing what I felt was important.

Finally, I found an alternative recovery method, Women for Sobriety. Unfortunately, there were no meetings I could get to. But, with a foundation of personal recovery based on writing to other sober women and using the philosophy outlined in the WFS literature—plus a year of sobriety—I started a group one year later.

I've found that learning to take care of myself (instead of focusing on everybody else), recognizing my own needs, and believing in myself have been critical to my sobriety. I think it's a travesty that AA is presented as the only viable way to sobriety. I find AA a tad cultish, and I have a real problem with anyone who believes in any kind of blind obedience and "one true way." That one true way didn't work for me. I had to find my own.

36 ▲ Ted

Treatment Scam

As I sit here and think about what has gone on in the last seven months, I shake my head in disbelief. I am stunned, shocked, amazed, and angered at what has happened. If someone had told me seven months ago that I would be carried into a world I never knew existed, to be treated the way I was, I would have said that they were crazy. This is the nineties—shit like that just can't happen.

It all started back in May 1998 when someone filed a complaint saying that they smelled alcohol on my breath while I was on my way to work. The company I work for refused to give me the details of the complaint. I was told only that someone smelled alcohol on my breath. My partner, who traveled with me for some hours on the way to work, and other people at work, stated that they did not smell alcohol on my breath or notice any changes in my behavior that night. From the time I left my home until the time I arrived with my partner at work, nine hours of travel time had passed, with no consumption of alcohol.

After the job was completed and I returned home (some two days later), I was called into the office for a meeting with our directors. They asked if I was drinking or drunk prior to reporting for work. I said *no*, I was not drunk and that I had drank a few beers before dinner and a couple with dinner, but did not work until some nine hours later. Our company guidelines are no alcohol consumption for at least eight hours before work, and I didn't breach that rule. I was then told that I had to go see the company EAP counselor for an "assessment," and if I refused to go, I would be fired. I agreed to see the counselor, for I had nothing to hide, and I wanted to keep my job. The following week I went to see her.

I had never been to see a counselor of any kind before. I was a little apprehensive about what was going to take place, so I approached the interview carefully. I thought the two interviews I had with her went quite well, but of all she said to me, what sticks in my mind the most is that she kept telling me that the process was completely confidential. The company would know absolutely nothing of what was going on. They would never use my name, even when billing. I could be assured that no one would know anything about this. She must have told me that a half a dozen times, and I believed her.

At the end of the second interview, she told me that I was going to return to work. She thought everything was OK and that I was fine, etc. *But,* she said, *first we'll get you to see our medical doctor because you need a medical certificate to return to work since you are on sick leave benefits. Dr. Baker,* she continued, *is very approachable and you'll like him.* She said it as though she was infatuated with Baker. I didn't care who he was, I just wanted to get my clean bill of health and get back to work.

I was to phone and make an appointment with Dr. Baker, so I phoned up Baker's office, explained who I was, and made an appointment. The receptionist gave me one for about three weeks later, then asked me to send a check for fifteen hundred dollars. *Fifteen hundred dollars, for a medical exam!,* I exclaimed. She also said I had to have blood tests and other tests, and the exam would take a couple of hours. I said, *Well I'm not paying that; send the bill to my company,* and hung up the phone.

I phoned the company EAP and said that the appointment to see Dr. Baker was unacceptable because I was scheduled back to work at the end of the month, and I wanted my medical exam done before that so I wouldn't miss any work. She managed to get me an appointment with Dr. Baker in two weeks by making a personal call to him.

Waiting for Dr. Baker on the appointment day, I was given a handful of forms asking various psychological questions. Dr. Baker came in, and I went in his office. He seemed like a reasonable guy; however, I felt uneasy about being there so I was guarded in my answers, not really offering any more that direct answers to his questions. He asked very personal questions ranging from those about drug and alcohol use to health, sex, and my family's health history. I was a little upset at the depth to which he was probing my family's health history and my wife's family's health, but I didn't want to seem uncooperative with him. I needed his approval (or so I thought) to return back to work.

He continually assured me of the complete confidentiality of my exam, and that no one would be privy to this information. Dr. Baker then performed a few medical examinations—blood pressure, stethoscope stuff, etc., and asked if he could talk to some of my friends, co-workers, family doctor, and my wife. I reluctantly said sure, having really nothing to hide. Something inside was telling me *this is not right*, but I figured I'd better agree if I wanted to go back to work. He also asked me to take a urinalysis test and a blood test, which I did. He said he would send his results to me in a week.

This "exam" took about thirty minutes to complete, and I left his office feeling relieved that it was over, but also quite uneasy about the questions I was asked and the way I was blindsided by his inquiries. I also was somewhat intimidated by him. I answered his questions correctly and honestly, but divulging that much personal information to anyone *felt wrong*. But he was a doctor, and I had to do it, knowing that he held the keys to my return to work. I didn't want to screw that up.

About ten days later, a call came in the morning from Dr. Baker, waking my wife from a dead sleep. While she was still half asleep in bed, he started asking her questions about me and my drinking habits, as well as personal questions about her and her family. After five minutes of his questions she hung up the phone. A week went by and I hadn't heard anything from anyone. Ten days passed, and I started to wonder what was going on.

After two weeks, I called the EAP's office and left messages, but my calls were not returned. Twenty days after seeing Dr. Baker, the day I was to return to work, I called one of the company directors and asked if I was going back to work. He said somewhat emphatically, *You're not going back to work!*

What do you mean? I asked. *Hasn't anyone talked to you?*, he asked. *No. How come I'm not going back to work?* He started to give me an explanation, then cut himself off in mid-sentence and said, *I'd better not say anything until they talk to you,* and hung up.

I put in a call to the EAP's office and left another message. I called a few more times and left messages, and I also called the EAP counselor and left messages with her answering machine. I didn't receive any replies to my calls until July 6th, when the EAP counselor called and left a message saying: *If this is about Dr. Baker's report, I have read it.* When I heard this I thought, *what report, what is she talking about?*

Amy T., the EAP counselor, called on July 6th. *Dr. Baker has said you must attend a four-week residential treatment program because he has diagnosed you as alcohol dependent,* she announced. This was to be followed up by biweekly visits to Dr. Baker.

I was shocked.

She went on to say that Dr. Baker recommends the Pacifica treatment center. *We have a bed waiting for you on July 11th.* I said, *I don't believe this, what's this all about? I can't just drop everything and run into some treatment center for four weeks, I've got obligations to fulfill and a business to run.* I asked, *Why do I have to go into a treatment center?*

She went on to say that I was alcohol dependent and I had to go because Dr. Baker said I must. We argued for a minute about going into treatment and I said, *I've got to talk to Baker on this,* and hung up.

I put a call into Dr. Baker's office asking for him to call me. I got the runaround about him not returning calls; I would have to make an appointment and so on. But I just told the receptionist this was an emergency and he'd better call me back.

Dr. Baker called that afternoon from his cell phone. I asked him what was going on and why he was insisting I go to a treatment center.

He said, *Well, there's some evidence of dependency.* He said I needed to go through an intense four-week program with a follow up of bi-weekly visits to him, and weekly AA meetings. He went on to say that if I was in any other job I would not have to go through this process. As I started to ask questions he just brushed them off and disconnected his phone. He did ask me one question before he hung up. He asked if I did do the urine and blood samples because he never received the results. I assured him that I had given samples the very day of our first meeting.

By this time I was pissed off, because I couldn't understand what was going on and I couldn't get any answers.

On the morning of July 8th, I met with two of the directors of my company. I am an equal shareholder in my company, and directors are also shareholders who are elected to run the company business. These directors are nothing more than equal shareholders and co-workers, not my employers.

In the meeting, I was confronted by two co-workers (who happen to be directors) and was asked questions concerning my not wanting to attend the treatment center. I said I thought this meeting was to discuss medical benefits. At that point the "meeting" turned into a series of threats, which included loss of employment. I was told my pay was cut off as of the last day I worked, back in May, and the money that I'd been paid in benefits was treated as a loan and would have to be paid back to the company. The loan would be paid by working it off day for day or paying it back in cash. I was also told that my license to earn my living would be suspended by the governing board, and I might never get it back.

I was calm and polite in dealing with their threats, but I felt I had to remain passive and compliant because I was very concerned that if I told them the real reason why I didn't want to go to treatment, they might threaten me with that as well. My wife and I were in the process of adopting a child, which was due to be born at the end of July. It would be the culmination of a very long, hard, and emotional journey which had begun 12 years ago. I was determined that nothing would interfere with our adopting this baby.

But as the threats and badgering persisted, I finally alluded to the fact that I was involved in an adoption and would be available to attend a treatment center in a couple of weeks. I decided to comply with going into treatment, fearing that if I became unemployed, and the adoption agency found out, our hopes of finally having our first child would end. That statement seemed to catch them off guard for a second, but as soon as their thoughts caught up with this new information, I could see wheels begin to turn, and some veiled threats about the adoption started floating out.

At that point my anger started to emerge. I surprised them by showing anger, which put them on the defensive. One of the directors, in attempting to quell my anger, blurted out, *Well, Dr. Baker told us that you are only in the very early stages of dependency and you have a better than ninety percent chance of a full recovery!* I looked at him and said, *How did you know that?* He said, *Well the doctor and Amy T. had a meeting with us and told us that you were alcohol dependent and stand a good chance of a full recovery.*

What he said didn't really register because I was more concerned about getting through this little crisis and not jeopardizing the upcoming adoption. I wanted to question him further on his statement; the alarm bell was ringing in my head, but my instinct said let it slide. As it turns out, his statement is a key to this whole thing.

I left this meeting feeling scared, saying that I would get into another treatment center in a couple of weeks. I knew that I would have to stall them until we completed our adoption, but I was under tremendous pressure to go into the treatment center.

I called the directors on Monday and told them I wanted to go to another treatment center. I also asked what my liability to the company was going to be regarding the treatment, and how it would affect my future work. I wanted to know if I was going to be hauled in and go through a treatment center whenever someone suspected I was under the influence, or, if I was involved in a minor incident, if I was going to be subjected to testing and that sort of thing. I was fishing for some clue as to what they might have planned for me after I completed treatment, or whether they were going to leave me alone. I told the director I wanted to see one of the company lawyers to discuss my case with him.

The director became irate and defensive about my seeing a company lawyer, whose pay in part comes out of my wages. *You can't see our lawyer,* he said. I started to argue with him, trying to put a spin on it like it was for the benefit of the company. He was becoming more adamant about my not seeing our lawyer and tried to talk to me out of it, saying that I didn't need to see a lawyer. Finally he said, *Well, if you want to see a lawyer you can pay for it yourself,* and hung up.

I called our lawyers and made an appointment with a guy whom I heard was good. The next day I went over to see him. I discussed my situation and how it would affect my future employment, and other issues I was concerned about, including the treatment order. He was, I thought, sincere with his advice, and said he wasn't going to charge me for his time. We ran out of time, and we arranged to meet a couple of days later.

He called me early the next day and asked if I could meet him for lunch. He said there was someone he knew who could help and that he would meet us for lunch. I asked who this person was and my lawyer didn't answer. He said, *Just get down here.* I though nothing of it, but felt elated.

We met his friend for lunch. I felt uncomfortable telling this guy about my situation, but was assured he was there to help me. I thought, *Well maybe this guy was a lawyer at one time or was some union negotiator or something,* but I absolutely was not prepared for what came out of his mouth. As I was telling him my story and how I was seeking assistance in protecting myself from any further sanctions or punishment, he didn't seem at all interested in what I was saying. I stopped talking and looked at him and my lawyer like, OK, what's this all about?

Then his friend starts on about being an alcoholic, about how he nearly lost everything he had to booze, how he found help through going to meetings, and how he'll take me to a meeting.

I was stunned. I basically said, *yeah, yeah,* and left, pissed off. After I thought about what went on, I became incensed. I had told this guy personal and confidential stuff with my lawyer sitting there—someone whom I'd put my trust in and who is supposed to act professionally on my behalf. And he set me up. *What the fuck is this?* I brushed it off but filed it away to deal with it at a later date. I still was concerned about the adoption falling through.

Over the next week I called a few other treatment centers and did some inquiring. I also set up a meeting with someone at Pacifica and booked a spot for August 16th. Another center I inquired about wanted $6000, a six-to-eight-week commitment, and $150 a day if I needed more time. Another center was booked. I felt I had done my part to appease those who were going to extreme lengths to get me into a treatment center.

In the meantime, I was getting calls from Amy T. almost daily, asking me what I was doing about getting myself into treatment. I told her that I'd inquired about another center, which was listed in the phone book. She said that that center did not use the 12 steps, and Dr. Baker wanted patients in 12-step centers. I said, *What's the difference what kind of a center it is?* I didn't know there was any difference. She became very defensive and was adamant that I had to comply with Dr. Baker's orders.

I had no idea what "12 step" meant or what it entailed. This was the first time I had ever heard the term used, but I didn't question it. I had decided that I better go along with this whole thing because the adoption was the primary goal. I convinced myself to view the process that was taking place with the doctor, my fellow workers, and this treatment order as an inconvenience, even though it turned out to be much more.

A few days later I received a call from a director, and he asked me in a somewhat sarcastic manner, *Don't you realize that you have a problem?* I said, *Excuse me?* He said, *Don't you realize you're sick and have a problem?* I said, *Is that all you called for?* He said, *Well don't you?* I said, *Go fuck yourself* and hung up. I immediately called the EAP counselor, Amy T., and verbally tore a strip off her about this taunting phone call from the director, and all the phone calls from her. After that, neither one called again. I felt better that I'd unloaded on her, but I was pissed off about the way I was being treated, and I still couldn't figure out why. Inside I kept telling myself that I was OK and didn't have a problem.

On July 22nd, I had an interview with one of the Pacifica treatment center counselors to see if I would be accepted for admission. The counselor started by asking a few questions about my drinking habits and use, but when it came around to questions about my family history involving alcohol, drug use, or drug abuse, she became perplexed that I had no family history of abuse of any kind. She looked disappointed, and her voice relayed that. *Are you sure?,* she asked. *Do you have a drinking problem?* She also asked, *Why are you here?* I answered, *To keep gainfully employed, I am required to attend this facility for four weeks.* At that point the interview was over and I was accepted to be a client of Pacifica starting August 16th.

The next week we were on pins and needles waiting for the baby to be born. We met the birth mother who had picked us as the parents-to-be, and asked when she was due to have the baby. She said, *I think this weekend.* This was Wednesday and we didn't even have a diaper. Hopefully, she would be late, but not too late for my date with Pacifica. It might get tricky to juggle all this at once, but I had made up my mind that baby came first.

Friday morning, two days before I was to begin treatment, the baby was finally born. A boy. I have a son. Great, this might just work. I could get the paperwork done on Saturday and make it in on Sunday. But we found out we couldn't do any paperwork until after the weekend. They don't work weekends. Shit! I phoned the treatment center and gave them a song and dance about my son having problems, and asked what's the latest time I could show up. They gave me until Monday midnight. If I wasn't there Monday by midnight, my spot would be gone. It wasn't much time, but it was better than Sunday night. On Sunday morning we got a call to come over to see the baby as soon as possible, the birth mother had left the hospital. It was a three-hour journey, but we got there on Sunday afternoon and saw the baby, our son. With all this shit falling around us, it didn't matter, because we were as close as we had ever gotten to a child in the last 12 years; he was in our arms. The plan was to sign papers on Monday, get the baby home, and show up at the treatment center.

On Monday morning there was a snag. The birth mother, although she'd left the hospital, didn't want to release the baby just yet. Someone had to stay in the hospital with the newborn. So I had to fly back home. I left my wife by herself in a strange city with a new baby, who may or may not be ours, while I sat through four weeks in a treatment center. I was not pleased, to say the least.

I dragged my body into this "treatment" center 15 minutes before my deadline Monday evening. *What the fuck am I doing here?* I asked myself as I walked through the door. I found myself asking that question often throughout the stay at the treatment center. I had no clue about what to expect. I was pissed off about letting things get to this point, but since I had no choice in the matter, I was committed to getting through it, because if I didn't, I knew I would be unemployed.

Somewhat curious to find out what treatment was all about, I was astonished by the number of repeat customers who were attending this treatment center. Some of the other clients were telling me that this was their second time through, third, fourth, sixth, and for one young woman it was her *eleventh* time in a treatment center. They all seemed like normal people to me. They just looked like they were having problems dealing with some aspects of their lives. I figure about 80 percent of the 33 people that were there had been through this process before.

I thought to myself, *Why aren't these people getting this? Why are they coming back?* After about the third day in there, I had it figured out—and my perception of treatment got progressively more negative. Of the 33 people who started, 12 either left or were thrown out for drinking or using during treatment. When I arrived, I was given a rah-rah talk on how this treatment center boasts a 95 percent success rate, and how great and helpful their program is. What bullshit. If it's so great, then why were these people coming back all the time?

The "program," I felt, was presented in a very seductive, peaceful, and mesmerizing way. On about the third day, when we were getting a massive dose of a seminar on *denial* and all the traits associated with it, I started to clue in. I thought, *Hold on a minute here, this can't be. These counselors are stripping people of their personalities and beliefs, making people shit scared about themselves and their surroundings.* Then the counselors were trying to install some off-the-wall personality trait, which clients were desperately trying to understand but just couldn't.

I heard it over and over again from other clients: *I'm going to get it this time,* or, *I was told I better get it this time,* or just plain, *I don't get it.*

I consider myself somewhat intelligent and educated, and *I* couldn't get it. There were so many twisted meanings, so many cliches, so much warped thinking. No wonder they keep coming back! I made up my mind I was not going to be any part of this.

I started writing a chronological journal of the events which led up to my sitting locked up in there. *Something was wrong.* I didn't have time to think about it before, but when I had time to put things down on paper and see what had actually happened, I didn't like it. I was

212 ▲ Treatment Scam

going to deal with it when I got out. I didn't know how, or what I was going to do—but I'd find a way.

When I returned home in mid-September, I greeted my wife and brand new son. We spent some dearly missed time together and I was very glad that this ordeal was over.

Ten days after I was released from the treatment center, my company's EAP called and told me to go see Dr. Baker to get a return-to-work certificate. I made an appointment and saw him on September 23rd.

When I saw him, he started to play a little hardball with me. He began ranting in this concerned tone that I was supposed to see him within 48 hours of being released from the center. He started on about the very high percentage of relapses immediately following treatment, and how very lucky I was not to have relapsed. I thought, *Well then, why do people go to treatment if they relapse as soon as they get out?* I knew why, but I didn't say anything; I just sat there all meek and mild, just smiling away like I was so very grateful to him for saving me.

After a brief conversation, he said that I must enter into a contract with him and one with my company. I said, *What contract?* He said, *It's a therapeutic contract between me and you and you're going to do certain things for me. If you are in violation of our contract then the employer will be notified and you'll have to answer to them. This is what you are going to do for me:*

First you will attend at least three AA meetings a week. You will be involved with a weekly step group and a weekly home group. You will get yourself a sponsor. You will provide us with urine and blood samples on a regular and random basis at my lab. You will see me every two weeks until I feel you're doing all right, then we'll increase the time in between visits. Oh by the way, you are responsible for all the associated costs. This contract is for two years, and you're lucky because there are some who get five-year contracts.

I asked, *When am I supposed to work if I'm going to all these meetings?* He said, *You can average them out, if you miss two meetings one week you can go to three meetings in one day or do five or six meetings the next week.*

Where's this contract?, I asked. *Well they're still working on it,* he said. *Fax it over to me when it's done,* I said. I asked him for a copy of his medical report on me. He said he couldn't give me a copy because he didn't own it. I said, *What do you mean you don't own it?* He told me someone purchased his service and whoever that was owns my medical report, and I would have to get it from him or her. I said, *Well who owns the report?* He said, *The person who referred you, probably Amy T.*

Really?, I said, and left his office. I called the EAP counselor, Amy T., that afternoon and left a message on her answering machine saying I wanted the medical report as soon as possible.

The next day I received a fax from Dr. Baker's office. There was a copy of the contract that he had outlined during his visit. The other was a contract with my company, which dovetailed with Baker's, but had sanctions added to it for noncompliance. The bottom line was that if I signed Baker's contract and was in noncompliance, then I would become unemployed. I could be dismissed for as little as missing an AA meeting. But I couldn't go back to work unless Baker OKed my return, saying I was medically fit.

I went to see a lawyer who worked with contract law. He reviewed all the material that I had collected along with company policies, and we drafted a letter asking for a number of things, including a copy of Dr. Baker's medical report.

While my lawyer was working on our letter, I received a phone call from one of the directors. In a very aggressive manner, obviously trying to intimidate me, he blurted out, *Amy T. just called and said you wanted the medical report.* I said, *Yes.* He shouted, *You can't have it! It's not yours, it's ours and you can't have it! We own it and you can't have it!* I was going to unload on him on the phone, but I thought I would play stupid so as not to tip him off about doing any more inquiring. I just said I wanted to look over the things that Dr. Baker and I had discussed. He was somewhat eased by my explanation but still refused to give it up.

The letter from my lawyer hit the office on October 3rd. An acknowledgment of the letter was received on October 7th. I waited and waited for a response.

Finally, on October 20th, there was a phone call from the company lawyer to my lawyer. The company issued an ultimatum through their lawyer. (I, as a partner, happened to be paying a share of his bill.) I also received a fax copy of a letter from the company president to Amy T., the EAP counselor, releasing to me any information I required. I called Amy T.'s number and said that I wanted Baker's medical report ASAP. She didn't call back.

The ultimatum was to sign the contracts with Baker by Monday or face a disciplinary hearing under our company articles, which could lead to expulsion from the company. To make things worse, my lawyer told me he was changing jobs and was unable to continue with my case.

With a deadline over my head, I ran around trying to find another lawyer. I found one who works for the union I belong to and made an appointment to see him the next day.

I dropped everything into his lap and told him what had been going on. He couldn't believe what was happening to me. He thought that someone was out to get me. My first lawyer had had the same feeling. To a great extent I also believe that someone was trying to screw me. We discussed the fact that to fight this thing to the end would become extremely expensive. We also discussed the possibility of negotiating another contract with another doctor, which would not include any mandatory AA participation. The company was trying awfully hard to paint me into a corner, but as my lawyer pointed out, the most important thing was for me to get back to work.

I phoned Rational Recovery and talked to Lois Trimpey, who gave me the name and number of a coordinator in our city. Through him I found Carol Francey, an alcohol and drug referral specialist. She was a tremendous help in supplying me with names and numbers of people who could assist me. After numerous calls to people I didn't even know, I got the name of a local doctor. I was very relieved. Without Carol's help I would have been dead in the water.

The doctor I found had considerable experience in the addiction field and was not an AA member. He was against AA and any 12-step group for a number of reasons, including having seen serious disorders caused by AA attendance. He had seen over 12,000 patients over seven years as head of a detox unit, as well as hundreds of patients with substance abuse problems in his own private practice. He was more than qualified.

I saw him on October 23rd and October 26th, and drafted another contract with him. It was similar to Baker's, but substituted a secular recovery group meeting one time a week for the five meetings a week Baker wanted. He did his own assessment of me for alcohol addiction and unsurprisingly did not find me "addicted to alcohol." I was not, in his judgment, the sick and diseased person that Dr. Baker had said I was. I wasn't even close. I now had to have Baker's report. My lawyer contacted the company lawyer to inform him that I was prepared to enter into a contract with another doctor.

In the meantime, the first deadline passed. The company lawyer was adamant about keeping the deadline. My lawyer was getting pissed off at the tack the company was taking. I was too, but I'd been pissed off for five months now.

Two days later, on October 28th, my lawyer received a letter from the secretary-treasurer of my company. Another deadline had been imposed. I had to sign my contracts by 4:30 p.m. that day or I would face the disciplinary committee, which could lead to expulsion from the company. The deadlines and threats were all designed to coerce me to sign this contract with Dr. Baker, since they didn't know I had another contract already in place. It was Baker or else. My lawyer fired back a letter stating I had already entered into a contract with another doctor and copies were on their way to the office.

I called Amy T. first thing in the morning. To say she was surprised to hear from me is an understatement. I asked where Dr. Baker's report was. She gave me an excuse that she had just returned from out of town and knew nothing of my request. I reminded her of the order from the company president to release the report to me, and she said she would mail it. I told her I wanted it now and to fax it. She then said she didn't have it, that it was somewhere else, but she would be able to fax it over to me after 4:30 p.m. I said fax it to me today or we'll meet before a judge, and he will decide when I should get it. I hung up.

Then I thought, *after 4:30? What a coincidence!* Just happened to be after the deadline that was imposed. She was stalling, thinking that I would be signed with Baker before the deadline. Baker's medical report was faxed over at 5:00 p.m.

I looked over Baker's medical report and saw why he didn't want me to see it. I sent a copy of it to my lawyer along with a list of inaccuracies, misstatements, and outright lies that were contained in the report. I couldn't believe it.

I also contacted psychologist and attorney Stanton Peele, who agreed to view the material I had and to evaluate Baker's report. Peele's expertise, from what I have read, is unmatched in the addictions field. I sent Stanton all the material I had to date, including the legal correspondence.

Meanwhile, the communication between lawyers was fast and heavy—they never expected that I would find another qualified doctor and have another contract drawn up before their deadline. My lawyer and I were both mystified as to why the company was exerting so much pressure on me to sign with Baker. When any telephone conversations took place between lawyers, the company lawyer became extremely defensive when questioned about the heavy-handed tactics being used.

A letter came back on October 30th from the company lawyer. Without going into great detail, they essentially accepted Rational Recovery as an alternative in one sentence and discounted it in the next sentence. They also said that the doctor I had selected simply wasn't qualified. They rejected him and the contracts. They simply discounted any alternative proposed, which would leave me only the option to sign with Baker.

Most importantly, they stated in the letter that I had a diagnosis of "addiction to alcohol." How did they find that out? I wondered who had released that personal information to them. They also included a list of ten doctors that the company regarded as experts in addiction medicine. Along with the list was the customary deadline to sign with one of these doctors within two days. Two days! It took me two weeks just to get in to see Dr Baker. We fired back another letter asking who had given them the information on the diagnosis and stating that I wanted all relevant material so that I could properly defend myself in the disciplinary hearing.

In the meantime I took the list of experts down to the doctor I had just signed the contract with, hoping he would know one of them. He said he had heard of most of them, but said all but one were 12-step members. The other one, he said, was doing good things, but he added, *You don't want to go see him, he runs an open clinic for injection drug users and AIDS patients down in the dregs of downtown.*

I said, *Then that's the guy I want to see.* He called the doctor and set up an appointment. I went down to see this doctor that afternoon. It's true, he has a clinic for IV users and AIDS patients in a very tough and dangerous part of town, but I didn't care. Anything would be better than AA meetings five days a week. We had a talk and he said he really wasn't set up to do this kind of work for me. I literally pleaded with him to draw up a contract that would save me from the 12-steppers. He finally agreed. My lawyer drew up the paperwork and faxed it down so we could sign it the next day.

This new doctor questioned me about how I managed to end up on his doorstep. He was floored by my ordeal. But most importantly, he was amazed by the fact that I was labeled as addicted to alcohol. He said, *You don't need to be here.* I told him that this was necessary for me in order to return to work, because I had run out of money.

The next day we signed the contracts and sent them down to the company lawyer. We made the deadline with some breathing room.

As I expected, there was no response from the company lawyer for four days. As I found out later, Dr. Baker had supplied the ten names of "addiction specialists" that the company had sent to me. Nine were 12-step believers, and half of them worked for Baker. They all worked in nice, modern offices with pretty receptionists. The one who was not a 12-stepper used motivational interviewing and harm reduction with his patients, and worked in the asshole of the world. The company had taken a chance by including him in among the 12-steppers, just to show that they had made an attempt to have all forms of treatment available, in case the matter ended up in court. I don't think they believed that in a million years I would have found the one diamond in the rough.

But I did. Now they were fucked. Not only had I beaten their deadline and had a contract in place, but I did it with one of their doctors and it didn't include AA. Now who were they to question one of their own recommended experts? I finally had something to smile about. It was nice having them scramble for a change, as I knew they were.

We didn't hear anything for nine days except an acknowledgment of the receipt of the contract. At that point, as I expected, they tried to manipulate the contract. They tried to get us to change everything back to the original way that Baker had set it out.

Out of money, and seemingly out of luck, I dug my heels in. I had come to the point where I was prepared to go to court.

In hindsight, I should have gone to court at the outset. On November 14th I received a copy of Stanton Peele's evaluation. I was truly shocked. His summary of Dr. Baker's so-called assessment was incredible. Dr. Baker's assessment didn't prove anything other than that he'd talked to me. His diagnosis of alcohol dependence appeared to be a case of deliberate misdiagnosis, a case of deliberate malpractice.

I now had some ammunition. On November 17th they sent a letter back saying the agreements were in order and I would be cleared to return to work when all the documents were signed. Just over six months to the day after my ordeal began, I returned to work. I have to keep my head down for a while until the adoption goes through, then it'll be my turn.

I won. Now it's time to deal with the conspiracy to deprive me of my livelihood and the deliberate medical misdiagnosis.

37 ▲ Tammy
Forced Programming

When I think of AA horror stories, a young woman named Dee comes to mind. I heard her story while working as her counselor in a DUI program.

Dee worked for the county in the department that handles retirement and other benefits and insurance claims. When I met her, she had been working there for about 12 years.

She got her DUI citation because she had been pulled over by the sheriff's department while driving intoxicated. Apparently, in a tipsy effort to be cute, she teased the deputies with comments about what she could do to their retirement accounts if they didn't watch out. I guess they didn't think it was too cute, because there were major repercussions to her statement.

Bear in mind that this was a simple DUI; there was no accident or other involvement. It was her first DUI and her blood alcohol concentration was just over the limit. For most folks, this would have meant a couple of hours in jail, a healthy fine, a couple of days on a work project, and a 90-day DUI program. In Dee's case, that was only the beginning. She was forced onto administrative leave from work and ordered to enter a year-long alcohol abuse program. Failure to complete the program meant she would lose her job.

She had to contact and collaborate with the alcohol abuse program providers. She was also ordered to attend daily (yes, daily) AA meetings for a year. In order to "pass" the alcohol abuse program provided through her medical insurance, it was necessary for Dee to "admit" she was alcoholic—which she was not. She was monitored very closely, and weekly reports were sent to her boss, even though she was still on administrative leave.

By the time she started attending counseling in the DUI program where I came into contact with her, she was getting pretty good at lying that she was indeed an alcoholic. After filling out an assessment questionnaire one day, I put down my pen and looked into Dee's eyes. *Dee*, I said, *do you believe that you are an alcoholic?* She hesitated and asked whether I wanted the real truth. I assured her I wanted the real truth.

No, she said. *I have been to six months of weekly classes at the hospital and daily AA meetings, where I must admit I am an alcoholic or lose my job. But after all the time I've spent listening in both those places, I am absolutely certain that I do not fit the criteria for alcoholism.* I agreed with her that I did not think she fit the profile of an alcoholic. *I have gotten pretty good at it,* she said. *I really almost believe that I am the person I pretend to be.* She went on to explain the tricks she played in her mind to "become" an alcoholic when she walked into treatment or AA meetings.

I was appalled and saddened by her story. By admitting she was alcoholic, she could *recover* and be allowed to maintain her job. In the meantime, she was treated like someone with a disease and not permitted to work. She was, however, required to subject herself to reviews of her "progress," which were grueling and dehumanizing. I asked her how she managed to submit to these degrading things, and she replied that she closed off herself and adopted a persona which was able to agree with and acquiesce to this torture.

To satisfy part of the review, she was forced to become someone's *sponsee* in AA and *work the steps* to the satisfaction of her boss. Dee managed to do it, and as she approached the end of the year as a model *recovering alcoholic*, the folks at work started to put on the pressure.

She had been permitted to return to work in a demoted status and was subjected daily to abuse from her boss. After all these concessions to retain her position, she attended her last hospital treatment session and was attacked verbally by the program director. He told her she was going to flunk the program for discussing issues he didn't feel relevant. This meant, of course, that she would lose her job, which she did in fact lose.

I believe this story says something about the way in which AA is being used as a punitive tool by the courts and employers. Twelve-step programs are supposedly based on rigorous honesty. How in the world can you expect honesty from people ordered into a program or blackmailed into a program? And while these people are present in AA, they are a part of it. This affects the whole organization and has greatly changed its nature. We now hear it said at AA and NA meetings, *It doesn't matter how you got here, it only matters that you are here.* I sincerely doubt that.

38 ▲ Dean

Treatment Anger

I don't know where to begin, but I know I have to. My name is Dean X., and I was introduced to the 12 steps back in 1989.

Up until my ex-wife put me in a hospital on the West Coast, I knew zero about AA or the steps. The place I went to was one of the better-known hospitals/treatment centers, and I was glad to be there. I had never tried any kind of addiction treatment and was absolutely clueless as to what the treatment would be.

It was a typical treatment center—addicts smoking, drinking coffee, and telling war stories in between eight to ten hours of groups and meetings per day. The counselors literally had to convince us that we had a disease because of the so-called *denial* that kept us from seeing just how sick we really were. We were the last to know, according to them.

They convinced me that I was ill. They said I had come to the last house on the block. Of course, this now seems ludicrous, seeing as how I never stopped at the any of the houses before theirs. They didn't care; they knew better than I did—I was sick and insane, not to mention that even if I did go *into recovery,* my disease would keep on progressing even after I stopped using.

They also told me how my ego had to be smashed or "humbled," and that only by believing in God as I understood him could I ever find any hope to stop my using. They told me that only people with the disease can understand, and that *normies*—the rest of the human race—could never, ever understand us. I felt good. I felt at home. I'd found friends.

Sobriety lasted for about six months. Then I used periodically, but it eventually caught up with me. So, back in I went, same place, same treatment. It *worked* again. This time I saw a psychiatrist and a clinical psychologist, Dr. D., every day for 21 days and then on a regular basis for the next six years. I stayed sober for the next seven years, thanks to the excellent treatment from Dr. D. I attended meetings for a while, but got very upset with the "fellowship" and its rhetoric. Eventually my insurance ran out, and I couldn't afford to pay for therapy on my own, so we ended it. I was fine for the next year or so, and then I relapsed.

I had been in school and was extremely tired, stressed out, and worried about my future. I made a bad choice. I used. It was a small amount. I did not use anywhere near the amount that I used to. My "disease" had not progressed into a wild beast with horns. Then I used again after two or three months—same small amount. I did this for about one year and then checked myself into an outpatient program. I was again feeling desperate and really did not want to go back to using regularly.

This time I told them up front about my feelings about the steps and that Big Blue Book they read at every meeting. No problem, Dean. Trust us, you're sick. So I joined up and had a couple of relapses while in treatment. Even though I said I didn't like their rhetoric, I was convinced to be more "open minded" this time and to *live and let live*. I tried. Nothing would derail my spiritual program. Then it really hit me about the third month into treatment—I started to think about what they were saying, and my eyes suddenly opened. I realized that *the 12 steps made me feel really bad about myself.* I felt bad, not because I had a drug problem; it was because I hated every word that came out of their mouths.

To me, 12-steppers looked like the walking dead. Sober *zombies* stalking the earth in search of alcoholics to suck dry. I began to cringe when I heard other steppers talking in acronyms (KISS—*Keep It Simple, Stupid*—etc.). Talking about God, Jesus, praying, our sins, amends—what in the hell happened to being an addict or alcoholic? Did I miss that group? I was in real trouble now. I could no longer listen to the crap that was being called *treatment*, but I didn't know anything else existed—until I looked.

What an idea.

I looked and found really good resources for recovery without the superstition and folklore that was being called treatment. I left the group and am now drug free and sort of happy.

I know now that it will take time to get this junk out of my head. It does not just stop the moment you leave. It lingers on, like a fungus. One thing that is really true about the 12 steps is that the program will mess up your using. That is true, but what they do not tell you is that it can screw up your head.

I have a lot of anger about the package of lies and deceit that is called treatment. I would never recommend the 12 steps to anyone. I hope that others who read this will see it as a warning. If you want to stay sick forever, label yourself as insane, believe you have a disease that has a mind of its own, and believe that only a belief in God will help you, then by all means the 12-step program is for you. Me, I choose to be well.

I still have a very difficult time getting rid of the 12-step philosophy. I constantly have to check my feelings because of the negative crap that was put into my head by the less-than-knowledgeable people who call themselves professionals. I wish to God (if there is one) that I had never been introduced to the 12-step powerless way of life. It has truly complicated and delayed my recovery from substance abuse. My goal is to speak out at every opportunity I get about the mindless, punitive, and degrading tactics used by 12 steppers. Refuse to engage them in their idiotic lingo. Call them on their lunatic fringe philosophies. I urge any person who is new and has questions to get answers. Do not let anyone ever again tell you to *take the cotton out of your ears and put it in your mouth.* Do not use slogans to explain away human suffering. Do not let anyone tell you how to live, what to believe, or what to think. Use your brain. Whatever you're told by these quacks and charlatans, do the opposite and you will get well real fast.

My name is Dean X. and I'm a human being.

39 ▲ Carrie
The Disease?

I am an ex-AA member. For the past two years, I have been trying to get fully and permanently sober again. I'm willing to try any means, *except AA*. Although I've occasionally known reasonably sane AA members, they're hard to find. It seems the mentally, emotionally, or spiritually healthier members stop going to meetings. I found the meeting goers to be controlling, condescending, and into unwanted and inappropriate self-disclosure. Many use alcoholism as an excuse for their behavior—*Oh, it's my disease talking.* They seem to be in this state most of the time—*staying in the disease,* not getting healthier. Just sober, that's all. I got so tired of the brain-dumping in AA meetings, and the sickness of the thinking, that I eventually stopped going to meetings. It's too bad, because a small percentage of AA members are sane, lucid, and really nice to be around.

Five years ago, my ex-sponsor told me to start dating at seven months sober, *so we would have something to work on.* She said she found me boring when I got sober, because I had no big hangups, no major problems, and was grateful and happy almost every day. I was competent at work and was getting promotions and raises. I did all my steps in about four months, so she thought I should start dating.

Of all people, the chosen "nice guy" was her husband's sponsee with 15 or so years sober, a shame-filled manic depressive. He saw a psychologist and took his medication in secret because his sponsor didn't approve. I've heard many AA members say their sponsors were pushing them to get off their medications. It's commonly thought in AA that prescribed medication is just another addiction or is masking problems, and is therefore standing in the way of being able to do real step work and achieve true sobriety.

Some women cried in the meetings over the guilt and fear and confusion as to what to do, who to listen to—doctor, or sponsor. The attitude was that if you did your steps and your inventory regularly, you wouldn't need any such "non-spiritual" help.

40 ▲ Denise

They Said I Couldn't Promise Myself Sobriety!

When I went to my first AA meeting, I was in a five-day state-run detox center in Alaska. I was 29 and had been a hooker, addict, and alcoholic in that town since the age of 16. I was 23 when I met my husband and got out of the street life, although I had not given up drugs and alcohol.

When I arrived at the meeting, I immediately recognized the majority of the people present, especially the men. This meeting took place in a small town with a *big* memory, and everyone at the meeting knew exactly who I was and what I'd been involved in. I had slept with most of the men at the meeting at some time or another before my marriage, and most of the women knew it.

At the meeting, I said that I was an alcoholic/addict and that nothing could ever be so horrible in my life as to ever make me do drugs or drink again. The people at the meeting were hostile to me and told me I didn't know that I would never again drink or use, and so I couldn't say that.

I told them that for 29 years I'd been living down to everyone else's destructive expectations, and now that I was finally setting a healthy goal for myself they were saying I couldn't do it. I felt attacked and humiliated. I was extremely uncomfortable there, and I knew the members were squirming in their seats just thinking about me telling my drunkalogs—they were in most of them! None of the women there would volunteer to be my sponsor. I felt the organization was negative, religious, and extremely male dominated. After the meeting, I asked my counselor to take me to the bookstore.

I felt there had to be other approaches to recovery. That's when I found Dr. Jean Kirkpatrick's books *Good-Bye Hangover, Hello Life* and *Turnabout*. The rest of my recovery is history: 11 years clean and sober, and no AA.

41 ▲ Sven
Swedish AA

I started using alcohol at about 18 years of age, and I found it was a great door-opener for relationships and fun living. I drank on the weekends, and there were no problems with it.

I began university classes in 1990, and in that social context I started to drink on week nights. But I completed my studies and moved back to the town where I now live. Times had changed and it was hard to get a job. I felt bad and bored, and drank more than before, but not daily.

In 1995, I searched for help with depression, and spoke out about my drinking. I then stayed sober on my own for some months and felt all right about that. But in the summertime, I started to drink again. My only really bad period was in 1996–1997, and it ended one day when I came drunk to my job

I realized then, on my own, that I had to do something about the situation, and searched for more help. I had heard about AA and started to go to meetings on a regular basis. The first meeting was okay, but I couldn't identify with all the people or their stories. I had drunk a lot, and had been in some trouble, but not to the same degree as most of the other people I met. They told me that I had the same disease as them, but that mine hadn't progressed as far, yet.

At the time, I was confused and felt that I had lost some control over my alcohol situation. Therefore, I easily accepted their analysis and went to meeting after meeting. Sometimes I felt good, but there were times when I felt something rotten in the air. One thing I will say is that while I liked some AA people, others were very strange and intolerant.

I had some "relapses," but always came back and told the others. They told me to keep coming to meetings and working the steps. The strange thing was that *the times I drank as a member of AA, my drinking was more destructive and out of control than it had ever been before.* I had been told I was helpless, and my "relapses" seemed to confirm it.

After some months, I got into non-12-step treatment. But by that time I was already brainwashed by AA, and rejected those parts of treatment which did not fit with the AA program.

After that, I became more involved in AA. I went to meetings every day and started to work in AA service. I was not treated extremely badly in the group, but the old-timers said that I was a *dry drunk* and that I must *let go* and *come down in the program.*

In the summer of 1998, I took the old-timers' advice and started to read all the AA literature and really analyze it. Ironically, this was the beginning of my end in AA. The more I studied the books and the program, the more I realized that there were many contradictions as well as lousy "scientific" conclusions in the texts.

I started questioning, and sometimes I shared that I disliked the program. I'll never forget one woman who works at a 12-step treatment center. She told me to get rid of my ego and let God do the work. I had never liked her, but I accepted her advice. I was too afraid not to.

I left AA in September 1998. I had begun to feel that something in AA was very wrong, but I was scared and confused and continued to try to get answers inside the program. But the only answers I got were: *It's your disease,* and *Your ego is playing tricks on you.*

One day I searched for AA sites on the net and found a Swedish anti-AA site. I read it and was very upset, but I saw that the information on the site was right, and AA was not. But AA was still deep in my mind, and I thought, *maybe I'm in denial.*

Then I read Ken Ragge's *The Real AA.* That book made my brain work again. I have studied social science and am trained in critical thinking, and have always had a rebellious attitude. AA had nearly killed that. I never returned to AA after reading Ken's book.

My way out of AA included re-reading existential literature, and making contact with alcohol researchers to get a scientific view on addiction and recovery. Of much importance has been contact with people who have thought the same way and managed to get out of AA, and live their own lives using their own minds. This process has made me more secure, and has helped me to take power over my own life. Now, I don't feel addicted to drinking—or to AA. I'm free!

People need both freedom and security. When you are totally free, the world is full of possibilities, but in many ways it is an insecure and dangerous place. Some people find it too hard to see themselves as free and responsible for their own lives, and search for a doctrine to rely on. AA's doctrine is to give up freedom and submit to another's will—your sponsor's, a Higher Power's, or the group's—in order to get the world under control and to feel that someone else will take care of everything.

When you're lonely and confused, it's easy to shut your eyes to facts that don't fit in with AA doctrines. Some of the AA slogans, program, and culture scare members into becoming uncritical conformists. They use the old religious trick of telling people that turning their minds over and submitting will make them free.

I'm glad that I can write down these thoughts today. There are many still out there fighting for the right to live their lives as self-governing individuals with power over their own minds.

42 ▲ Gerald

My Religion Wasn't Allowed

I was court ordered into treatment after a DUI arrest. Yes, I was guilty, but I'm now 10 months alcohol free.

I belong to a non-Judeo-Christian religion called Asatru, which is a reconstruction of pre-Christian Teutonic and Scandinavian beliefs. All other people at the treatment center were allowed to keep their Bibles and other religious literature of a Judeo-Christian nature, while I was denied the right to *any* books on my religion. I was told, *Talk to your counselor about it next week.*

A week went by, and I talked to my counselor. I presented her with literature explaining my religion, its beliefs and practices. The next day, I was told by this so-called counselor: *This is not a religion, it's a hobby.* The arrogance of that remark alone, dismissing an entire religion as a hobby, is inexcusable. This counselor also pushed a fundamentalist Christian viewpoint down our throats during "therapy" sessions.

I really think she expected me to give up and admit defeat, but I took it to the director of the treatment center, who *finally* allowed me access to two—and only two—of the books which I had brought to treatment with me. Actually, it's probably fortunate for them that they did cave in to a degree. At that point, I had already gotten a list of attorneys and was prepared to file a civil rights lawsuit for violation of my First Amendment right to freedom of religion. The center's rules specifically and categorically stated that they weren't allowed to discriminate on the basis of religion. This, of course, wasn't the case in reality.

I was also punished for not participating in the Lord's Prayer at the end of meetings, even though as a part of my own beliefs I cannot in good conscience pray to the gods of another religion. I have to admit that I caved in to the degree that I finally stood up and joined hands but would not pray, because I would never be granted the privilege of being allowed visitors unless I did so.

43 ▲ Cliff Walker
NA Suicides

I was court ordered to NA. When I objected to that, on religious grounds, I was put in jail on a 30-day hold. I was not in a position to fight at that time. There had been no such cases before, and my lawyer said: *You're right, but we don't have anything to work on—I'm just a defense attorney here.*

After I got out of jail, I went to NA. I got used to it, and decided to make the most of it. I didn't like a lot of what I saw in NA, so I got involved with the literature committee. One guy had said: *This is where you can make changes, and there's no one on the literature committee but me; if you join, there will be two of us.*

So, there I was on the literature committee. I like to write, and I learned to write properly. The NA WSO (World Service Organization) sends out literature they are proposing to the literature committees, and they wanted us to comment on it. I loved doing that; I like to straighten things out, to look at something and give it my best. I'd found my niche in Narcotics Anonymous.

I started out at the local level, and later I became part of the NA service structure on the state level. I worked on a couple of very long projects myself, and I sent reviews and analyses to WSO as an individual. The smaller projects were pamphlets, the kind you see on the racks at NA meetings. The big projects were books and service manuals. WSO did not give us much time to review final projects, and quite often we didn't even have time to schedule a review meeting, so I would review many of the projects by myself. I was very stringent in my reviews.

I had to be stringent; some of the material they sent us was shockingly religious, dogmatic, and fundamentalist. There was one passage I recall—and this one actually made it into the *Basic Text* —that if you don't work the fourth step (the searching and fearless moral inventory) you *will* relapse. I know that most people who get clean and sober—and I knew this back then—don't even go through 12-step programs. So that was just plain *false.*

Of course most of the folks in NA are deeply religious; they believe in a supernatural, rescuing deity. Also, you can't take religion out of the steps, because, really, religion is what the steps are about. You can say, *I believe my Harley can restore me to sanity.* You can believe in the ashtray or the light bulb as your Higher Power. But by the time you get up to step six—*We became entirely ready to have our Harley remove all our defects of character*—you aren't talking about some abstract concept anymore. It doesn't fit step six. It doesn't fit step seven, and it doesn't fit step eleven. Like Jack Trimpey says—*it's a bait-and-switch head game.* It's not for me anymore, and if you push most people, they'll now admit that 12-step programs aren't the only thing that works.

But because of my beliefs, some of the NA steppers want to accuse me of being a *murderer.* These fundamentalists aren't usually the respected folks of mainstream NA—rather, they are those who often hold leadership positions in rural areas or isolated communities, and they're also well represented in the committees. Because the representatives on the committees are usually hard-core NA loyalists elected by the individual groups, you find a lot of fundamentalists in them.

I spent about 11 years in NA, although for many of those years I was also highly involved with Rational Recovery. I quit just before my 11th-year anniversary. I was basically driven out of NA by whisper campaigns. All this time, however, I was, and still am, supportive of NA as part of American culture; I still think it helps more people than it hurts, so it deserves to exist. But I don't have a black-and-white outlook on NA; my view of it can't be reduced to a bumper sticker. So, anyone like myself who tries to make changes ends up with fundamentalists in their face saying: *If yer not fer us, yer agin' us.*

Many people develop an approach to the 12-step model where they think the 12 steps are all you need. They won't talk to people who are on psychiatric meds. They won't go to their clean-and-sober anniversaries because they think those people are "on drugs" and "not working the program" because they are on prescription medications. There are many who think you need to turn in your clean and sober key tags if you're on pain medication as well.

These kinds of groupers told a man I knew that he needed to abstain from *all* drugs—including psych meds. He followed their advice and eventually pulled his own plug. They had a big NA meeting after the funeral and were so sad. But nobody brought up the meds issue. There are lots of steppers who still believe this: *Don't take psych meds, because they are drugs.* Some of them kill themselves when they can't handle depression.

There was a piece of literature, "In Times of Illness," that WSO proposed as a replacement for an older piece, "The Use of Medication in Recovery." This new pamphlet was supposed to give detailed "dos" and "don'ts" about using medication. One of the statements in this proposed pamphlet was: "Your brain does not know the difference between over-the-counter medications and street drugs." But they said nothing new about the proper use of prescription drugs. I wanted them to add something I thought was very important: There are two things about prescription drugs you must remember—follow the prescription instructions as written, and don't stop taking any prescription without first consulting the doctor who prescribed it.

Several of us from Portland thought this was so important that we drove about 100 miles to a meeting in Salem to help hammer out the directions in this pamphlet. We spent much time on this one proposal about following the prescription instructions and to avoid deviation or termination without consulting the doctor. But WSO just ignored it.

This ties in with one of my earlier experiences with NA in 1983 in San Diego. I was on antidepressants, and group members told me in no uncertain terms that I was not working the program if I remained on those drugs. I was on those drugs for depression and suicidal ideation. I see my depression differently now, but I think if someone is going to go off prescription drugs, they need to talk to the doctor who prescribed them first, and to be a real stickler about following the doctor's instructions. I think that added recommendation would have been very helpful, particularly for those who tend toward fundamentalism, those who want someone to tell them what to do. Without such written instructions, they're going to do what their sponsors tell them. The whole 12-step philosophy encourages that way of thinking —*don't trust your own thinking; get a sponsor; rely on a higher power*. If the WSO would be specific about sticking to the doctor's instructions when it comes to psych meds or any medication, a large number of people could be helped.

Within a year after WSO ignored our recommendations concerning the drug pamphlet, yet another group member—someone who had previously been helped by psych meds, but went off them—killed himself. That's not uncommon in NA. Ironically, he had been the husband of one of the women who drove down to

Salem and fought hard for the changes that could have helped save guys like her husband.

Though I was, as I've said, run out of NA by a whisper campaign, it was, of course, ultimately my decision to leave. That decision was based on *how much abuse am I willing to endure vs. what am I getting out of this, and what can I give?* If someone comes up with a whisper campaign, and it isn't true, but it is something most of the others in the NA community believe, what good can I do there? Someone said I went on TV and said 12-step programs ruin lives. I challenged the rumor monger and told him I'd get a copy of the TV program and we'd sit down and watch it. But it's very hard to fight NA fundamentalism. I finally said, *My friends are right. I shouldn't be involved in this.* And I stopped.

When I left, I was preparing to recommend to the NA Board of Trustees that they recommend to the groups that they stop signing attendance slips of those forced to attend AA by the courts, because it is compromising the tradition of voluntarism inherent in all 12 traditions: *We are here voluntarily.* As long as we're signing these forms, we're telling the agencies who coerce people into attending NA that it's okay if they force people to come to our program.

This is unlikely to change. The groups want to survive, and coerced attendance helps them get members, so they use the excuse: *Any way you can get people in here and exposed to this might help someone.* So what I had to say about this was *viciously* unpopular. These guys would come into this meeting I loved. As soon as I showed up, this one guy would leave. Then he'd be back in 10 minutes with a bunch of bikers. They'd wait until after I spoke, then one by one they'd start talking— they'd hog the baton, and just denounce me, openly threaten me in the meeting. And so I stopped going to that meeting. At the same time, I was still hanging around the local committee meeting, but it was no fun because I was not elected; I was just there because someone had resigned. Every time I made a report, this one gal would, month after month, make these niggling corrections. Finally, because of the whisper campaign, the bikers, etc., I told myself: *No, there's a limit. I've hit it. If I give everything, I won't have anything left to give.*

44 ▲ Jane

AA Suicides

I had been sober almost four years when my boyfriend's "sponsee" committed suicide. John was 24 years old and had been in the program for about two years. He mainly hung out with a group of extremely hard-line AAs who were half-jokingly referred to as *The Trudgers*—as in *trudge the Road to Happy Destiny*. (from the Big Book)

John asked my boyfriend to be his sponsor, because his previous sponsor, a Trudger, had called him a "wimp" and an "asshole" whenever John tried to discuss personal problems. Apparently the Trudgers' line of thought was that if you were working the program rigorously and correctly you wouldn't have problems, such as not being able to talk to girls. And if you did, these problems shouldn't matter because the program was supposed to be your entire life. It was an attitude shared by the Trudger crowd, along with a certain arrogance—after all, they were the ones who were working it correctly. In other parts of the country, such groups or individuals are often referred to as "AA fundies" or "AA fundamentalists."

John emptied the medicine cabinet into himself and hopped the first streetcar out of his neighborhood. He was found on the waterfront unconscious, having drunk a bottle of vodka to wash down the pills. He was taken to a local hospital. Since no pill bottles were found on him, an assumption was made that he was just drunk, so they didn't pump his stomach. He died a few hours later.

I went to his funeral, and the Trudger crowd was there, including that rat-bastard ex-sponsor. Everyone was standing around in the lobby of the funeral home, and here were these AAs hanging out as if it were just another meeting. None of them looked so much as sad. John's family was sitting off to one side of the room, and on the other were AAs analyzing amongst themselves just why John had done himself in.

I heard a lot of talk over the next few weeks that maybe he'd held something back in his fourth step, or maybe had something else he just couldn't face, and I felt my own rage building up. A lot of things that had merely irritated me about the Program and the way people interacted within it began to seriously piss me off. I went to meetings for another four months but, eventually, I had to abandon AA.

John had been ill served by the Program when alive, and his memory was found wanting by its members after he was dead. He'd been a sweet, bright kid. He'd been rather immature, but he certainly didn't deserve to die. Also, he'd had wide mood swings, and I think he could have been helped by medication. But, had he taken it, the self-designated recovery experts in AA would have stood smugly by and told him he wasn't sober.

Another tragedy occurred with Tess. She had been in AA for a number of years before a cab driver beat the living shit out of her one night for refusing his advances. He beat her so badly she had to have vertebrae in her neck and back fused, and she was in constant pain the entire time I knew her. Some days she'd be hysterical with it.

She wouldn't take the painkillers she'd been prescribed, because she didn't want to "lose her sobriety." But the attitude toward her in the meetings was that Tess was a "drama queen" who wanted a lot of attention, when, in fact, she was half out of her mind with pain.

Finally the Catch-22 got her. She took her prescribed medication —all at once. A small group of her close friends were genuinely affected by her loss, but the general attitude of the same people who thought of her as a hysterical attention-seeker was that she just didn't work the program hard enough.

Fuck, yes, I still "have a resentment."

Because of these kinds of tragedies, I left AA after four-and-a-half years. I had no money, no real job prospects, and although San Francisco was a big city, I couldn't go anywhere without running into another AA. So I ended up doing a *geographic cure*. It was the best move I could have made. I moved to a town where I knew absolutely nobody; I had to rebuild my entire social life from the ground up. It was terribly lonely for the first year, and if I'd known the job market was as bad as it was, I might have done things differently.

But after four years here, I can honestly say that I made the right choice. I got to remake myself in my own image, and I was able to make friends with a pretty cool bunch of people just by showing up for Saturday morning coffee at the same place every weekend. I have told my friends about my time in AA, and none of them can figure out why I ever thought I was an alcoholic.

I remember being incredibly depressed as I was leaving AA. I couldn't continue in it, yet I hadn't really found anything to replace it (although school helped). I felt cut off from the entire human race, so I ended up contacting a couple of people I used to drink with in my bad old days, mainly because I could recall better times with them than I could with my AA cronies. They've turned out to be great friends after all; they remember me at my worst, and forgive it.

If you really think moving elsewhere will help, it probably will. Even if adjusting to a new place is tough, it beats having to deal with the same old shit—the expectations people can load on you. If you want to be *new and improved*, it really helps to get as far away from the old patterns as possible. So, if you think it's right, *go for it*. Trust yourself.

45 ▲ Teresa
We Will Love You, They Said

I had a favorite joke during my 15 years in AA: whenever I was asked to lead, I referred to it as the *blind leading the blind*. I thought that was funny. In fact, there was more truth in it than I cared to admit. Eventually, there was no humor in it and, sadly, it became a statement of fact to me.

They said, *We will love you until you can love yourself.* Please tell me how a bunch of dysfunctional people in a cult know how to love in the first place! How can you know how to love if you were never shown? You sure wouldn't be sitting in AA meetings, that's for certain. The people who love you would be helping you!

There were many, many contradictions within the AA program, but I didn't question or examine them during my first years in AA. I started going to meetings in 1982, and I was so damned glad I had found relief from my drinking that I blindly went to the *90 meetings in 90 days.*

I kept going to meetings because they told me I had to, or I would drink, go insane, or die. I made coffee, sat on steering committees, was a secretary for an AA convention in my state, and so on. I was doing regular fourth and fifth steps, being honest at the tables, and going to therapy when I felt I needed it. Yet, I never felt a part of the whole picture. It seemed like there were people who really *got* the program—the "AA gurus"—and I seemed to be trudging my way through. *Working the program* seemed more difficult for me, for some reason. I found out why later, while working the steps.

I began to have the feeling that there had to be more to life than sitting in AA meetings. I was barely a year clean when my stepfather asked me how I wanted to be remembered after my death. At the time, I could see no further than endless membership in AA. I knew there had to be something outside those smoky rooms that was *better*. I wanted to be so much more than a recovering drunk. I wanted to make a difference. A *big* difference.

As the result of one of my fifth steps, I ended up suing a man who molested me as a child. The case lasted a few years and at one point I was deposed for five hours in front of the perpetrator and his attorney. It was one of the most triumphant days in my life. Was there anyone in AA there with me? No.

Unfortunately, the court of appeals eventually ruled against me, citing their interpretation of the statute of limitations. It was a technicality to my understanding, and it could have been defined in a myriad of ways. Still, it was a grave disappointment to me. I tried to share this at meetings, and was met with glazed looks. Nobody was really listening, nor did they care. They were just waiting for their turn to talk about themselves.

I had hoped my case would set a precedent and pave an easier road to justice for other survivors, and I hoped that it would help me heal in some way. I felt some healing, but realized that I needed to address behaviors that were a result of the abuse, and I wasn't getting any help from AA in that sense. In fact, I was asked to look at "my part" in the abuse. I had been three years old at the time—how could I have any part in the blame? That question always bothered me. Now I know why. It's just wrong to suggest that anyone who has been attacked has *any* part in the blame. I am still looking for peace in the fractured 12-step philosophy, because AA played such a big part in my life for so long. I have only begun to remove the blinders. But I will continue to search for a comfortable place within myself, rather than in a cult or organized religion.

I believe I drank because of the pain associated with residual behaviors resulting from childhood abuse. That is a lot simpler than I was led to believe in AA, but it's *my* truth. I was told many times that AA was a *selfish* program. How many interpretations are contained in that short sentence! I still am very confused about that one. They said they would love me, but they're practicing a *selfish program.* How can you love and be selfish at the same time?

There were many times throughout my AA career when I expected to be *loved.* When I called someone in the middle of the night, afraid and unable to sleep, or in the hospital, in pain, I expected to be listened to, and I'd do the same if the situation were reversed. Of course, if I mentioned these situations or negative feelings of any sort in an AA meeting, my feelings would be interpreted as *sitting on the pity pot* (more AA selfishness?), or I would be classified as a *dry drunk.* Couldn't it just be asking someone to show love or compassion?

My second marriage was to a man in AA. Throughout our marriage, he abused prescription drugs, going from doctor to doctor and clinics all over the state, using aliases and cash to get drugs, yet going to meetings the entire time—high. I knew he was not *sober,* but never seemed to be able to prove it. I thought I was in love. But it was not love. In fact, the entire time I was in AA, I did not have any idea what love of any kind really was. Not until I walked away.

When my husband finally crashed and I put him in treatment, I questioned my situation. He had never really been honest with me about himself or anything in his past. Today, four years later, I am discovering and realizing things about his activities that make me want to smack myself on the forehead with disbelief. Why didn't I see it? I refused to see so much; I refused to admit something was wrong. His sponsor was a pillar of the community, sober *decades* and the director of a local treatment center. This man, I strongly suspect, lied in a court of law in an embezzlement case. I know he lied later, when he testified against me when I divorced his sponsee.

Before the divorce, my ex-husband beat me. He had a teenage son from a previous marriage and visited him three or four times a year. Now *sober,* he wanted his drug-addicted, molested, cigarette-smoking 13-year-old in our house every weekend. Around our six-year-old daughter! I told him I could not deal with the stress of having his son over every weekend. He ended up screaming and swearing and beating on me one day because I would not back down from trying to work out a compromise. He felt so guilty and desperate about his son that he lost control of himself. It was not the first time, but it was the last time he ever hit me.

As I look back, I see things that happened all around me in AA that I closed my eyes to. I watched a few people in AA commit suicide or die senseless deaths—all of them sober for more than ten years.

"Danny" came into AA in 1982. He had tried to commit suicide by shooting himself in the chest. He finally succeeded in 1994. He overdosed on Prozac.

"Chester" was sober about 27 years when he supposedly passed away from complications of diabetes. Like hell. Chester was only in his fifties when he died. He could never hold a job as long as I had known him. He did not care about himself, and I really believe he had a death wish. He smoked and abused his diet to the point that he went into insulin shock twice while renting a small apartment from me. But he didn't miss a meeting. I was disgusted by his followers hanging on his every word and defending him: *He has such **good** things to say!*, they would exclaim. I knew how he lived and pretty much how he died. This god had clay feet . . . but I was being *judgmental.*

"Bill" had a very bad time trying to recover. He could not seem to get it together after a freak car accident. He was driving a carload of people to an AA meeting in the winter and lost control of the car, slid off the road, and sideswiped a tree. A young man sitting in the backseat was ejected out the side window and killed instantly. Bill tried for years to go to AA meetings and live with the guilt of the young man's death. He began using drugs but still went to meetings for a few more years. The end finally came when he was shot in the head by a drug dealer.

These three men had serious problems and thought AA was the only way to solve them. It ended up killing them. AA degraded them with guilt and shame. It worked for a while because of the *pink cloud* effect (which is a temporary reprieve from guilt and shame often experienced after being introduced to AA). But because the core issues behind the guilt and shame were not addressed and/or resolved, the pain cycle continued to the point of suicide.

My last meeting was my 15th sober anniversary. I really didn't know it would be my last meeting. I had been chastised for bringing my own cake; they already had one—for about six people at a 100-person meeting! The tiny cake had been some kind of twisted tradition for as long as I could remember, and I thought it was time to share. The person who bought the little cakes by the dozen on sale and froze them told me she spent a whole $2.50 on the cake, and why didn't I call her and tell her I was bringing a cake? A petty little thing, I agree, but the last straw. I walked out of that meeting and never went back.

I know I am never going to be perfect. I thought all those fourth and fifth steps were going to make me perfect, if I did them right. All the time I was in AA, I thought if I got rid of all my imperfections I would finally be lovable. I'm still a little afraid of confronting or being confronted, but I don't back down. And I continue to ask questions. A lot of questions.

Days before I was to be married this year, my husband's son was tragically killed. I loved the boy and had adopted him as one of my own children. The pain was, and still is, a very big hurt. I am learning how to deal with grief and loss without shoving it under the rug or using inane slogans that don't mean jack squat and don't change the way I feel. I would not trade what I have experienced for anything.

Being able to feel deeply and accept life with its gray areas are the biggest changes I've undergone.

Since leaving AA, I have felt the greatest joy of my life, as well as the deepest sorrow. These have been lessons long in coming. I am at peace with myself now that I know there are many more people out there like me that question an institution like AA—and actually *disagree* with what it represents and teaches.

I doubt if I will ever drink. My life is good, so why take the chance? It is not a life-or-death issue for me anymore. I have continued my abstinence and see no reason why it will not continue. I have encountered many stressful situations and have not had to fall back on going to meetings, drinking, or even smoking. I am capable of standing on my own two feet. If I were to need help, there are many places I'd go before I'd go back to AA.

46 ▲ Jim

One Man's Journey
Out the Door Marked "Exit"

I have chosen this title because I believe that AA indoctrination has little to do with not drinking, but much to do with disempowering the individual. I speak from years of personal experience around the halls of the *chosen ones,* as they like to refer to themselves at times, and I have a story to tell that could be of benefit to those trying to get the gum off their shoes and leave the collective hive of AA.

I was raised in a religious home, but had a predisposition toward skepticism. One of the reasons I originally chose to drink, at age 11, was the feeling that I was being lied to about alcohol's evils. Around the age of 13, I ran into a guy who was doing martial arts. Since I was growing up in L.A., learning self-defense seemed like a pretty rational thing to do. So, I was introduced to martial arts—a way of life that honors vigorous individual effort, respect for the well-being of oneself and others, and, above all, personal responsibility for one's actions. I was and still am enamored of such beliefs. (No thanks to AA there.) Through that experience I gained a confidence in my own integrity that I sensed lacking in many of the adults around me.

One of my early dreams was to be a world traveler. I used to sit on the beach in Southern California and look out across the ocean and tell myself traveling was what I wanted to do. I managed to navigate to over 18 countries by the time I was 25, and ingesting intoxicating substances was a part of my lifestyle. It wasn't, however, the biggest, most important part of my life. But then some tragedies occurred: in rapid succession, I experienced the realities of death, divorce, and loss of fortune.

It started when I was living overseas and I got a telex (no faxes in those days) that my father had cancer. I spent a small fortune traveling back and forth to watch him slowly die. Then, like dominoes falling, my mother, my grandmother, my brother, and my best friend all died. My business was stolen out from under me, and my lovely wife hit the road. It is one thing to hit a bump in the road, but quite another to go bumpity, bumpity, bumpity crash. To put it mildly, I was devastated—and I spent the next few years on a mission of self-medication. I was living again in L.A., a place where I really had no desire to be.

I came to believe that life sucked, and mine was beyond repair. I believe that today mental heath professionals would label me as suffering from post traumatic stress disorder. For years, I felt a soup of dark emotions swirling about like a swarm of nasty bees.

But eventually I thought I might see daylight again. I began to believe the constant, habitual ingesting of intoxicants was severely working against me. Enter AA. I was introduced to AA by a well-meaning friend. In those days, there was no other place offering help.

Since I believed the trauma of severe losses in my life had damaged me for good, the AA philosophy of labeling myself as a diseased person, crippled within for life, agreed with me at that time. As a human being I have a tendency to go out of my way to prove my thinking right. That is natural, but when you are trying to prove wrong thinking right, problems are sure to follow. And problems did, indeed, follow.

I succumbed to the AA indoctrination process. Meetings, meetings, meetings till you drop. Sponsorship, which consists of trusting that just because some bozo says he has been sober for X amount of years he must be qualified to guide you out of your intoxicated haze. Read, read, read the Bi- Bi- Big Book. Up the steps, down the steps. Write moral inventories. Be of service, you selfish, self-centered, diseased twit. Write about it again. Forgive everyone for everything and be free, free, free. Write some more and always tell your sponsor everything.

My first sponsor was an ex-con who had a voice like sandpaper and the demeanor of a drill sergeant. He had neither the sensitivity nor the education to properly give sound advice. His guidance was merely the stock: *Go to meetings, read the Big Book, work the steps, write inventories, be of service, forgive everyone for everything. Call me every day, and don't drink between meetings. If you do drink don't call me until you're sober. Now go be of service to someone and get out of yourself.*

I later found a more suitable, but passive-aggressive sponsor. He would ask nice things like, *How is your face?* to be followed by, *Because it sure is hurting me.* Implying that I was still a *newborn* who had a lot of meetings to go to, inventories to write . . . well you get the picture. That's how it went for a few years, until I had managed to become another edition of a walking Big Book.

Out of desperation, I had adopted a persona full of the righteous witticisms of AA lore, complete with my very own personal story of debasement by the most powerful of demons—alcohol—and my subsequent rescue. I had all the answers, though none were truly mine. I believed I could not trust my own thinking, that if I didn't stay close to the center of the herd the wolves of John Barleycorn would snatch me back into alcoholic oblivion. Hell on earth would be my fate as the penalty for straying.

So I stuck, and stayed stuck. The gum of AA grew from the bottom of my shoes up my legs. Then, at around three years into the collective briar patch, I lost my high-paying job as a corporate executive. I went through a divorce and joined the ranks of unemployed ex-senior management types.

But hey—I still had AA and, hallelujah, I was sober. Now I could go to the noon meetings, claiming I had something to be grateful for. This went on for a couple of years. Then one day I got a phone call from an old friend asking me what I was up to and if I would consider helping him out in a new business overseas. With my years of experience working outside the U.S., all the pieces fit. So hasty plans were made, and I was sent off by the hive with a loud cheer and held up as a miracle of the program. Little did I know that phone call would eventually put me back at home plate, and that I was about to hit a home run.

Meanwhile, in my mind, a sneaking suspicion was growing. Had I actually been on a downward spiral by spouting beliefs and engaging in behaviors that were robbing me of personal integrity, disempowering me, and molding me into a two-dimensional cardboard cutout of my former self?

It took awhile. I sought out AA in my new country, but meetings were hard to get to, and the most I could usually manage was once a week. Besides, it was different than the AA I had known—the people seemed weird, and I just wasn't getting the juice anymore. I got the AA withdrawals. I tried to adapt, but I was, nevertheless, jonesing. Actually—unknown to me—I was getting healthier.

I decided I needed to go back to the U.S. and go to my old home group. So I did just that. I met some old groupers at a coffee shop before the big event. Among them was a guy who was always criticizing the program yet could not stay sober for any appreciable length of time. I berated him with steppism and Big Book lore. I admonished him for his lack of honesty in not working a good and proper program. Then we headed over to the ol' meeting hall. I walked in and felt the old rush. The chorus of cheers met my ears and I knew I was going to be picked to share. Then as I sat there looking around at some familiar faces, I took notice of the disoriented new catch of the month arranged around the room. I saw myself so many years ago. Weak and vulnerable, crying inside, begging for relief from my confusion and pain.

Then I looked at the faces of the old-timers with their smug, know-it-all grins, and I saw a pack of predators ready to pounce and shove the steps, meetings, the Big Book, and all the rest of the rigid dogma and ritual down the gullets of the new birds. I remembered the recent altercation in the coffee shop where I too had armed myself with AA dogma and ritual and beaten a guy over the head with it. I looked again at those sanctimonious old-timers with their looks of authority in dispensing their beliefs in their "God-given" solution to substance abuse. As my mind fast-forwarded, I saw a new sight that ripped my guts out. I saw me.

I realized that *I* was one of those authoritative old-timers dispensing my AA wisdom like some overly well-behaved child. I had qualified myself based solely on the fact that I wasn't drinking, to assign an imaginary cause (AA) to an observable event (being sober), and to preach some gobbledygook of disease, powerlessness, rituals and dogma to every unsuspecting person down in the dumps over an addiction problem. Talk about a moment of clarity. Man, I was on fire inside. The moment at the plate came and I hit that home run.

I got up before I was tagged to share my pearls of wisdom, wiped the gum off my shoes and walked out. One of my old AA buddies, having noticed the lack of star-struck luster in my eyes, followed me out with that feigned look of concern and asked the same old question: *Are you all right?*, which translated to mean, *Is your program all right?* I looked at him as I actually held back a few tears of joy and said, *I just can't do it anymore, it's a **cult** and I don't want anything to do with it. For whatever it's worth, I think you're an OK guy and maybe someday you'll see what I just saw in there, but it is time to move on. Good-bye.*

Back in my new overseas home I began to see life in a progressively clearer light. I had taken my girlfriend to a meeting at one time and introduced her to my AA friends. A couple of years had passed and we had gotten married. Then one day I asked my new wife (who speaks English as a second language, but has never been a substance abuser) if she thought AA was a cult. I had really begun to see clearly that my behavior and my beliefs in AA had kept my personal integrity in a fog for years. Without hesitation, in her heavy accent, she said, *of course.* How simple it all became, and how obvious it also became now that I had returned to health and was out of the group loop. Now that is what I call a step. I gained, and continue to seek, clarity.

Recently I learned that my favorite uncle died. There was that old deja-vu feeling, being overseas, getting a message about another one gone. Yet this time I didn't even think of calling anyone except my cousin to offer my condolences. I didn't even think about going to a meeting and sharing my feelings. I took some private time and went down by the local river and thought about him and how he was a player in my life. I paid my respects and said good-bye. I felt good, at peace with it, and glad to be alive and taking a stand in life quite different than that old AA way.

Nowadays, I endeavor to reach for the things that wise old *sensei* passed my way so many years ago when I learned martial arts. Things like personal integrity, self-responsibility, self-confidence, discipline, respect for oneself and others, compassion for suffering, to relax, to play, to give myself, as well as the other guy, a break—and many other empowering things.

To take a stand in the drift of life—to say I know sometimes things just are not fair, and sometimes I will screw things up, is part of what makes me human. I am not diseased.

But don't take me wrong here. Not everyone in AA is going to have the same experience. Just try not to get confused like I did and think that the steps, the Big Book, and the whole lot really has anything to do with freedom from alcohol, or freedom period. I actually did meet some really nice people along the way. But if you are in there and you hear a knock on the door, you might want to take a look at those mushrooms that have been growing in the basement of your mind. You might want to walk up those steps, open the door, and step out into the fresh air of your own integrity. You might want to devise your own program for living.

I'm glad I stopped selling myself out. I'm glad I rejoined the human race. I'm glad I'm living my life again.

Secular Self-Help Groups

There are five important alternative (to AA) self-help groups in the United States. Unfortunately, none of them have been subjected to controlled studies, so there is no proof yet of their efficacy. We strongly suspect that *all* of them are more effective than AA (if for no other reasons than that attendance at them is overwhelmingly voluntary and because they do not inculcate the harmful 12-step "powerless," "disease," and "loss of control" concepts); but, at present, there is no scientific evidence to support this belief.

At the same time, it's important to realize that a large majority of those with alcohol problems solve those problems without participating in *any* self-help group or formal treatment. It's also important to realize that recovery from alcohol problems via moderation is at least as common as recovery via abstinence.*

A brief description of the alternative groups, in alphabetical order, follows:

Moderation Management: MM, founded in 1994, suggests guidelines and limits for moderate drinking, and provides professionally advised meetings for those attempting to moderate. MM provides a supportive mutual-help environment that encourages people who are concerned about their drinking to cut back or quit drinking before their drinking problems become severe. For more information, or for groups in your area, call (310) 275-5433, or write to Moderation Management, c/o Addiction Alternatives Inc., Beverly Hills Medical Tower, 1125 S. Beverly Drive, Suite 401, Los Angeles, CA 90035. E-mail: habitdoc@msn.com Web site: http://www.moderation.org

Rational Recovery: RR, founded in 1986, is based on Addictive Voice Recognition Technique (AVRT®), and is a total abstinence program. RR advises that participation in recovery groups is not necessary for

---

* For further discussion of these issues, see *Resisting 12-Step Coercion: How to Fight Forced Participation in AA, NA, or 12-Step Treatment,* by Stanton Peele, Charles Bufe, and Archie Brodsky.

those who learn AVRT. For this reason, several months prior to the publication of this book, RR founder/president Jack Trimpey ordered all RR self-help groups to disband. For more information, call (530) 621-2667 or write to Rational Recovery, P.O. Box 800, Lotus, CA 95651. Web site: http://www.rational.org.

Secular Organizations for Sobriety: SOS, founded in 1985, believes that alcoholism is a disease, and thus takes a strict abstinence approach. Its program consists largely of the "Sobriety Priority," which is a daily acknowledgment that staying sober is one's highest priority. For more information, or for groups in your area, call (310) 821-8430, or write to SOS, 5521 Grosvenor Blvd., Marina del Rey, CA 90066. Web site: http://www.unhooked.com

SMART Recovery (Self-Management And Recovery Training): SMART was incorporated as a non-profit in 1992, and states that its teachings "are based on scientific knowledge, and evolve as scientific knowledge evolves." SMART is a time-limited, free, professionally advised abstinence program that views addictive behavior as learned behavior that can be unlearned by correcting inaccurate and self-defeating thinking. For more information or for groups in your area call (440) 951-5357, or write to SMART Recovery, 7537 Mentor Ave. #306, Mentor, OH 44060.
Web site: http://www.smartrecovery.org

Women for Sobriety: WFS is the oldest—founded in 1975—of the modern (non-12-step) programs, and is dedicated to helping women overcome alcoholism and other addictions. WFS accepts the disease model and is an abstinence program. Its "New Life" program is specifically designed for women. For more information or for groups in your area call (215) 536-8026, or write to Women for Sobriety, P.O. Box 618, Quakertown, PA 18951.
Web site: http://www.womenforsobriety.org

For a more thorough discussion of the self-help alternatives to AA, see *Alcoholics Anonymous: Cult or Cure?* (2nd ed.), by Charles Bufe, which contains detailed descriptions (in most cases self-descriptions) of the self-help groups listed here.

Bibliography

Bufe, Charles. *Alcoholics Anonymous: Cult or Cure? (2nd Ed.)* Tucson, AZ: See Sharp Press, 1998.

Ellis, Albert and Velten, Emmett. *When AA Doesn't Work for You: Rational Steps to Quitting Drinking.* Secaucus, NJ: Barricade Books, 1992.

Hassan, Steven. *Combatting Cult Mind Control.* Rochester, VT: Park Street Press, 1988.

Kirkpatrick, Jean. *Goodbye Hangovers, Hello Life.* Quakertown, PA: Women for Sobriety, 1991.

Peele, Stanton. *Diseasing of America: Addiction Treatment Out of Control.* Lexington, MA: Lexington Books, 1989.

Peele, Stanton, and Brodsky, Archie. *The Truth About Addiction and Recovery.* New York: Simon & Schuster, 1991.

Peele, Stanton, Bufe, Charles, and Brodsky, Archie. *Resisting 12-Step Coercion: How to Fight Forced Participation in AA, NA, or 12-Step Treatment.* Tucson, AZ: See Sharp Press, 2000.

Ragge, Ken. *The Real AA: Behind the Myth of 12-Step Recovery.* Tucson, AZ: See Sharp Press, 1998.

Schaler, Jeffrey. *Addiction Is a Choice.* Chicago: Open Court, 1999.

Tate, Philip. *Alcohol: How to Give It Up and Be Glad You Did (2nd Ed.)* Tucson, AZ: See Sharp Press, 1996.

Trimpey, Jack. *Rational Recovery from Alcoholism: The Small Book.* Lotus, CA: Lotus Press, 1989.